Graduate Students' Research about Community Colleges

This book brings together a collection of chapters with different research designs that explore the research, practice, and policies of community colleges.

The chapters in this book are the result of the graduate students and their faculty mentor's scholarly work, and a rigorous special issue's peer review process. Furthermore, this book offers recommendations on how to mentor graduate students, in the absence of research and mentorship on how to publish for graduate students and practitioner-scholars, as well as recognizing that graduate programs and professional associations are important on the socialization of practitioner-scholars.

Each book chapter addresses the implications for practice and future research, policy for community colleges, and recommendation for change indicated by the research results. Five broad research themes, higher education policy, leadership practices and roles, network community, student success, and technology emerged from the empirical articles and critical reviews. A final chapter shares advice and lessons learned from the 30 authors and mentors.

With the exception of Chapter 14, the chapters in this book were originally published as a special issue of the *Community College Journal of Research and Practice*.

Deborah L. Floyd is a Professor of Higher Education Leadership at Florida Atlantic University, Boca Raton, USA. She is Editor-in-Chief of the *Community College Journal of Research and Practice*. Her research focuses on leadership, community colleges, student affairs, and baccalaureate models.

Cristobal Salinas Jr. is an Associate Professor in the Educational Leadership and Research Methodology Department at Florida Atlantic University, Boca Raton, USA. His research promotes access and equality in higher education for historically marginalized communities.

Ethan C. Swingle is a recent doctoral graduate of the Higher Education Program at Florida Atlantic University, Boca Raton, USA. His research interests include intercollegiate athletics, with a focus on student athlete transfer experiences.

María-José Zeledón-Pérez is an Assistant Professor in the Communication Studies Department and Co-Director of the World Cultures Program at San Diego City College, USA.

Sim Barhoum is the Coordinator for the Department of Humanities and Writing Center, San Diego Mesa College, San Diego, CA, USA. His research examines active learning, relational equity practices, students of color, and educational models.

Gianna Ramdin is the Associate Editor of the *Community College Journal of Research and Practice*. Her primary research area is the study of campus greening and sustainable initiatives implemented on university and college campuses.

Graduate Students' Research about Community Colleges

A Guide for Publishing

Edited by
Deborah L. Floyd, Cristobal Salinas Jr.,
Ethan C. Swingle, María-José Zeledón-Pérez,
Sim Barhoum and Gianna Ramdin

LONDON AND NEW YORK

First published 2021
by Routledge
2 Park Square, Milton Park, Abingdon, Oxon, OX14 4RN

and by Routledge
52 Vanderbilt Avenue, New York, NY 10017

Routledge is an imprint of the Taylor & Francis Group, an informa business

© 2021 Taylor & Francis

All rights reserved. No part of this book may be reprinted or reproduced or utilised in any form or by any electronic, mechanical, or other means, now known or hereafter invented, including photocopying and recording, or in any information storage or retrieval system, without permission in writing from the publishers.

Trademark notice: Product or corporate names may be trademarks or registered trademarks, and are used only for identification and explanation without intent to infringe.

British Library Cataloguing-in-Publication Data
A catalogue record for this book is available from the British Library

ISBN13: 978-0-367-43710-7

Typeset in Minion Pro
by codeMantra

Publisher's Note
The publisher accepts responsibility for any inconsistencies that may have arisen during the conversion of this book from journal articles to book chapters, namely the inclusion of journal terminology.

Disclaimer
Every effort has been made to contact copyright holders for their permission to reprint material in this book. The publishers would be grateful to hear from any copyright holder who is not here acknowledged and will undertake to rectify any errors or omissions in future editions of this book.

Contents

Citation Information vii
Notes on Contributors x

1 Publishing Graduate Students' Research About Community Colleges 1
 Deborah L. Floyd, Cristobal Salinas Jr., and Gianna Ramdin

2 Transformational Leadership and the Proliferation of Community College Leadership Frameworks: A Systematic Review of the Literature 12
 Daniel Tarker

3 Do Community College Students Demonstrate Different Behaviors from Four-Year University Students on Virtual Proctored Exams? 30
 Tammi Kolski and Jennifer L. Weible

4 Faculty of Color Unmask Color-Blind Ideology in the Community College Faculty Search Process 42
 Luke J. Lara

5 Case Studies of Women of Color Leading Community Colleges in Texas: Navigating the Leadership Pipeline through Mentoring and Culture 58
 Maria Yareli Delgado and Taryn Ozuna Allen

6 "Where are My People At?": A Community Cultural Wealth Analysis of How Lesbian, Gay, and Bisexual Community College Students of Color Access Community and Support 70
 Melvin A. Whitehead

7 Evolving Narratives about College: Immigrant Community College Students' Perceptions of all Four-Year Degree in the Great Plains 83
 Moises Padilla, Justin Chase Brown, and Elvira Abrica

8 Crossing the Shapeless River on a Government Craft: How Military-Affiliated Students Navigate Community College Transfer 96
 Saralyn McKinnon-Crowley, Eliza Epstein, Huriya Jabbar, and Lauren Schudde

CONTENTS

9 Historically Black Community Colleges: A Descriptive Profile and Call for Context-Based Future Research 110
   Kayla C. Elliott, Jarrett B. Warshaw, and Crystal A. deGregroy

10 Two-Year Institution and Community College Web Accessibility: Updating the Literature after the 2018 Section 508 Amendment 125
   Z. W. Taylor and Ibrahim Bicak

11 A Document Analysis of Student Conduct in Florida's Community Colleges 136
   Allyson Miller and Cristobal Salinas Jr.

12 Experiential Learning as a Strategy for Student Completion and Course Success in the Community College 143
   Carolyn Walker

13 Texas Community Colleges Respond to the Threatened End of DACA: A Document Analysis 147
   Nicholas Tapia-Fuselier and Jemimah L. Young

14 Reflections on Publishing Graduate Students' Research: Advice and Lessons Learned 152
   Deborah L. Floyd, Cristobal Salinas Jr., Ethan C. Swingle, María-Jose Zeledón-Pérez, Sim Barhoum, and Gianna Ramdin

   Index 155

Citation Information

The following chapters were originally published in the *Community College Journal of Research and Practice,* volume 43, issue 10–11 (2019). When citing this material, please use the original page numbering for each article, as follows:

Chapter 1
Publishing Graduate Students' Research About Community Colleges
Deborah L. Floyd, Cristobal Salinas Jr., and Gianna Ramdin
Community College Journal of Research and Practice, volume 43, issue 10–11 (2019)
pp. 661–671

Chapter 2
Transformational Leadership and Proliferation of Community College Research Framework: A Systematic Review of the Literature
Daniel Tarker
Community College Journal of Research and Practice, volume 43, issue 10–11 (2019)
pp. 672–689

Chapter 3
Do Community College Students Demonstrate Different Behaviors from Four-Year University Students on Virtual Proctored Exams?
Tammi Kolski and Jennifer L. Weible
Community College Journal of Research and Practice, volume 43, issue 10–11 (2019)
pp. 690–701

Chapter 4
Faculty of Color Un mask Color-Blind Ideology in the Community College Faculty Search Process
Luke J. Lara
Community College Journal of Research and Practice, volume 43, issue 10–11 (2019)
pp. 702–717

Chapter 5
Case Studies of Women of Color Leading Community Colleges in Texas: Navigating the Leadership Pipeline through Mentoring and Culture
Maria Yareli Delgado and Taryn Ozuna Allen
Community College Journal of Research and Practice, volume 43, issue 10–11 (2019)
pp. 718–729

Chapter 6
"Where are My People At?": A Community Cultural Wealth Analysis of How Lesbian, Gay, and Bisexual Community College Students of Color Access Community and Support
Melvin A. Whitehead

Chapter 7
Evolving Narratives about College: Immigrant Community College Students' Perceptions of all Four-Year Degree in the Great Plains
Moises Padilla, Justin Chase Brown, and Elvira Abrica

Chapter 8
Crossing the Shapeless River on a Government Craft: How Military-Affiliated Students Navigate Community College Transfer
Saralyn McKinnon-Crowley, Eliza Epstein, Huriya Jabbar, and Lauren Schudde

Chapter 9
Historically Black Community Colleges: A Descriptive Profile and Call for Context-Based Future Research
Kayla C. Elliott, Jarrett B. Warshaw, and Crystal A. deGregroy

Chapter 10
Two-Year Institution and Community College Web Accessibility: Updating the Literature after the 2018 Section 508 Amendment
Z. W. Taylor and Ibrahim Bicak

Chapter 11
A Document Analysis of Student Conduct in Florida's Community Colleges
Allyson Miller and Cristobal Salinas Jr.

Chapter 12
Experiential Learning as a Strategy for Student Completion and Course Success in the Community College
Carolyn Walker

Chapter 13
Texas Community Colleges Respond to the Threatened End of DACA: A Document Analysis
Nicholas Tapia-Fuselier and Jemimah L. Young
Community College Journal of Research and Practice, volume 43, issue 10–11 (2019) pp. 807–811

For any permission-related enquiries please visit:
http://www.tandfonline.com/page/help/permissions

Contributors

Elvira Abrica Educational Administration, University of Nebraska-Lincoln, USA.

Taryn Ozuna Allen Educational Leadership & Policy Studies, University of Texas at Arlington, USA.

Sim Barhoum San Diego Mesa College, USA.

Ibrahim Bicak Department of Educational Leadership and Policy, The University of Texas at Austin, USA.

Justin Chase Brown Educational Administration, University of Nebraska-Lincoln, USA.

Crystal A. deGregory Academic Affairs, Kentucky State University, Frankfort, USA.

Maria Yareli Delgado Educational Leadership, University of Texas at Arlington, USA.

Kayla C. Elliott Educational Leadership and Research Methodology, Florida Atlantic University, Boca Raton, USA.

Eliza Epstein Department of Educational Leadership and Policy, The University of Texas at Austin, USA.

Deborah L. Floyd Department of Educational Leadership & Research Methodology, Florida Atlantic University, Boca Raton, USA.

Huriya Jabbar Department of Educational Leadership and Policy, The University of Texas at Austin, USA.

Tammi Kolski Teacher Education and Professional Development, Central Michigan University, Newaygo, USA.

Luke J. Lara Department of Administration, Rehabilitation, and Postsecondary Education, San Diego State University College of Education, USA.

Saralyn McKinnon-Crowley Department of Educational Leadership and Policy, The University of Texas at Austin, USA.

Allyson Miller Educational Leadership and Research Methodology, Florida Atlantic University, Boca Raton, USA.

Moises Padilla Educational Administration, University of Nebraska-Lincoln, USA.

Gianna Ramdin Department of Educational Leadership & Research Methodology, Florida Atlantic University, Boca Raton, USA.

Cristobal Salinas Jr. Department of Educational Leadership and Research Methodology, Florida Atlantic University, Boca Raton, USA.

Lauren Schudde Department of Educational Leadership and Policy, The University of Texas at Austin, USA.

Ethan C. Swingle Higher Education Program at Florida Atlantic University, Boca Raton, USA.

Nicholas Tapia-Fuselier Department of Counseling and Higher Education, University of North Texas, Denton, USA.

Daniel Tarker Adult and Higher Education in Community College Leadership, Oregon State University, Corvallis, USA.

Z. W. Taylor Department of Educational Leadership and Policy, The University of Texas at Austin, USA.

Carolyn Walker Department of Administrative Office Technology, Greenville Technical College, Greenville, USA.

Jarrett B. Warshaw Educational Leadership and Research Methodology, Florida Atlantic University, Boca Raton, USA.

Jennifer L. Weible Teacher Education and Professional Development, Central Michigan University, Mount Pleasant, USA.

Melvin A. Whitehead Department of Counseling and Human Development Services, University of Georgia, Athens, USA.

Jemimah L. Young Department of Teaching and Learning, University of North Texas, Denton, USA.

María-José Zeledón-Pérez Communication Studies Department and Co-Director of the World Cultures Program at San Diego City College, USA.

Publishing Graduate Students' Research About Community Colleges

Deborah L. Floyd, Cristobal Salinas Jr., and Gianna Ramdin

ABSTRACT
Unlike many graduate education disciplines such as science and engineering, graduate education programs specializing in the study of community colleges have not focused their efforts on preparing future faculty. Rather, these programs focused on the scholarly and practical study of community college education and leadership, education, and programs with research requirements for doctoral degrees, but with little emphasis on publishing works. That is changing, however, as more graduate students and faculty alike value the processes and benefits of students learning how to publish their research, often with the guidance and mentorship of faculty advisors.

Publishing as a graduate student or as a faculty member has an established history in higher education starting with an increase in publishers during the 1960s and 1970s (McGuigan & Russell, 2008). Since then, publishing has been employed to demonstrate one's academic talent to colleagues and to increase the likelihood of finding a professoriate job or the chances of obtaining tenure (Coggburn & Neely, 2015; Sweeney, 2000). Although publishing has been ingrained in the culture of graduate school and professorship, limited studies have been conducted to understand how to publish in academic journals.

Increasingly, evidence-based research that informs practice is valued among community college practitioners and scholars alike. Initiatives and programs, such as Achieving the Dream, College Promise, and Civitas Learning, focus on utilizing research and data to help advise policies and practices. While the *Community College Journal of Research and Practice* (*CCJRP*) has published numerous articles about community college evidence-based research projects, we know that many more practitioner-scholars would like to publish their work if they knew how, and received mentorship and support during their efforts. This is as more graduate students are aspiring to university graduate faculty positions either immediately upon graduation or as a part of their career after assuming community college teaching or administrative roles (Tolman, McBrayer, & Evans, 2019).

In this paper, we provide an overview of the literature on the socialization to becoming practitioner-scholars. Then, we provide an overview of the development process and a brief description of each article published in this issue on publishing graduate students' research about community colleges. Last, we offer recommendations for graduate programs, professional associations, and faculty on how to mentor graduate students and tips for graduate students and recent graduates on how to publish their works. In this paper, we use the term *practitioner-scholars* to refer to individuals that are working full time as administrators or faculty members, as well as graduate students that aspire to become an administrator or faculty member.

The purpose of this paper is to (1) discuss and provide recommendations to graduate students on how to publish in academic journals, and (2) provide mentorship guidance and suggestions for faculty members when helping their colleagues and graduate students. Specifically, this paper provides a guide to graduate students on how to publish in peer-reviewed journals, regardless of their career track as practitioner-scholars.

Socialization to becoming practitioner-scholars

While publishing is an essential component of graduate school, especially in graduate education programs, limited studies have been conducted on the process or understand the importance of publishing. Pasco (2009) suggested that each field requires different amounts of publication to have a truly beneficial experience but emphasized the importance of having at least one to two published articles before graduation. Van Cott (2005) addressed the different types of articles that can be published by graduate students such as seminar papers, conference papers, book reviews, and full journal articles. Van Cott also discussed the process for graduate students to collaborate with faculty and noted that it is important to understand the process of publishing before submitting an article to an academic journal. However, understanding the process of publishing an article comes with practice and mentorship.

Another area of research on graduate student publishing is their perceptions of electronic journals. In their study, Li Liew, Foo, and Chennupati (2000) discovered recent graduate students utilized electronic journals more than print journals, had a positive perception about publishing, and participants were optimistic about new electrotonic journals. Although students are optimistic about publishing and appear to understand the importance of publishing, it is evident to focus on whether graduate programs are doing enough to help make the most of the opportunity of graduate school and to transition graduate students into new careers.

Offstein, Larson, Mcneill, and Mjoni Mwale (2004) discovered that doctoral students' experiences are intensively stressful and programs across the nation need to support these students in order to help them accomplish their practitioner-scholar goals. One valuable strategy is effective mentorship between faculty and students to address the expectations of each student and teach the process of publishing in academic journals (Offstein et al., 2004). Further, building on the importance of faculty and graduate student mentorship, Lechuga (2011) found that mentorship can increase the productivity of both graduate students and faculty, and allows for learning moments to occur for both parties. Therefore, graduate programs should invest more time in developing faculty-graduate student mentorship programs to support more publishing opportunities that focus on developing a research plan, writing strategies, selection of a peer-review journal to submit a manuscript, and the process of submitting a manuscript for review.

Last, Ducheny, Alletzhauser, Crandell, and Schneider (1997) posited graduate students need to understand how publishing affects their professional development and how one's individual professional development needs to change throughout their journey. While the academic and professional needs of graduate students have changed over time, so, too, has publishers' guides on how to publish in their journals. Another change surrounding the publication process is many publishers are providing guidance to potential authors. To further illustrate, Taylor & Francis Author Services offer suggested steps from preparing your paper to what to expect during the peer-review process and promoting your research. As publishing continues to impel academic and professional elements of higher education, we provide a general overview of the steps applied in the publication process and a brief description of each article publishing in *Graduate Students' Research About Community Colleges*.

The publication process of this special issue

In 2017, the editorial team of the *CCJRP* decided to pursue a new special issue featuring graduate students' research about community colleges. In 2018, editors and reviewers were recruited, a customized call for papers was prepared, and a process to encourage submissions was launched.

We were exceptionally pleased with the response and quite encouraged that papers were submitted from graduate students representing a variety of ages, geographic locations, and institutions on numerous important topics about community colleges. We believe that this special issue makes a wonderful contribution to the literature and that this is evidence that our profession benefits greatly when perspectives are expanded. *Graduate Students' Research About Community Colleges* details the publishing process used to curate this special issue and offers as an added benefit the opportunity to provide guidance and suggestions on the subject of graduate students' desire to be mentored on how to publish in academic journal.

This is the first (and we hope not the last) *CCJRP* special issue featuring papers authored by graduate students. All first authors are currently graduate students or were graduate students within the past year. An important aim of this project was to encourage mentorship in the publishing process and toward that aim, some papers include faculty as co-authors, but only in a secondary capacity. Graduate students and recent graduates of master's and doctoral programs were strongly encouraged to receive mentorship and assistance from faculty. This special issue is one of the first of its kind that allows graduate students to be the first author and publish in a peer-reviewed journal on community colleges.

Our hope was that this special issue would bring together a diversity of experiences and perspectives of the context and complexity of community colleges. A call for papers for this special issue – *Graduate Students' Research About Community Colleges*, was distributed via e-mail to community college graduate programs, academic conferences' listserves, and social media. The call for proposal stated the special issue's purpose, deadlines for submission, review process and publication, guest editors' contact information, and instruction on the guidelines and how to summit a paper for review.

Throughout the process, graduate students were afforded opportunities to be engaged in the editorial process from the submission and review stages, through the production stages, and finally to publication and dissemination. Students learned how to shape their ideas into articles and to follow the published guidelines for papers, including specifics about formatting. Submitting papers in a *blind* format via the ScholarOne Manuscript management system was also an important part of the process and a learning experience for some graduate students. Reviewing submissions without knowing the authors' and receiving feedback from anonymous reviewers are processes professors know well, but were new experiences for most graduate students. For some, numerous rewrites, revisions, and responses to editorial queries may have been frustrating, but eventually resulted in a quality publication. For some, however, the review process resulted in feedback and a decision that the paper would not be accepted for this issue. For all, we hope that this process was a positive learning experience and that all who bravely submitted their works for *blind* review benefited.

Fifty-three manuscripts were submitted to ScholarOne by the submission deadline. A total of 85 authors affiliated with 32 U.S. higher education institutions and one Australian higher education institution contributed research to this special issue (U.S. higher education institutions: Ashland Community and Technical College, Ball State University, Bellarmine University, Central Michigan University, College of San Mateo, Colorado Mountain College, Florida Atlantic University, Georgia Southern University, Greenville Technical College, James Madison University, Kingsborough Community College, Mississippi State University, North Seattle Community College, Rutgers University, San Diego State University, San Francisco State University, Texas State University, University of Arizona, University of Colorado, University of Georgia, University of Illinois at Urbana-Champaign, University of Massachusetts Amherst, University of Minnesota, University of Nebraska-Lincoln, University of North Texas, University of South Carolina, University of Southern California, University of Texas at Arlington, University of Texas at Austin, Wake Technical Community College, Western Michigan University, and Wingate University; Australian higher education institution: University of Tasmania). Before manuscripts were sent to the four expert external guest reviewers for the initial review, each one of the manuscripts had to meet the criteria required for this special issue, which were the first authors self-identify their student status (i.e., either a current graduate student or a recent graduate of a master's or doctoral program), the manuscript had to match the *CCJRP*'s Aim & Scope, the manuscript must meet the *CCJRP*'s plagiarism benchmark, and the manuscript must be free of author-identifying information. Therefore, 39.6% of the papers submitted were desk rejected for not meeting the published criteria for this special issue. Thirty-two (60.4%) of the initially submitted manuscripts authored by 41 graduate students or recent graduates of a master's or doctoral program, and 13 faculty mentors were sent for the first external peer review. The authors of 17 manuscripts were asked to make further revisions and resubmit the manuscript for a second quadruple-blind peer review. Twelve articles – nine full-length articles and three Exchange articles – authored by 15 graduate students or a recent graduates of a master's or doctoral program, and 9 faculty mentors from 10 institutions (Central Michigan University, Florida Atlantic University, Greenville Technical College, North Seattle Community College, San Diego State University, University of Georgia, University of Nebraska-Lincoln, University of North Texas, University of Texas at Arlington, and University of Texas at Austin) were accepted after an eight-month editorial process. Therefore, the acceptance rate for this special issue is 22.6%.

Each accepted manuscript underwent two rounds of copy editing. A preliminary copy editing carried out by the *CCJRP*'s editorial team, followed by a second round of copy editing completed by Taylor & Francis. Authors were responsible for responding to copy editing queries when submitting their corrections. Once manuscripts are batched to Taylor & Francis production department, they are entered into the Central Article Tracking System (CATS). Authors received an email notification concerning the publishing agreement and when the manuscript's proof was ready for review.

CCJRP publishes two types of papers: (1) scholarly and research full-length manuscripts and (2) exchange manuscripts. For this special issue, all submission for scholarly and research full-length manuscripts were generally 20–25 pages long. Both scholarly and research papers addressed implications for practice and future research and policy for community colleges and recommendation for change indicated by the research results. The exchange manuscripts were short-length manuscripts of 5–8 pages long. These manuscripts focus on featuring thought-provoking and scholarly succinct manuscripts with a focus on research and practical applications for community colleges. The articles published in this special issue are the result of the graduate students and their faculty mentor's hard work, and a rigorous special issue's peer review process. Five broad research themes, higher education policy, leadership practices and roles, network community, student success, and technology, emerged from the empirical articles and critical reviews.

The papers selected for publication

The first full-length article by Daniel Tarker explores how transformational leadership and the five-factor model inform community college leadership frameworks such as the American Association of Community Colleges' Competencies for Community College Leaders. The review of literature focused on the skills, knowledge, traits, experience, and training the contemporary community college leader would require. The findings revealed both theories have the potential to lessen the barrier of construct proliferation and lead to the development of a comprehensive theory of leadership.

Next, Tammi Kolski and Jennifer Weible compared student behaviors displayed while completing a virtual proctored exam. Archived recordings of higher education students taking eLearning exams were used to provide a window into displayed student behaviors. Findings from this study add to the research in several areas: the majority of all students utilized virtual proctoring and displayed similar behaviors, and when comparing the frequency of behaviors observed between the community college and four-year university students, more similarities than differences were found.

The third and fourth full-length articles consider the importance of community colleges and People of Color. Luke Lara examines the community college full-time faculty search process from the purview of the Faculty of Color who participate in racial justice advocacy. Critical race theory is the guiding framework, and the study's participant interviews reveal the assertion of color-blind ideology. The findings also reveal that dominant ideologies are challenged by leadership and the agency of faculty of color, to support the hiring of faculty of color. Maria Delgado and Taryn Ozuna examine the personal and professional experiences of women of color who currently hold higher-level administrative positions at a Texas community college district. The qualitative study obtained data from a variety of sources. The study's finding demonstrates women of color were successful in their roles because they were able to draw upon their minority culture and shared the importance of developing an extensive mentoring networking.

The fifth full-length manuscript by Melvin Whitehead explores the experiences of self-identified LGB Students of Color attending a community college. Findings described how the study's participants used the two forms of capital that were most prevalent – social capital and navigational capital – to access community, support, and needed resources. Limited visible representation of those who shared the participants' identities emerged as a theme and served to limit the participants' ability to find meaningful communities.

The next two full-length articles focus on various aspects of student success. Justin Brown, Moises Padilla, and Elvira Abrica explore immigrant community college students' perceptions of the utility, viability, and value of the four-year degree. This study is part of a larger qualitative research study focusing on the career decision-making of immigrants and children of immigrants attending community colleges in the Great Plains region. The dominant narrative of the study's participants situates community colleges above four-year institutions in relationship to their own academic pathway and a broader societal shift. Saralyn McKinnon-Crowley, Eliza Epstein, Huriya Jabbar, and Lauren Schudde investigate the factors which contribute to the successful transfer of military-affiliated students. This article draws from three years of longitudinal qualitative interviews to investigate the transfer journey of 16 veterans and active duty soldiers. The results found that military benefits assisted these students in the transfer process.

The eighth full-length manuscript by Kayla Elliott, Jarrett Warshaw, and Crystal deGregory begins with a historical context of Historical Black Community Colleges (HBCC), followed by a descriptive reporting of the current state of HBCCs' organizational characteristics. The authors provide topical and theoretical recommendations for future research based on the extant HBCC literature and characteristics.

The final full-length article expands the research on technology. Zachary Taylor and Ibrahim Bicak broaden the research on website compliance for students with disabilities. Tenon™ accessibility software was applied to test web accessibility errors and their HTML locations. The study suggests students with disabilities may experience varying levels of web accessibility when navigating community college websites.

The three Exchange articles present practical and thought-provoking research in the following areas: policy and curriculum. Allyson Miller and Cristobal Salinas Jr. examine the history of student conduct and conducted a documented analysis of the mission statements of student conduct offices at Florida community colleges. Through their document analysis, the authors hope to create an exchange of ideas and start the conversation surrounding the value of student conduct offices and their role in student learning. Carolyn Walker explored experiential learning as a curriculum strategy to improve student completion rates. Comparison results between experiential and non-experiential learning participants yielded positive benefits for the experiential learning participants. Nicholas Tapia-Fuselier and Jemimah Young strongly acknowledged that the decision to address essential policy choices is complex and propose an Undocu-Competent Institutional Response (UCIR) Framework for administrators to consider when crafting institutional responses about issues impacting undocumented students.

Publishing recommendations for mentors

Through the publishing process of this special issue for graduate students' research about community colleges, we were able to engage students and faculty. The most common forms of questions that we received from graduate students were around "How do I publish? How do I submit my paper for publication? How do I know if my paper fits within the *CCRJP* aims and scope?". It was clear that graduate students had various questions about the publishing process, and that their graduate programs did not provide them with the resources, support, and mentorship on how to publish. In the absence of research and mentorship on how to publish for graduate students and practitioner-scholars and recognizing that graduate programs and professional associations are important on the socialization of practitioner-scholars, in this section we offer recommendations on how to mentors graduate students.

Professional associations

- Include various sessions that would allow graduate students to engage with editors of journals.
- Host webinars to teach step-by-step guidance on selecting the right journal for an article, using third-party material in an article, etc.
- Professional associations should include a section on their website for academic-blog posts and white-papers presented at their associations.

Graduate programs

- Mainstream their curriculum to teach graduate students on how to write papers that could become future publication papers. In this process, graduate students should experience how to publish for research journals, research and policy briefs, academic blogs, news, and grant writing.
- Offer resources, such as workshops, online coaching, writing groups, and writing centers, to assist students with academic writing and publishing.

Faculty mentors

- Faculty mentors are ideally positioned to teach students and mentees about the processes to publish an article from conceptualization, selecting a journal or publisher, writing the article, submitting the article for review, responding to reviewers and editors' feedback, revising the article, and handling rejection.
- Provide timely and constructive feedback on papers students are preparing for publication.
- Advise students when to publish and how much they should publish as graduate students.
- Graduate students should seek mentorship and publishing opportunities.
- Faculty mentors should develop a culture of writing group among graduate students.

Graduate students

- Follow the mentor's advice; read recommended publications and give feedback about the usefulness of the mentor's suggestions.
- Seek opportunities to work with a mentor on research, scholarly, and creative writing projects; professional presentations; editorial reviews of publications; and grant proposals.
- Give appropriate credit to mentors and fellow collaborators in publications and presentations.
- Invest in writing skills by reading and reviewing examples of papers that are in the graduate student's areas of research interest.
- Develop a writing group with other graduate students and faculty members.
- Make writing a daily habit.

Recent graduates

- Extracting peer review journal articles or book from your dissertation for publication. While your dissertation is a publication, the preparation, style, and formatting of a journal article for submission for review to a peer journal differs from the dissertation writing process. Taylor &

Francis offers tips on converting your thesis or dissertation into an article for publication (https://authorservices.taylorandfrancis.com/3-tips-for-getting-your-dissertation-published/).

- Set goals and work plans for writing for a publication that is aligned with your post-graduate work. For instance, a goal of those working in administration could be to publishing something at least every two years, while those in a faculty position would need to publish more often.
- Find publishing opportunities in your field of work; consider publishing in research journals, research and policy briefs, academic blogs, and news.
- Stay connected and collaborate with faculty and mentors; they can also provide additional publishing opportunities.
- Continue to engage in a writing group; this could be with your colleagues in graduate programs and with others interested in publishing.

Tips for publishing your research

Taylor & Francis (2019) encourages practitioner-scholars to practice the four As: aims, audience, awareness, and articulation. First, the aims of the journal can help authors choose a peer-review journal to publish their research. Second, understanding who the audience is and the research interest of the audience is important, since policymakers, practitioners, faculty members, educators, or the general public have different concerns and needs. This leads to getting familiar with a journal's scope and guidelines, as each journal focuses on in a particular scope, or particular community or region. Another important practice is awareness. It is important that potential authors contextualize their work around published policies, debates, and research within their topic to avoid duplication and plagiarism. Lastly, it is salient to articulate the logic of the work being submitted for review and does the paper meet the guidelines and requirements of the chosen journal before submission (Taylor & Francis, 2019).

Taylor & Francis (2019) offers potential authors support, and a range of resources and guides on the preparation of manuscripts through their Author Services website (https://authorservices.taylor-andfrancis.com/). Taylor & Francis also offers a full range of fee-based editing services to help authors maximize the impact of their research and improve the quality of their manuscript. Authors can select from the following services, which include: English language editing, translation with editing, manuscript formatting, plagiarism check, and technical review by visiting Taylor & Francis Editing Services website (https://www.tandfeditingservices.com/) (Taylor & Francis, 2019).

The publication process begins with choosing the right journal to publish your research. Taylor & Francis (n.d.) recommend authors ask themselves the following 10 questions when selecting a journal:

(1) Is the journal peer reviewed? What is the peer review policy?
(2) Is the journal print, online, or both? What's your preference?
(3) Is your research international? If so, does the journal have an international audience?
(4) Who is the Editor-in-Chief? Who is on the editorial board?
(5) Who published this journal?
(6) Who reads it?
(7) What's the journal's Impact Factor?
(8) Is it published by an international association or learned society?
(9) Is the journal Open Access, or does it have an Open Access option?
(10) What's the submission process? (p. 2)

Once a journal is selected, the author should carefully read the Instructions for Authors for guidance on formatting, style, and word limit. Each journal has its own, specific set of detailed instructions, which can be found on the journal's web page. Authors are also encouraged to read articles published in the selected journal so they know who they are writing for, the interests of the audiences, and the style of the journal before beginning to writing the first draft. Next, the author can begin preparing the first draft of the

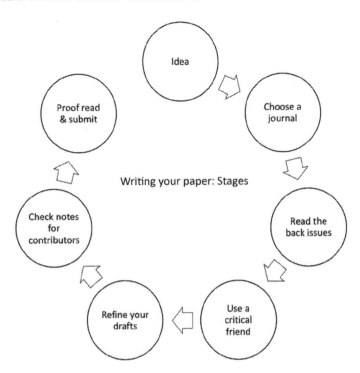

Figure 1. Taylor & Francis Author Services Writing your paper. Adapted from "Tips for publishing your research," by Taylor & Francis Group.
(n.d.), p. 4. Retrieved from https://authorservices.taylorandfrancis.com/wp-content/uploads/2015/07/AS-tips-for-publishing-your-research.pdf. Adapted with permission.

manuscript, which includes an introduction, a methodology, a finding, and a discussion section. During the writing process, the author have a critical friend read the draft and provide feedback. Then, the feedback should be used to refine the manuscript before submitting it to a journal. In addition, the author should ensure all third-party material is properly cited and listed in the references, and that figures, graphs, and tables are formatted according to the journal's style guide. Often times the final steps an author completes before submitting an article is to write the abstract and title. This allows the author to optimize the discoverability of the paper through careful selection of a title this is concise, accurate, and informative, as well as write an abstract that describes the research and grabs the readers' attention. Figure 1 outlines the various stages of writing the manuscript goes through before it is ready to be submitted to a Taylor & Francis journal (Taylor & Francis, n.d.). The writing process outlined in Figure 1 may be more detailed when compared with other peer review journals, but the figure includes the potential steps that can occur.

Taylor & Francis (n.d.) has developed a checklist for authors ready to submit their manuscript to ensure that critical items are not overlooked. The checklist includes eight components which are as follows:

(1) Is the article clear, concise, and accessible?
(2) Have you stuck to the article length specified in the journal's instructions for authors?
(3) Have you included an abstract and keywords, highlighting your article's key points?
(4) Have you included the name and affiliation of any/all co-authors?
(5) Is your article formatted to the style required by the journal?
(6) Are all the references made to the literature included in your references section?
(7) Have you got written permission for the reproduction of any images/figures/tables, etc.?

(8) Have you checked your chosen journal's peer-review policy (on the Aims & Scope or Instructions for Authors), as you may need to make your paper anonymous?(p. 5)

Once you are ready to submit your manuscript, the Instructions for Authors will guide you through the submission step. The *CCJRP* uses ScholarOne Manuscripts management system for online submission and manuscript tracking. A couple of essential elements to remember that are often overlooked when submitting a manuscript are it is essential to research into the blinding process of the selected journal and have a cover letter prepared. A link to a sample cover letter can be found on Taylor & Francis Author Services (https://authorservices.taylorandfrancis.com/writing-a-cover-letter/).

All manuscripts submitted to the *CCJRP* undergo editorial screening, which includes manuscripts matches the *CCJRP*'s Aim and Scope, manuscripts are free of author-identifying information (submitted blind), and manuscripts meet the *CCJRP*'s plagiarism benchmark. All manuscripts are submitted to a plagiarism check using Crossref Similarity Check Powered by iThenticate. Once the manuscript has been assessed for suitability by the editor, it will then be sent out for double-blind peer review by independent, anonymous expert referees. Peer review allows the manuscript to be evaluated and commented by independent experts who work within the same academic field. Figure 2 illustrates the peer review process (Taylor & Francis, n.d.). Reviewers are asked to read the manuscript and advise the Editor-in-Chief whether to publish the manuscript in that journal through comments, suggestions, and recommendations. This feedback is then given to the authors, telling them if any changes need to be made before the manuscript is ready for publication. If an author is given the opportunity to revise and re-submit the manuscript, then they can amend their article based on the reviewers' comments, resubmitting it with any or all changes made. Authors may be asked to make further revisions or the paper may be rejected if the editor thinks that the revisions made are not adequate. A revised article will go to the same reviewers, who will assess the updated article and make recommendations to the Editor-in-Chief (Floyd, 2019, p. 3). The

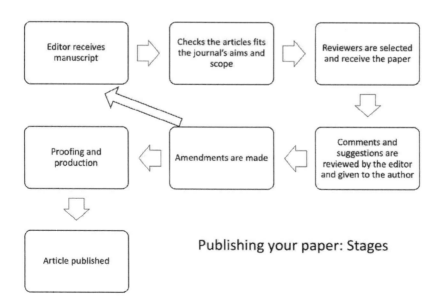

Figure 2. Taylor & Francis Author Services the peer review process.
Adapted from "Tips for publishing your research," by Taylor & Francis Group. (n.d.), p. 7. Retrieved from https://authorservices.taylorandfrancis.com/wp-content/uploads/2015/07/AS-tips-for-publishing-your-research.pdf. Adapted with permission

journal's Editor-in-Chief will collate reviews and make the decision whether to reject your article, ask for further revisions, or accept it (Floyd, 2019, p. 3).

If your submission gets rejected, do not give up! Ask the Editor-in-Chief for reader feedback, if this information has not been sent to you already. Also, consider a revision which takes into account the objections and recommendations of these reviewers. If, however, your article is accepted, it undergoes a preliminary round of copy editing by the *CCJRP* editorial team. Then, the manuscript is sent to the Taylor & Francis production department where it is entered into Taylor & Francis' Central Article Tracking System (CATS) and will receive a second round of copy editing. Authors will receive email notifications on the publishing agreement and when the manuscript's proof is ready for review. When checking proofs, it is recommended that authors respond to all queries when submitting the manuscript's corrections. Authors should check the proofs against the original text for accuracy as well as inspect that all figures, graphs, and tables are correct.

The final phase of the publication process is how to maximize your manuscript's readership. Taylor & Francis' iFirst online manuscript system provides an opportunity to post articles on *CCJRP* online shortly after the last production approval. Articles are given a Digital Object Identifier (DOI) and then posted online. iFirst articles can be cited instantly using the DOI. In effect, this lengthens the citation window and provides opportunities to increase the manuscript's Impact Factor (Floyd, 2019). Taylor & Francis also offers a variety of tools and tips to maximize the impact of authors' research (https://authorservices.taylorandfrancis.com/ensuring-your-research-makes-an-impact/). Through Taylor & Francis Online, each published author receives 50 eprints to share giving colleagues and friends free access to your article (Taylor & Francis, n.d.). To further support the promotion of *CCJRP* articles, Taylor & Francis Online offers authors the capability to track article-level metrics, which includes the number of downloads, citations (on Web of Science, CrossRef, and Scopus), and the Altmetric Attention Score (Floyd, 2019).

Conclusion

We are confident that this special issue makes a valuable contribution to the study of community colleges and to the literature on how to publish a peer review article. With this inaugural special issue: *Graduate Students' Research About Community Colleges*, we believe that our aim of helping to create a space to support graduate students and their research, encourage sustainability of publishing works throughout faculty and practitioners careers alike, and encourage mentoring of graduate students have been successful. The special issue offers guidance, developments, tips, and recommendations for practitioner-scholars at all stages of the publishing process on preparing a manuscript, selecting a journal, information on what to expect during peer review, production, and once the article is published. This article also offers the added insights on mentorship on how to publish in a peer review journal. Additionally, we hope the *CCJRP* reader gains greater awareness on how to navigate the publication process.

References

Coggburn, J. D., & Neely, S. R. (2015). Publish or perish? Examining academic tenure standards in public affairs and administration programs. *Journal of Public Affairs Education*, *21*(2), 199–214. doi:10.1080/15236803.2015.12001828

Ducheny, K., Alletzhauser, H. L., Crandell, D., & Schneider, T. R. (1997). Graduate student professional development. *Professional Psychology: Research and Practice*, *28*(1), 87. doi:10.1037/0735-7028.28.1.87

Floyd, D. L. (2019). Supporting and sustaining community college scholarship and research. *Community College Journal of Research and Practice*, *43*(1), 1–4. doi:10.1080/10668926.2018.1522830

Lechuga, V. M. (2011). Faculty-graduate student mentoring relationships: Mentors' perceived roles and responsibilities. *Higher Education*, *62*(6), 757–771. doi:10.1007/s10734-011-9416-0

Li Liew, C., Foo, S., & Chennupati, K. R. (2000). A study of graduate student end-users' use and perception of electronic journals. *Online Information Review*, *24*(4), 302–315. doi:10.1108/14684520010350650

McGuigan, G. S., & Russell, R. R. (2008). The business of academic publishing: A strategic analysis of the academic journal publishing industry and its impact upon the future of scholarly publishing. *E-JASL: the Electronic Journal of*

Academic and Special Librarianship, 9(3). Retrieved from http://southernlibrarianship.icaap.org/content/v09n03/mcguigan_g01.html

Offstein, E. H., Larson, M. B., Mcneill, A. L., & Mjoni Mwale, H. (2004). Are we doing enough for today's graduate student? *International Journal of Educational Management, 18*(7), 396–407.

Pasco, A. H. (2009). Should graduate students publish? *Journal of Scholarly Publishing, 40*(3), 231–240. doi:10.3138/jsp.40.3.231

Russell, R. D. (2008). The business of academic publishing: A strategic analysis of the academic journal publishing industry and its impact on the future of scholarly publishing. *Electronic Journal of Academic and Special Librarianship, 9*, 3.

Sweeney, A. E. (2000). Tenure and promotion: Should you publish in electronic journals? *Journal of Electronic Publishing, 6*, 2. doi:10.3998/3336451.0006.201

Taylor & Francis. (2019). *What to think before you start to write a journal article.* Retrieved from https://authorservices.taylorandfrancis.com/category/making-your-submission/

Taylor & Francis. (n.d.) *Tips for publishing your research.* Retrieved from https://authorservices.taylorandfrancis.com/wp-content/uploads/2015/07/AS-tips-for-publishing-your-research.pdf

Tolman, S., McBrayer, J. S., & Evans, D. (2019). Educational leadership doctoral faculty academic qualifications and practitioner experiences in Georgia. *International Journal of Doctoral Studies, 14*, 85–104. doi:10.28945/4179

Van Cott, D. L. (2005). A graduate student's guide to publishing scholarly journal articles. *PS: Political Science & Politics, 38*(4), 741–743.

Transformational Leadership and the Proliferation of Community College Leadership Frameworks: A Systematic Review of the Literature

Daniel Tarker

ABSTRACT

Due to a significant turnover of community college presidents, considerable research has emerged on the topic of community college leadership in recent years. What competencies, skills, knowledge, behaviors, and traits do community college presidents need to possess – especially when they face an unprecedented number of challenges including increased accountability, changing government funding models, and pressure to adopt significant curriculum reform to improve student completion and success rates? An unintended result of the expansion of the literature may be the emergence of a research phenomenon called construct proliferation. Construct proliferation occurs when multiple, competing theories and frameworks are developed to explain a similar phenomenon, which can impede research. One solution to this problem may be to use transformational leadership theory and the five-factor model as theories to help synthesize these multiple constructs. This article reviews the literature on community college leadership published since 2005 to demonstrate how transformational leadership and the five-factor model can inform community college leadership frameworks like AACC's Competencies for Community College Leaders and the major themes that have emerged in the literature on community college leadership over the past two decades. Findings indicate that both theories may be useful in addressing the issue of construct proliferation in the community college leadership literature.

A considerable amount of research has emerged over the past two decades on the leadership role of the community college president in the 21st century. This has been driven by multiple factors. One is the increasing turnover in community college presidents, in which experienced leaders are handing over the reins of their institutions to emerging leaders (Eddy, Sydow, Alfred, & Garza-Mitchell, 2015; Ellis & Garcia, 2017). Other factors involve the changing and uncertain postsecondary educational environment. These factors include declining enrollments, criticism over low completion rates, changing government funding models, growing accountability issues, and pressure to adopt major curriculum reform to increase student success and completion rates (Eddy, 2010; Phelan, 2016).

Since the founding of Joliet Junior College in Chicago 117 years ago, community colleges have been characterized as disruptive organizations within the United States higher education system (Nevarez & Wood, 2010; Phelan, 2016). By embracing open access policies, these historically two-year colleges have become the gateway to postsecondary educational opportunities for an increasingly diverse and non-traditional student body (Philibert, Allen, & Elleven, 2008). They have adopted a comprehensive educational mission that includes transfer degree pathways, workforce training, and community enrichment (Dadgar & Trimble, 2015; Vaughan, 2006). Over the past two decades, some have even expanded their offerings to include Bachelors of Applied Science (BAS) degrees, distance learning options, corporate training, international education, and more (Floyd, 2006; Kasper, 2003; Parrott, 1995; Romano, 2002). Yet, today community colleges face multiple existential threats as some question the ability of these complex educational organizations to maintain the very features that have made these institutions unique in the world of higher education – primarily their open access mission and comprehensive educational offerings (Phelan, 2016).

Recognizing the tumultuous and uncertain climate many community college presidents are entering as they take executive leadership roles at their institutions, numerous researchers (Eddy, 2012; Kezar, 2001a; McNair, 2009) have examined significant leadership themes that inform the contemporary community college presidency. In addition, advocacy organizations like the American Association of Community Colleges (AACC) (2005, 2013, 2018), The Aspen Institute & Achieving the Dream (2013) have sought to identify what personality traits, behaviors, competencies, values, and knowledge community college executives need to lead their organizations in a future that promises to be full of change and uncertainty (Eddy, 2010; Ellis & Garcia, 2017).

As happened within the broader field of leadership studies, this growing body of research on community college leadership has produced a phenomenon known as construct proliferation (Le, Schmidt, Harter, & Lauver, 2010). Construct proliferation occurs when multiple, competing theories are developed to explain the same phenomenon (Banks, Gooty, Ross, Williams, & Harrington, 2018). This can inadvertently impede research by creating a barrier to developing cumulative knowledge about a topic of inquiry (Shaffer, DeGeest, & Li, 2016).

Transformational leadership is one theory that researchers repeatedly return to when attempting to overcome the challenges of construct proliferation in leadership studies (Grove-Heuser, 2016; Robison, 2014; Roueche, Baker, & Rose, 1989). Developed as a theory for understanding political and organizational leadership, the behaviors described by transformational leadership theory have been thoroughly researched in educational settings within multiple cultural and geographic contexts around the world (Dumdum, Lowe, & Avolio, 2013). Findings consistently show that transformational leadership produces positive results within educational settings especially when measuring its impact on organizational innovation, organizational commitment, organizational citizenship behaviors, employee satisfaction, and perceptions of leadership effectiveness (Nguni, Sleegers, & Denessen, 2006). Therefore, it makes sense that transformational leadership theory would continue to be a dominant construct that researchers return to when attempting to synthesize all the frameworks around community college leadership.

In an effort to deepen understanding of transformational leadership, researchers have extended their inquiry to examine whether specific personality traits could be predictors of the emergence of particular behaviors associated with this leadership approach (Judge & Bono, 2000; Lim & Ployhart, 2004). One construct they have used to examine this relationship is the five-factor model (FFM), which measures five personality traits in subjects: *extravertism, openness to experience, neuroticism, conscientiousness,* and *agreeableness* (John & Srivastava, 1999). Using the five-factor personality traits model, researchers have found correlations between certain personality traits and distinct transformational leadership behaviors (Deinert, Homan, Boer, Voelpel, & Gutermann, 2015; Judge & Bono, 2000). This growing body of evidence indicates that transformational leadership theory could be enhanced by examining the specific personality traits that may predict the potential emergence of particular transformational leadership behaviors. In turn, transformational leadership and the five-factor model may be able to provide theoretically grounded insights into some of the major themes that recur throughout the literature on contemporary community college leadership. They may also be useful theories to inform research on the current iteration of AACC's (2018) *Competencies for Community College Leaders.*

Purpose of the literature review

The purpose of this systematic review of the literature is to explore how transformational leadership and the five-factor model can inform some of the dominant frameworks and themes that have emerged in the growing body of literature on community college leadership. It does this by providing a theoretical dimension to enhance understanding of presidential leadership in the community college context. In addition, it begins to address the issue of construct proliferation in the community college leadership literature by highlighting areas where different constructs or themes have the potential to be synthesized. After reviewing the methods used to review and analyze the literature, I will share the major findings and then discuss suggestions for future research, recommendations for practice, and the limitations of this study.

Methods

Systematic literature reviews provide a synthesis of the salient themes and issues on a topic of inquiry (Ridley, 2012). The purpose is to distill knowledge from a large body of research into a manageable article (Mulrow, 1994). To capture the dominant themes and issues on community college presidential leadership, the following methods were used to determine the research to include in this review of the literature and analyze the findings.

Inclusion and exclusion criteria

I primarily searched for articles, books, and reports published by peer-reviewed journals, academic publishing houses, or community college advocacy organizations between 2005 and 2018. I chose the year 2005 since that is when the American Association of Community Colleges (AACC) published its *Competencies for Community College Leaders*. This was a starting point for discussion about what skills, knowledge, traits, experience, and training community college leaders would require in the 21st century. I included research prior to 2005 to give context to themes that emerged like transformational leadership, which has been a subject of academic inquiry since the 1970s. For this review of the literature, I also analyzed book-length research by some of the leading scholars in community college leadership published since 2005.

Search methods

To identify research articles, I followed Webster and Watson (2002) recommendations to focus primarily on research published in leading journals, examine work from a broad spectrum of academic disciplines, and utilize the citations from one source to backtrack to another. Ridley (2012) described the latter as a snowball method of literature research. In addition to using Google Scholar as an academic search engine, I used a variety of journal databases including Academic Search Premier, JSTOR, and ProQuest to find relevant articles through the Oregon State University library. In order to develop a comprehensive view of the literature around community college leadership, I engaged in an iterative process refining the specificity of my searches as my research evolved, beginning with broad search terms like "leadership" and "community college leadership". As my search progressed, I narrowed my searches using a Boolean approach using terms like "transformational leadership" AND "community colleges". I continued this until I felt that I had achieved saturation, signaled by my increasing familiarity with the names of key researchers in this area of inquiry and the recurrence of similar themes.

Data analysis

I collected information on articles and books chosen for inclusion in a database with the relevant themes from each summarized. I coded the data until dominant categories emerged. As transformational leadership and the five-factor model began to recur as theories that could potentially inform AACC's leadership competencies and other community college leadership themes, I gave additional attention to identifying specifically how these constructs intersected with the dominant community college leadership themes in the literature.

Findings

The findings section is divided into three parts. The first shares background information on the issue of construct proliferation in the leadership literature and uses AACC's (2005, 2013, 2018) leadership competencies and the Aspen Institute and Achieving the Dream's (2013) *Crisis and Opportunity* framework to demonstrate how this phenomenon is impacting community college leadership studies. The second describes how transformational leadership theory and the five-factor model can be used to inform and synthesize AACC's leadership competencies and other emerging themes in the literature on community college leadership. Finally, the third section reviews other dominant themes in the literature on community college leadership with attention paid to how transformational leadership theory and the five-factor model can be used to expand our understanding of them.

Construct proliferation within community college leadership studies

One of the most significant challenges facing research on the phenomenon of leadership is the issue of construct proliferation (Dinh et al., 2014; Shaffer et al., 2016). Construct proliferation results from the development of multiple overlapping or competing theories or constructs to explain the same phenomenon (Le et al., 2010). This can create a barrier to the development of a comprehensive theory of leadership because the competing theories or frameworks may overlap or contradict one another (Banks et al., 2018).

The study of community college leadership is not exempt from this challenge. The following is a brief list of some of the theories that have been used to explore community college leadership: pervasive leadership (Strange & Banning, 2001), adaptive leadership (Randall & Coakley, 2007), situational leadership (Malm, 2008), servant leadership (Fulton-Calkins & Milling, 2005), participatory leadership (Kezar, 2001b), and democratic leadership (Nevarez, Wood, & Penrose, 2013). In addition, several advocacy organizations have developed their own community college leadership frameworks. To illustrate this phenomenon, two of the most prominent community college leadership frameworks will be examined – AACC's (2005, 2013, 2018) *Competencies for Community College Leaders* and the Aspen Institute and Achieving the Dream's (2013) *Crisis and Opportunity: Aligning the Community College Presidency with Student Success* report.

AACC's competencies for community college leaders

A brief exploration of the evolution of AACC's (2005, 2013, 2018) leadership competencies will demonstrate the challenge of developing a comprehensive leadership framework for community colleges. Examining the three iterations of AACC's (2005, 2013, 2019) *Competencies for Community College Leaders* framework revealed three overarching themes. One is an epistemological position that the leadership competencies described in the framework can be learned over time. Two is a broadening conception of leadership in community colleges that embraces participatory leadership approach rather than a hierarchical one. Third is a struggle to construct a framework with a manageable number of competencies that addresses all the skills, knowledge areas and personal traits that community college leaders need to develop as they advance through their careers.

The first iteration of AACC's (2005) competencies framework, which was developed through a series of Leading Forward summits with community college leaders and scholars between 2003–2005, consisted of a list of six competency areas (McNair, Duree, & Ebbers, 2011; Ross, 2017). The competencies included organizational strategy, resource management, communication, collaboration, community college advocacy, and professionalism (American Association of Community Colleges, 2005). Many of the themes that have informed subsequent iterations of this framework were established in this initial document. These include its position that leadership can be learned, a recognition that future leaders need to be developed to fill positions vacated due to retirement, and an awareness of the importance of transformational leadership behaviors.

The second iteration of AACC's (2013) leadership competencies extended the framework's epistemological position that leadership skills and knowledge areas can be learned over time (Eddy & Mitchell, 2017). It extends this position by constructing a three-stage timeline for what aspects of these competencies should be developed over a community college president's career. The first stage was the emerging leader on the pathway to a presidency. The second was the new CEO with up to three years of experience as a president. Finally, the third stage was the CEO with three or more years of experience in the position (American Association of Community Colleges, 2013). This feature of the construct has persisted in AACC's (2018) latest framework with the recommendation that the document should be used by aspiring community college leaders as a tool to identify which competencies they need to develop during each stage of their careers in order to move forward as organizational leaders.

The third iteration of AACC's (2018) leadership competencies expands the framework further by extending the participatory leadership focus embedded in the language of previous iterations. Participatory leadership is a collectivist theory of leadership that emphasizes teamwork, connectedness between different parts of the organizational system, empowerment rather than control, the importance of embracing diverse perspectives, and collaborative learning (Kezar, 2001b). The latest version of AACC's (2018) leadership competencies extends this approach by expanding the framework to address three additional employee groups: faculty, mid-level leaders, and senior-level leaders. In addition, the framework continued to offer guidance to aspiring CEOs, New CEOs with up to two years of experience as president, and CEOs with three or more years of experience as a president.

Another theme that emerged when examining the evolution of AACC's (2005, 2013, 2018) leadership competencies was a struggle to distill the competencies into a manageable framework. AACC's (2013) second iteration of the core competencies framework did not deviate significantly from the first version in terms of the competency categories except that it eliminated the professionalism competency, which was the area that most directly addressed the need for transformational leadership. The second iteration, therefore, reduced the competencies it focused on from six to five: organizational strategy; institutional finance, research, fundraising, and resource management; communication; collaboration; and community college advocacy.

Based on research conducted by its Commission on Leadership and Professional Development, the third iteration of AACC's (2018) competencies organized the competencies under 11 focus areas: organizational culture; governance, institutional policy, and legislation; student success; institutional leadership; institutional infrastructure; information and analytics; advocacy and mobilizing/motivating others; fundraising and relationship cultivation; communications; collaboration; and personal traits and abilities. Under the first 10 focus areas, the framework listed and described specific competencies to develop. With this redesign, the number of competencies within the framework expanded from five to 50. In addition, the eleventh focus area of the framework provides a section listing nine personal traits and abilities each of the employee categories should develop throughout their careers.

The third iteration of AACC's (2018) leadership competencies addresses some of the limitations that have been raised about previous editions. The addition of the organizational culture focus area is likely informed by feedback from researchers who identified this as a gap in previous iterations of the framework (Eddy, 2012). As a result, American Association of Community Colleges (2018) leadership competencies framework provides an exhaustive list of focus areas for leaders to consider. As data were collected on the response to the revised framework, research may find that there is a need for further synthesis of the focus areas in order to create a more manageable construct.

The crisis and opportunity framework

Dream's (2013) *Crisis and Opportunity: Aligning the Community College Presidency with Student Success* offered another framework to provide guidance to current and future community college presidents. This construct was developed by collecting data through interviews with 23 community college presidents and a discussion of the findings with two focus groups comprised of 40 current and retired community college presidents who were either Aspen Prize winners or who led an Achieving the Dream Leader College. Some possessed both credentials.

As with AACC's second iteration of its competencies framework, *Crisis and Opportunity* divided the qualities a community college president should possess into five categories. One was a deep commitment to student access and success. Two was a willingness to take significant risks to advance student success. Three was the ability to create lasting change within the college. Four was a strategic vision for the college and its students. Five was the ability to raise and allocate resources in ways aligned toward student success (The Aspen Institute & Achieving the Dream, 2013).

From construct proliferation to transformational leadership

A brief comparison of AACC's (2018) leadership competencies and the Aspen Institute and Achieving the Dream's (2013) *Crisis and Opportunity* framework will demonstrate the challenges created by construct proliferation. Competing frameworks can create confusion by utilizing different terminology to describe the same concept (Shaffer et al., 2016). Comparing features of AACC's competencies and the Aspen Institute's *Crisis and Opportunity* frameworks highlight this aspect of construct proliferation. For example, AACC's (2005, 2013, 2018) competencies included a focus area devoted to collaboration. The definition of collaboration in all three iterations of the framework uses words like responsiveness, cooperation, and ethics while emphasizing broad activities like promoting the success of the college community and sustaining the college's mission. In the third iteration, collaboration is changed from a competency to a focus area (American Association of Community Colleges, 2018). The competencies listed under this focus area include interconnectivity and interdependence, working with your supervisor, institutional team building, and collective bargaining. The emphasis of the language is on paying attention to the interdependence of faculty and staff, keeping lines of communication open, developing teams, and understanding collective bargaining agreements. In contrast, the *Crisis & Opportunity* report placed collaboration underneath the "being able to create lasting change within a college" category (p. 7). Its definition used words like listening and communication while emphasizing specific actions like eliminating silos between faculty and student support staff. Though both frameworks acknowledge that community college leaders need to possess the ability to collaborate and encourage interconnectivity between the different areas of their organizations, each described this competency using distinctly different language.

Transformational leadership as a solution to construct proliferation in community college leadership frameworks

One solution proposed to address the problem of construct proliferation in the leadership literature is to explore the different frameworks and theories that may overlap and interact with one another (DeRue, Nahrgang, Wellman, & Humphrey, 2011). In reviewing the literature, one dominant theory that scholars repeatedly used to synthesize leadership constructs was transformational leadership (Banks, McCauley, Gardner, & Guler, 2016). For example, Hoch, Bommer, Dulebohn, and Wu (2016) meta-analysis of emerging positive leadership theories found that theories such as authentic leadership and ethical leadership were highly correlated with transformational leadership, indicating that these new frameworks may be creating redundancy in the literature and contributing to construct proliferation.

In some instances, transformational leadership theory was not explicitly stated in this review of the literature on community college leadership, but terms such as transformative, transformational, or transforming were repeatedly used when describing the necessary qualities of a contemporary community college executive leader (Eddy, 2010; Nevarez & Wood, 2010; Phelan, 2016). In other cases, the theory was explicitly used such as in several recent dissertations. Robison (2014) examined how transformational leadership theory intersected with the first iteration of AACC's (2005) competencies for community college leaders within in-house community college leadership training programs in the southern United States. He found that the community college advocacy and professionalism competencies were the most emphasized while the resource management competency was the least. Transformational leadership behaviors addressed in the training programs included empowering others, creating a shared vision, understanding organizational culture, rewarding innovation and change, and working ethically (Robison, 2014). In a similar vein, Grove-Heuser (2016) studied the leadership behaviors among 12 female community college vice-presidents using Kouzes and Posner (2013) transformational leadership model. She found evidence that the majority of her participants used transformational leadership behaviors such as modeling the way, inspiring a shared vision, challenging the process, and enabling others to act, but found little evidence of them using the encouraging from the heart behavior.

Transformational leadership behaviors

In order to frame this literature review around the concept of how transformational leadership and the five-factor model can inform the dominant frameworks and themes emerging in the exploration of community college leadership, a brief description of these two theories and how they intersect is necessary.

Transformational leadership is part of a continuum of leadership behaviors called the full range leadership theory, which includes transactional and laissez-faire leadership (Bass, 1999; Boga & Ensari, 2009). Although researchers often depict transformational leadership as the more positive set of behaviors, research shows that an effective leader must be able to utilize both transformational and transactional leadership behaviors (Dartey-Baah, 2015). In fact, research indicates that a solid transactional relationship needs to be established before the leader can use transformational behaviors to elevate followers to higher levels of performance (Judge & Piccolo, 2004).

Transactional leadership is the more managerial focused leadership approach on the continuum. It involves appealing to the self-interest of followers in a task-oriented exchange of benefits for services (Bass, 1999; De Hoogh et al., 2005). According to Judge and Piccolo (2004), transactional leadership consists of three primary behaviors. *Contingent reward* involves the leader establishing rewards for behaviors. *Management by exception – passive* involves the leader waiting for the follower to make an error before intervening. *Management by exception – active* involves the leader monitoring the performance of followers, anticipating problems, and taking action before an error occurs. Benefits exchanged for meeting or exceeding work performance standards can include increased wages, employment stability, and promotions (Boga & Ensari, 2009; DeRue et al., 2011).

On the other end is transformational leadership, which is a relational approach to leadership characterized by the four I's: *idealized influence, individual consideration, inspirational motivation,* and *intellectual stimulation* (Bass, 1999; DeRue et al., 2011). Idealized influence involves the leader acting as a role model and articulating a sense of vision and mission for their followers (Bass, 1999). Inspirational motivation concerns how the leader aligns the values of the followers with those of the organization (Bass, 1999). Intellectual stimulation speaks to how the leader motivates followers to solve problems in new and creative ways (Bass, 1999). Finally, individual consideration describes how the leader treats each follower like an individual and gives them personal attention (Bass, 1999). Some researchers identify the combination of idealized influence and inspirational motivation, i.e., being a good role model who speaks to higher order values, as charisma (Abbas, Iqbal, Waheed, & Naveed Riaz, 2012).

Numerous studies over the past four decades have produced compelling evidence that transformational leadership behaviors are strongly correlated to organizational effectiveness, change, and innovation (Eisenbach, Watson, & Pillai, 1999; Erkutlu, 2008). In their meta-analysis of studies using the Multifactor Leadership Questionnaire, Lowe, Kroeck, and Sivasubramaniam (1996) concluded that transformational leadership was more strongly associated with organizational effectiveness as evaluated by subordinate measures and organizational measures, especially in terms of the dimension of charisma. Similarly, in their study of employee perceptions of organizational success, Boga and Ensari (2009) found that employees working within organizations undergoing a great deal of organizational change perceived their organizations to be more successful when led by a transformational leader. Abbas et al. (2012) likewise identified strong correlations between transformational leadership and innovation in educational institutions. Additionally, Bateh and Heyliger (2014) found a more positive relationship between transformational leadership behaviors and faculty feelings of job satisfaction in higher education institutions than with transactional behaviors.

Transformational leadership and the five-factor model

Scholars have also begun studying the connection between personality traits and transformational leadership using the five-factor model. These studies have produced compelling findings to suggest that certain personality traits could be predictors of the emergence of specific transformational leadership behaviors (De Hoogh, Den Hartog, & Koopman, 2005; Judge & Bono, 2000; Lim & Ployhart, 2004). The personality traits in the five-factor model include extravertism, agreeableness, conscientiousness, openness to experience, and neuroticism (De Hoogh et al., 2005). O'Boyle, Forsyth, Banks, Story, and White (2015) used some of the following adjectives to describe each of these personality traits. Extravertism involves sociability, dominance, and excitement. Agreeableness is characterized by being cooperative and trusting. Conscientiousness is described as being dutiful, dependable, and achievement striving. Openness to experience is depicted as being creative and broad-minded. Finally, neuroticism, also referred to as emotional stability, speaks to the levels of confidence and anxiety a person possesses.

Research shows there is strong evidence to support the connection between specific personality traits described by the five-factor model and particular transformational leadership behaviors. Deinert et al. (2015) found that both openness to experience and conscientiousness were associated with the overall transformational leadership approach, but conscientiousness had limited impact on perceptions around each of the transformative leadership behaviors. Extravertism was highly associated with idealized influence, inspirational motivation, and intellectual stimulation, but was unrelated to perceptions around individual consideration. Agreeableness was positively associated with idealized influence and inspirational motivation, but this trait was negatively associated with intellectual stimulation. Neuroticism was negatively associated with transformational leadership overall.

De Hoogh et al. (2005) additionally examined the interrelation between the five-factor model and transformational/transactional leadership in dynamic and stable environments. Using trait activation theory as a framework, they studied how the environment impacts the expression of certain personality traits and leadership behaviors as well as how they are perceived by followers. They found a correlation between perceptions of effective leadership based on whether the environment was dynamic or stable. Transformational leadership was perceived by followers as more effective within dynamic contexts and transactional as more effective within stable ones. Giving credence to the importance of the environment on the perception of leadership effectiveness, they found that agreeableness and conscientiousness were more closely associated with transformational leadership by employees in a stable environment whereas these traits were seen as impeding transformational leadership in dynamic environments. Adding to the importance of examining the emergence and perceptions of leadership in situational contexts, Lim and Ployhart (2004) identified transformational leadership as an effective mediator between personality traits and team performance in high-stress contexts.

In terms of community colleges, much of the current literature describes these organizations as dynamic workplaces that need to undergo significant changes to survive in a more uncertain higher education environment (Eddy et al., 2015; Phelan, 2016). This is supported by the language used in AACC's (2018) leadership competencies framework, which emphasizes that leaders need to be open to continual change. Also, the addition of a section on the nine personal traits leaders need to develop suggests a potential connection to the five-factor model. For instance, the forward-looking philosophy behavior could be informed by the openness to experience trait in the five-factor model. Likewise, the self-management and environmental scanning behavior may be informed by the five-factor model's conscientiousness trait. Therefore, developing a greater understanding of how personality traits and transformational leadership may interact with the environment could also shed light on how these theories may inform AACC's (2018) competencies framework.

Transformational leadership with in the AACC framework

When examining AACC's (2005, 2013, 2018) competencies, transformational leadership can also be found throughout the language of all the iterations of the framework. However, it is most explicitly referred to in the professionalism competency of the first iteration and the organizational strategy section of the second iteration. The third iteration does not explicitly identify developing transformational leadership behaviors. However, the section focusing on what personal traits community college leaders should develop identifies several behaviors that fall within the transformational leadership construct: authenticity, emotional intelligence, ethics, and embracing change.

The usefulness of transformational leadership to inform AACC's (2005, 2013, 2019) leadership competencies is supported by research on previous iterations of the framework. Hawkins (2009) identified significant skill and ability areas where AACC's (2005) competencies framework and transformational leadership overlap: active visionary, goal-directed, intuitive, trustworthy, ethical, tenacious, selfless, politically aware, motivator, decision-maker, systems thinker, and advocate. Skills and abilities described in AACC's (2005) competency framework not described in the transformational leadership framework according to Hawkins include listener, communicator, and team builder. However, Hawkins (2009) findings should be questioned since research shows transformational leadership is effective in improving team cohesion and performance, and the ability to inspire others through shared values requires strong communication skills (Dionne, Yammarino, Atwater, & Spangler, 2004).

Duree and Ebbers (2012) connected transformational leadership to AACC's (2005) competencies for community college leaders, but their work does so broadly without correlating specific behaviors to competencies. Their study focused on determining the preparedness of community college presidents based on AACC's *Community College Presidency Demographics and Leadership Preparation Survey* in order to determine what competencies require most development for future leaders. Respondents reported feeling competent with organizational strategy, resource management, communication, community college advocacy, and professionalism, but did not feel as competent with the collaboration competency.

In terms of analyzing the findings through the lens of transformational leadership, Duree and Ebbers (2012) connected the communication competency with inspiring a common vision by fostering shared values within the group, which speaks to the idealized motivation transformational leadership behavior. The collaboration competency was connected to individualized consideration by emphasizing that community college leaders need to "understand the various roles that are played in resolving issues and to empower others to take an active part in making decisions, managing conflict, and working effectively with constituents" (Duree & Ebbers, 2012, p. 45). They also linked the competencies of resource management and organizational strategy to transformational leadership in terms of their ability to manage significant challenges and retain college personnel, but it is unclear what specific behaviors relate to these competencies.

Despite these limitations, Duree and Ebbers (2012) found that community college presidents perceived these competencies to be beneficial, and they linked specific competencies to transformational leadership behaviors. In their study of community college presidents' perceived confidence with each competency when they assumed their executive roles, Duree and Ebbers (2012) identified that respondents did not rate themselves highly in terms of creating a "sense of collaboration" (p. 45). Connecting this to transformational leadership, they observed we know that transformational leaders in the community college setting must be able to understand the various roles that are played in resolving issues and to empower others to take an active part in making decisions, managing conflict, and working effectively with constituents. (p. 45)

Their study additionally found that 80% of respondents identified themselves as transformational leaders, which the researchers in this context associated with the professionalism competency. They also found that "only slightly more than two-thirds rated themselves prepared to competently demonstrate transformational leadership when they assumed their first presidency" (p. 45). Although this study begins to lay the groundwork for an association between AACC's competencies and transformational leadership, one limitation to the study is that the researchers do not evaluate each competency within the theoretical lens of transformational leadership.

Contemporary themes in community college leadership

This section will briefly highlight some of the dominant themes that emerged from reviewing the literature on community college presidential leadership published since 2005. These themes included engaging in change and innovation, transforming culture to focus on student success, articulating a vision, creating a learning organization, and practicing ethical leadership. Each of these themes were also emphasized in AACC's (2018) *Competencies for Community College Leaders* framework, so the findings in this section have the potential to inform this construct as well.

Engaging in change and innovation

A prevailing theme in the literature on community college leadership over the past 20 years is the need for executives to be able to lead substantive change within their organizations. A search of some recently published books on community college leadership found that the term change occurs 67 times in Ellis and Garcia (2017) and over 100 times in Eddy et al. (2015). The terms innovate or innovation occurred over 100 times in Phelan (2016). The terms transform, transformation, or transformational occurred over 100 times in Eddy et al. (2015). Yet as Phelan (2016) asserted, community colleges have become calcified in their approach to delivering education, and that this once disruptive sector of the higher education environment must once again embrace its risk-taking and innovative past in order to respond to the multiple challenges it faces. Eddy (2010) suggested that community college leaders cannot conceptualize change within their institutions as an episode, but rather as a long term process that may be better described as an era within the institution's history.

Nevarez and Wood (2010) argued that leadership and change are inextricably linked. Administration and management are associated with concepts like maintaining the status quo and focusing on tasks and procedures, behaviors associated with the transactional end of the full range leadership continuum (De Hoogh et al., 2005). Leadership, on the other hand, is associated with being an architectural designer, re-structuring the community college to be more effective and prosperous, which is associated with the transformational end of the full range leadership continuum (Eddy et al., 2015; Nevarez & Wood, 2010).

Change can be a slow process at community colleges, which can be a frustrating aspect of the environment to organizational leaders (Ellis & Garcia, 2017). Change often involves transforming the culture of the organization and the values of the faculty and staff within the institution (Eddy et al., 2015). As Heifetz, Grashow, and Linsky (2009) argued, resistance to change is often rooted in a fear of loss among those who may be impacted, which may result in a defensive response. Noting that the largest barrier to change are employees who want to maintain the status quo, Phelan (2016) suggested that getting employees involved in the process early by communicating the necessity of change, soliciting feedback, and providing professional development around the change initiative is key to its success.

Individual consideration and idealized influence are two behaviors within the transformational leadership approach that have been associated with helping employees overcome their fear of loss and resulting resistance to organizational change. Moreover, De Hoogh et al. (2005) found a corollary between the five-factor model trait openness to experience and subordinate perceptions of transformational leadership in dynamic environments. They suggested that leaders who are open to new experiences may be more likely to question the status quo and "find new opportunities to reach organizational goals" (p. 858). This perception did not persist in stable environments, likely due to subordinates perceiving the questioning of the status quo as too disruptive.

Phelan (2016) differentiated change at community colleges into two categories, sustaining innovation and disruptive. The first described small, incremental changes that occur over time while the other described major, paradigm-shifting changes. It is clear from researchers like Eddy et al. (2015) that community college leaders need to be focused on major, institution-wide transformation. One major area of change that Ellis and Garcia (2017), and Phelan (2016) described centers around the changing expectations of students, who are seeking more personalized, high-tech, interactive, and flexible options in college. As Eddy et al. (2015) pointed out, these changing expectations translate into increased competition for community colleges as four-year colleges and proprietary institutions have shown a willingness to address these gaps in the higher education marketplace. Phelan (2016) argued that universities have taken the community college's place as innovators by becoming early adopters of educational technologies like massive open online courses (MOOCs). Yet, changing student expectations and increased competition are only but two of the issues facing community college leaders.

Transforming culture to focus on student success

Understanding organizational culture has been identified as an important competency for community college presidents (Eddy et al., 2015). Not only will leaders need to be able to read culture, but they will also need to be able to change the culture of an organization. Yet as Phelan (2016) argued, institutional culture is one of the most significant barriers to organizational change because people within the organization will often revert to the way things have been done in the past. According to Eddy et al. (2015), one of the key aspects to changing organizational culture is transforming organizational values to focus on new norms like student success. It may also require developing cultures within the organization that embrace change rather than resist it. Given that cultural change involves reshaping the values and norms of an organization, transformational leadership again is a useful theory due to its association with creating innovative and adaptive organizations (Bass & Avolio, 1993).

In terms of reshaping culture, researchers repeatedly stress how important it is for community college leaders to make student success the core value of their leadership approach (Ellis & Garcia, 2017; Nevarez & Wood, 2010; The Aspen Institute & Achieving the Dream, 2013). This makes sense given that one of the primary criticisms of community colleges has been their inability to retain students and their persistently low completion rates. Adding to this concern, community college leaders also need to be aware of the barriers that produce low completion rates among Black, Hispanic, and Native American students (Nevarez & Wood, 2010). Therefore, leaders need to have a comprehensive knowledge of student success initiatives and frameworks so that they can use them to make sense of low retention rates – especially among nontraditional student populations (Ellis & Garcia, 2017; Nevarez & Wood, 2010).

Overall, the recommendation is that community college leaders develop the skills to change the culture of their organizations to promote student success. This is where transformational leadership intersects with the need to change organizational culture to make it more student success focused. Transformational leadership has been linked to organizational innovation with certain leadership behaviors influencing organizational change characteristics (Abbas et al., 2012). Idealized influence was found to positively correlate to idea generation, work commitment and idea implementation. Inspirational motivation correlated with all of the innovative behaviors above as well as idea promotion. Intellectual stimulation positively correlated with all of the above except work commitment. Individualized consideration positively correlated to idea generation and idea implementation (Abbas et al., 2012). As a leadership framework that can produce innovative change within an organizational culture, transformational leadership has the potential to help community colleges make the necessary innovations to improve student success.

Articulating a vision

Vision is a recurring attribute throughout the literature on community college leadership (Duree & Ebbers, 2012; Nevarez & Wood, 2010). In order to change the culture of an organization, a leader needs to articulate and reinforce a clear vision for where the institution is going. Vision can thus be defined as a mindset that focuses on the future and what cultural and organizational changes need to be made in order to achieve an ideal state of being. Within the *Crisis and Opportunity* framework (2013), for instance, strategic vision is a necessary ability that leaders must possess in order to transform community colleges into more student success focused organizations. In terms of leadership theory, vision can be associated with the openness to experience within the five-factor model as well as inspirational motivation which is described as the leader's ability to articulate shared values in order to motivate followers within transformational leadership theory (Robison, 2014). One of the major strengths of transformational leadership theory is the focus on the leader's ability to motivate followers by articulating a vision based on shared values (Eddy et al., 2015; Nevarez & Wood, 2010).

Creating a learning organization

In order to promote an organizational culture that encourages innovation and change, leaders need to turn their colleges into learning organizations. First described by Senge (1990), the learning organization adapts to its environment through the process of learning in order to remain competitive (Bass, 2000; Zagoršek, Dimovski, & Škerlavaj, 2009). Organizational learning in order to self-diagnose and manage problems must become part of the culture (Arachchi, 2012). While numerous constructs have been proposed to describe learning organization, Zagoršek et al. (2009) proposed four pillars in their study of the association between transformational leadership and organizational learning. These include information acquisition, distribution of information, information interpretation, and the resulting behavioral and cognitive changes. Although Bass (2000) predicted there would be a close association between transformational leadership behaviors and the creation and maintenance of learning organizations, Zagoršek et al.'s (2009) study found inconclusive evidence of this. They found both transformational and transactional leadership had an impact on different dimensions of the organizational learning process, but transformational leadership did have the most impact on changing the behavior and cognition of followers, which is the most important stage of organizational learning. However, more research should be conducted in this area since many behaviors describing effective leadership in learning organizations parallel behaviors often associated with transformational leadership such as systems thinking, shared vision, team building, and developing individuals (Arachchi, 2012).

Practicing ethical leadership

Ethical leadership is another significant dimension of community college leadership that pervades the literature. Nevarez and Wood (2014) asserted that bringing ethical theory to practice will aid community college leaders in making more informed decisions. They advocated for using the following ethical lenses. *Ethic of justice* focuses on issues of fairness and equality (Simola, Barling, & Turner, 2010. *Ethic of critique* involves considering how factors such as race, gender, sexual orientation, disability, and privilege inform discourse and scholarly inquiry (Murray, 2009). *Ethic of care* is concerned with developing relationships, understanding the subjective experience of others, and finding creative solutions to meet people's needs (Simola et al., 2010). Finally, *ethic of community* emphasizes the interests of the community over the interests of the individual in moral decision making among educational leaders (Furman, 2004).

Since its inception as a model, one of the primary features of transformational leadership theory has been its emphasis on ethics. Burns (1978), who is largely credited with first conceptualizing transformational leadership theory, believed that the role of the transformative leader was to elevate followers through their moral development. Thus, a core dimension of the transformational leadership approach is to raise the performance of followers by speaking to shared values in order to help them transcend self-interest and work toward the overall benefit of the organization (Carlson & Perrewe, 1995). The behavior of idealized influence is often associated with the ethical dimension of transformational leadership since that describes the role modeling aspect of this theory (Brown, Treviño, & Harrison, 2005).

Discussion

The review of the literature on contemporary community college leadership theories and frameworks found that this niche area of leadership suffers from construct proliferation, the development of multiple, competing theories. This can limit research due to the numerous overlapping definitions and frameworks to explain the same phenomena. One solution to address this is to begin synthesizing the different proposed frameworks together. In reviewing the literature on community college leadership, transformational leadership and, to a lesser degree, the five-factor model were found to inform AACC's (2005, 2013, 2018) leadership competencies and other themes that emerged in the literature. This suggests that these theories can expand our understanding of the dominant community college leadership themes identified and discussed in this review of the literature.

Future research

Research on transformational leadership within community colleges should continue. In addition to building off previous work exploring associations between AACC's (2005, 2013, 2018) leadership competencies and transformational leadership, future studies may also consider extending their investigations using the five-factor personality traits model to determine if certain personality traits are predictors of transformational leadership behaviors within the community college setting. In addition, research could be conducted examining associations between ethical leadership, learning organizations, and transformational leadership behaviors within the context of community colleges. Another research opportunity involves exploring the gap in the literature regarding the relevance and usefulness of the Aspen Institute and Achieving the Dream's (2013) *Crisis and Opportunity* framework much like researchers like McNair et al. (2011) and Eddy (2012) have done with AACC's leadership competencies. In addition, there are at least four avenues for further inquiry regarding the third iteration of AACC's (2018) *Competencies for Community College Leaders*. One is to investigate whether the framework needs to be simplified. Two is to study if leaders within community colleges perceive the focus areas and competencies identified in the framework to be beneficial to their work. Third is to examine how the framework can be used for professional development in both graduate school and in-house leadership training contexts. Fourth is to research how the five-factor model may be able to inform specific behaviors in the personal traits section of the construct. Some traits that may potentially be informed by the five-factor model include courage, self-management and environmental scanning, time management, forward-looking philosophy, and embracing change. Finally, the issue of construct proliferation needs to be addressed by designing studies that can begin to synthesize these leadership frameworks and constructs into one comprehensive community college leadership theory.

Recommendations for practice

This review of the literature establishes that AACC's leadership competencies, transformational leadership, and the five-factor model could be useful in developing professional development programs for community college leaders. Therefore, it is useful to review how these findings can be used to inform graduate school, in-house mentoring, and other on the job leadership development programs for community college leaders.

Community college leadership training

Although graduate school is one clear avenue for developing AACC's (2018) leadership competencies and transformational leadership behaviors, many community college leaders report their graduate studies have limited impact on the development of these competencies and behaviors (McNair, 2009). However, they did see the potential of graduate school programs being able to help develop these leadership competencies. Therefore, more work should be done to embed AACC's core competencies and transformational leadership theory into graduate school programs for community college leaders.

McNair (2009) also found that community college presidents in her study identified on the job training and work experience as more beneficial than graduate school training. On the job training can come in multiple forms including in-house developed leadership programs, mentor-protégée relationships, and progressive work experience (McNair, 2009). In terms of in-house, grow-your-own leadership programs, research shows that these can have a positive impact in developing AACC's competencies and transformational leadership behaviors (Caldwell, 2016; Robison, 2014). Another option that research shows can be valuable is to develop mentor-protégée programs (Duree & Ebbers, 2012). These programs have the benefit of being more cost effective than an in-house leadership program, but they also require the participation of veteran leaders who can contribute their time and expertise to these efforts (McNair, 2009). Finally, progressive job experience was found to be the most effective way to develop AACC's competencies in future leaders in a study of the perceptions of deans, vice-presidents, and presidents within the Pennsylvania community college system (Boswell & Imroz, 2013). Therefore, community colleges engaged in developing in-house leadership development programs should consider how to integrate AACC's leadership competencies and transformational leadership into their curriculum or program.

Limitations

There are two limitations to this study. Given the constraints for the length of this article, a comprehensive presentation of all the findings about community college presidential leadership was not feasible. Therefore, this presentation of findings is not exhaustive, but rather highlights some of the most dominant themes identified. In addition, I chose to frame the literature review around the concept of using transformational leadership theory and to a lesser extent the five-factor model to address the issue of construct proliferation in the leadership literature. This approach also narrowed the focus of this literature review. It also introduces the potential for bias on the researcher's part. While this approach emerged as part of the research process, I understand other approaches should be explored to address the issue of construct proliferation in the community college leadership literature. However, I hope this review of the literature highlights the potential for future research and practice to focus on using transformational leadership theory and the five-factor model to inform constructs like the third iteration of AACC's (2018) leadership competencies and other emerging themes about community college leadership.

Closing

This systematic review of the literature explored the literature on community college leadership published by academic journals and advocacy organizations between 2005 and 2018. Considerable research has been conducted on community college leadership over the past two decades due to the retirement of senior leaders and the changing environment in which these organizations operate. Findings suggest that the multiple frameworks and theories that have emerged may be impacted by a research phenomenon known as construct proliferation. Researchers use construct proliferation as a term to describe the emergence of multiple theories and frameworks to describe the same phenomenon. This can negatively impact research efforts due to an inconsistency in the terms and definitions used to describe aspects of the subject of inquiry. Two community college leadership frameworks developed by advocacy organizations were explored to highlight this phenomenon. An examination of the three iterations of the American Association of Community College's (2005, 2013, 2018) leadership competencies demonstrated that the developers of the framework have struggled to synthesize all the dimensions of community college leadership into a simplified framework. Likewise, the Aspen Institute and Achieving the Dream's (2013) *Crisis and Opportunity* framework provides similar recommendations as the AACC construct, but the terminology used is inconsistent between the reports, contributing to the research challenges created by construct proliferation. In addition, the findings of this study identified transformational leadership and, to a lesser extent, the five-factor model as possible theories that can help mitigate the issue of construct proliferation in the literature on community college leadership. These theories were found to inform both the AACC (2018) competency framework and many of the major themes that emerged in the study of the literature on community college leadership. This review of the literature also identified that further research needs to be conducted exploring the intersection of transformational leadership, the five-factor model, and AACC's (2018) leadership competencies. In terms of practice, these constructs should be taken into consideration when developing or revising graduate curriculum and in-house programs on community college leadership.

References

Abbas, G., Iqbal, J., Waheed, A., & Naveed Riaz, M. (2012). Relationship between transformational leadership style and innovative work behavior in educational institutions. *Journal of Behavioral Sciences, 22*(3), 18–32. Retrieved from http://pu.edu.pk/home/journal/24

American Association of Community Colleges. (2005). *Competencies for community college leaders.* Retrieved from http://www.aacc.nche.edu/Resources/competencies/Documents/compentenciesforleaders.pdf

American Association of Community Colleges. (2013). *Competencies for community college leaders*, 2nd ed. Retrieved from https://www.aacc.nche.edu/wp-content/uploads/2017/09/AACC_Core_Competencies_web.pdf

American Association of Community Colleges. (2018). *Competencies for community college leaders*, 3rd ed. Retrieved from https://www.aacc.nche.edu/wp-content/uploads/2018/11/AACC-2018-Competencies_111618_5.1.pdf

Arachchi, K. C. (2012). Transformational leadership and learning organizations. *The Journal of Adyapana Sanwada, 4,* 71–89. Retrieved from http://192.248.16.117:8080/research/bitstream/70130/2191/1/Transformational%20leadership.pdf

Banks, F. C., Gooty, J., Ross, R. L., Williams, C. E., & Harrington, N. T. (2018). Construct redundancy in leader behaviors: A review and agenda for the future. *The Leadership Quarterly, 29*(1), 236–251. doi:10.1016/j.leaqua.2017.12.005

Banks, G. C., McCauley, K. D., Gardner, W. L., & Guler, C. E. (2016). A meta-analytic review of authentic and transformational leadership: A test for redundancy. *The Leadership Quarterly, 27*(4), 634–652. doi:10.1016/j.leaqua.2016.02.006

Bass, B. M. (1999). Two decades of research and development in transformational leadership. *European Journal of Work and Organizational Psychology, 8*(1), 9–32. doi:10.1080/135943299398410

Bass, B. M. (2000). The future of leadership in learning organizations. *Journal of Leadership Studies, 7*(3), 18–40. doi:10.1177/107179190000700302

Bass, B. M., & Avolio, B. J. (1993). Transformational leadership and organizational culture. *Public Administration Quarterly, 17*(3–4), 112–121. doi:10.1080/01900699408524907

Bateh, J., & Heyliger, W. (2014). Academic administrator leadership styles and the impact on faculty job satisfaction. *Journal of Leadership Education, 13*(3), 34–49. doi:10.12806/V13/I3/R3

Boga, I., & Ensari, N. (2009). The role of transformational leadership and organizational change on perceived organizational success. *The Psychologist-Manager Journal, 12*(4), 235–251. doi:10.1080/10887150903316248

Boswell, R. A., & Imroz, S. M. (2013). The AACC leadership competencies: Pennsylvania's views and experiences. *Community College Journal of Research and Practice, 37*(11), 892–900. doi:10.1080/10668926.2012.676497

Brown, M. E., Treviño, L. K., & Harrison, D. A. (2005). Ethical leadership: A social learning perspective for construct development and testing. *Organizational Behavior and Human Decision Processes, 97*(2), 117–134. doi:10.1016/j.obhdp.2005.03.002

Burns, J. M. (1978). *Leadership.* New York, NY: Open Road Integrated Media.

Caldwell, A. (2016). *Effectiveness of Arkansas community colleges'(ACC) leadership institute (LI) in competency development.* (Doctoral dissertation). Retrieved from https://search.proquest.com/openview/270d521c02ea4f2b8ed0e57b58ae6da4/1?pq-origsite=gscholar&cbl=18750&diss=y (Accession No. 10140645)

Carlson, D. S., & Perrewe, P. L. (1995). Institutionalization of organizational ethics through transformational leadership. *Journal of Business Ethics, 14*(10), 829–838. doi:10.1007/BF00872349

Dadgar, M., & Trimble, M. J. (2015). Labor market returns to sub-baccalaureate credentials: How much does a community college degree or certificate pay? *Educational Evaluation and Policy Analysis, 37*(4), 399–418. doi:10.3102/0162373714553814

Dartey-Baah, K. (2015). Resilient leadership: A transformational-transactional leadership mix. *Journal of Global Responsibility, 6*(1), 99–112. doi:10.1108/JGR-07-2014-0026

De Hoogh, A. H., Den Hartog, D. N., & Koopman, P. L. (2005). Linking the big five-factors of personality to charismatic and transactional leadership; perceived dynamic work environment as a moderator. *Journal of Organizational Behavior: The International Journal of Industrial, Occupational and Organizational Psychology and Behavior, 26*(7), 839–865.

De Hoogh, A. H., Den Hartog, D. N., Koopman, P. L., Thierry, H., Van Den Berg, P. T., Van der Weide, J. G., & Wilderom, C. P. (2005). Leader motives, charismatic leadership, and subordinates' work attitude in the profit and voluntary sector. *The Leadership Quarterly, 16*(1), 17–38. doi:10.1016/j.leaqua.2004.10.001

Deinert, A., Homan, A. C., Boer, D., Voelpel, S. C., & Gutermann, D. (2015). Transformational leadership sub-dimensions and their link to leaders' personality and performance. *The Leadership Quarterly, 26*(6), 1095–1120. doi:10.1016/j.leaqua.2015.08.001

DeRue, D. S., Nahrgang, J. D., Wellman, N. E. D., & Humphrey, S. E. (2011). Trait and behavioral theories of leadership: An integration and meta-analytic test of their relative validity. *Personnel Psychology, 64*(1), 7–52. doi:10.1111/j.1744-6570.2010.01201.x

Dinh, J. E., Lord, R. G., Gardner, W. L., Meuser, J. D., Liden, R. C., & Hu, J. (2014). Leadership theory and research in the new millennium: Current theoretical trends and changing perspectives. *The Leadership Quarterly, 25*(1), 36–62. doi:10.1016/j.leaqua.2013.11.005

Dionne, S. D., Yammarino, F. J., Atwater, L. E., & Spangler, W. D. (2004). Transformational leadership and team performance. *Journal of Organizational Change Management, 17*(2), 177–193. doi:10.1108/09534810410530601

Dumdum, U. R., Lowe, K. B., & Avolio, B. J. (2013). A meta-analysis of transformational and transactional leadership correlates of effectiveness and satisfaction: An update and extension. In *Transformational and Charismatic Leadership: The Road Ahead 10th Anniversary Edition* (pp. 39–70). Bingley, UK: Emerald Group Publishing Limited.

Duree, C., & Ebbers, L. (2012). The AACC competencies in action. *New Directions for Community Colleges, 159*, 41–52. doi:10.1002/cc.20025

Eddy, P. L. (2010). *Community college leadership: A multidimensional model for leading change*. Sterling, VA: Stylus Publishing, LLC.

Eddy, P. L. (2012). A holistic perspective of leadership competencies. *New Directions for Community Colleges, 2012*(159), 29–39. doi:10.1002/cc.20024

Eddy, P. L., & Mitchell, R. L. G. (2017). Preparing community college leaders to meet tomorrow's challenges. *Journal for the Study of Postsecondary and Tertiary Education, 2*, 127–145. doi:10.28945/3884

Eddy, P. L., Sydow, D. L., Alfred, R. L., & Garza-Mitchell, R. L. (2015). *Developing tomorrow's leaders: Context, challenges, and capabilities*. New York, NY: Rowman & Littlefield.

Eisenbach, R., Watson, K., & Pillai, R. (1999). Transformational leadership in the context of organizational change. *Journal of Organizational Change Management, 12*(2), 80–89. doi:10.1108/09534819910263631

Ellis, M. M., & Garcia, L. (2017). *Generation X presidents leading community colleges: New challenges, new leaders*. New York, NY: Rowman & Littlefield.

Erkutlu, H. (2008). The impact of transformational leadership on organizational and leadership effectiveness: The Turkish case. *Journal of Management Development, 27*(7), 708–726. doi:10.1108/02621710810883616

Floyd, D. L. (2006). Achieving the baccalaureate through the community college. *New Directions for Community Colleges, 135*, 59–72. doi:10.1002/cc.248

Fulton-Calkins, P., & Milling, C. (2005). Community-college leadership: An art to be practiced: 2010 and beyond. *Community College Journal of Research and Practice, 29*(3), 233–250. doi:10.1080/10668920590901176

Furman, G. C. (2004). The ethic of community. *Journal of Educational Administration, 42*(2), 215–235. doi:10.1108/09578230410525612

Grove-Heuser, J. R. (2016). Women as transformational leaders: Learning to lead in the community college (Doctoral dissertation). doi: 10.15760/etd.2702

Hawkins, C. (2009). Leadership theories-managing practices, challenges, suggestions. *Community College Enterprise, 15*(2), 39–62. Retrieved from: http://www.schoolcraft.edu/pdfs/cce/15.2.39-62.pdf

Heifetz, R. A., Grashow, A., & Linsky, M. (2009). *The practice of adaptive leadership: Tools and tactics for changing your organization and the world*. Boston, MA: Harvard Business Press.

Hoch, J. E., Bommer, W. H., Dulebohn, J. H., & Wu, D. (2016). Do ethical, authentic, and servant leadership explain variance above and beyond transformational leadership? A meta-analysis. *Journal of Management, 44*(2), 501–529. doi:10.1177/0149206316665461

John, O. P., & Srivastava, S. (1999). The big five trait taxonomy: History, measurement, and theoretical perspectives. *Handbook of Personality: Theory and Research, 2*, 102–138. Retrieved from http://t.personality-project.org/revelle/syllabi/classreadings/john.pdf

Judge, T. A., & Bono, J. E. (2000). Five-factor model of personality and transformational leadership. *Journal of Applied Psychology, 85*(5), 751–765. doi:10.1037/0021-9010.85.5.751

Judge, T. A., & Piccolo, R. F. (2004). Transformational and transactional leadership: A meta-analytic test of their relative validity. *Journal of Applied Psychology, 89*(5), 755–768. doi:10.1037/0021-9010.89.5.755

Kasper, H. T. (2003). The changing role of community college. *Occupational Outlook Quarterly, 46*(4), 14–21. Retrieved from: https://stats.bls.gov/careeroutlook/2002/winter/art02.pdf

Kezar, A. (2001a). Understanding and facilitating organizational change in the 21st century. *ASHE-ERIC Higher Education Report, 28*(4), 147. Retrieved from: https://files.eric.ed.gov/fulltext/ED457711.pdf

Kezar, A. (2001b). Understanding organizational fit in a participatory leadership environment. *Journal of Higher Education Policy and Management, 23*(1), 85–101. doi:10.1080/13600800020047261

Kouzes, J. M., & Posner, B. Z. (2013). *The student leadership challenge: The five practices of exemplary leadership*. San Francisco, CA: Jossey-Bass.

Le, H., Schmidt, F. L., Harter, J. K., & Lauver, K. J. (2010). The problem of empirical redundancy of constructs in organizational research: An empirical investigation. *Organizational Behavior and Human Decision Processes, 112*(2), 112–125. doi:10.1016/j.obhdp.2010.02.003

Lim, B. C., & Ployhart, R. E. (2004). Transformational leadership: Relations to the five-factor model and team performance in typical and maximum contexts. *Journal of Applied Psychology, 89*(4), 610–621. doi:10.1037/0021-9010.89.4.610

Lowe, K. B., Kroeck, K. G., & Sivasubramaniam, N. (1996). Effectiveness correlates of transformational and transactional leadership: A meta-analytic review of the MLQ literature. *The Leadership Quarterly, 7*(3), 385–425. doi:10.1016/S1048-9843(96)90027-2

Malm, J. R. (2008). Six community college presidents: Organizational pressures, change processes and approaches to leadership. *Community College Journal of Research and Practice, 32*(8), 614–628. doi:10.1080/10668920802103813

McNair, D. E. (2009). Preparing community college leaders: The AACC core competencies for effective leadership & doctoral education. *Community College Journal of Research and Practice, 34*(1–2), 199–217. doi:10.1080/10668920903388206

McNair, D. E., Duree, C. A., & Ebbers, L. (2011). If I knew then what I know now: Using the leadership competencies developed by the American Association of Community Colleges to prepare community college presidents. *Community College Review, 39*(1), 3–25. doi:10.1177/0091552110394831

Mulrow, C. D. (1994). Systematic reviews: Rationale for systematic reviews. *BMJ, 309*(6954), 597–599. doi:10.1136/bmj.309.6954.597

Murray, S. J. (2009). Aporia: Towards an ethic of critique. *Aporia, 1*(1), 8–14. Retrieved from https://www.researchgate.net/profile/Stuart_Murray2/publication/26645036_Aporia_Towards_an_Ethic_of_Critique/links/00b7d525d73793c73b000000.pdf

Nevarez, C., & Wood, J. L. (2010). *Community college leadership and administration: Theory, practice, and change* (Vol. 3). New York, NY: Peter Lang. doi:10.3726/978-1-4539-1712-1

Nevarez, C., & Wood, J. L. (2014). *Ethical leadership and the community college: Paradigms, decision making, and praxis*. Charlotte, NC: Information Age Publishing, Inc.

Nevarez, C., Wood, J. L., & Penrose, R. (2013). *Leadership theory and the community college: Applying theory to practice*. Sterling, VA:: Stylus Publishing, LLC.

Nguni, S., Sleegers, P., & Denessen, E. (2006). Transformational and transactional leadership effects on teachers' job satisfaction, organizational commitment, and organizational citizenship behavior in primary schools: The Tanzanian case. *School Effectiveness and School Improvement, 17*(2), 145–177. doi:10.1080/09243450600565746

Parrott, S. 1995. Future learning: Distance education in community colleges. *ERIC Digest*, Retrieved from https://files.eric.ed.gov/fulltext/ED385311.pdf

Phelan, D. J. (2016). *Unrelenting change, innovation, and risk: Forging the next generation of community colleges*. New York, NY: Rowman & Littlefield.

Philibert, N., Allen, J., & Elleven, R. (2008). Nontraditional students in community colleges and the model of college outcomes for adults. *Community College Journal of Research and Practice, 32*(8), 582–596. doi:10.1080/10668920600859913

Randall, L. M., & Coakley, L. A. (2007). Applying adaptive leadership to successful change initiatives in academia. *Leadership & Organization Development Journal, 28*(4), 325–335. doi:10.1108/01437730710752201

Ridley, D. (2012). *The literature review: A step-by-step guide for students* (2nd. ed.). Thousand Oaks, CA: SAGE Publications Inc.

Robison, G. E. (2014). *The utilization of the American association of community colleges leadership competencies in public community college leadership development programs in the Southern United States* (Doctoral dissertation). Retrieved from http://thescholarship.ecu.edu/bitstream/handle/10342/4382/Robison_ecu_0600E_11159.pdf?sequence=1&isAllowed=n

Romano, R. M. (2002). *Internationalizing the community college*. Washington, DC: Community College Press.

Ross, J. C. (2017). *Leadership competencies for the community college department chairperson* (Doctoral dissertation). Retrieved from http://aquila.usm.edu/dissertations/1208

Roueche, P. E., Baker, G. A. I. I. I., & Rose, R. R. (1989). *Shared vision: Transformational leadership in American community colleges*. Washington, DC: The Community College Press.

Senge, P. (1990). *The fifth discipline: The art and science of the learning organization*. New York, NY: Currency Doubleday.

Shaffer, J. A., DeGeest, D., & Li, A. (2016). Tackling the problem of construct proliferation: A guide to assessing the discriminant validity of conceptually related constructs. *Organizational Research Methods, 19*(1), 80–110. doi:10.1177/1094428115598239

Simola, S. K., Barling, J., & Turner, N. (2010). Transformational leadership and leader moral orientation: Contrasting an ethic of justice and an ethic of care. *The Leadership Quarterly, 21*(1), 179–188. doi:10.1016/j.leaqua.2009.10.013

Strange, C. C., & Banning, J. H. (2001). *Educating by design: Creating campus learning environments that work*. San Francisco, CA: Jossey-Bass.

The Aspen Institute & Achieving the Dream. (2013). *Crisis and opportunity: Aligning the community college presidency with student success*. Retrieved from https://assets.aspeninstitute.org/content/uploads/files/content/upload/CEP_Final_Report.pdf

Vaughan, G. B. (2006). *The community college story* (3rd ed). Washington, DC: Community College Press.

Webster, J., & Watson, R. T. (2002). Analyzing the past to prepare for the future: Writing a literature review. *MIS Quarterly, 26*(2), xiii–xxiii. Retrived from http://www.jstor.org/stable/4132319

Zagoršek, H., Dimovski, V., & Škerlavaj, M. (2009). Transactional and transformational leadership impacts on organizational learning. *Journal for East European Management Studies, 14*(2), 144–165. Retrieved from https://www.econstor.eu/bitstream/10419/84118/1/766754006.pdf

Do Community College Students Demonstrate Different Behaviors from Four-Year University Students on Virtual Proctored Exams?

Tammi Kolski and Jennifer L. Weible

ABSTRACT
eLearning instruction has become an accepted means of delivering a quality education to higher education students, with community college online learning enrollment rates rising annually. Consistent with the desires of eLearning students for convenience and flexibility, educators utilize virtual proctored exams to safeguard against academic dishonesty behaviors in their students. Research is absent in exploring the actual behaviors displayed by students while taking their online exams under the watchful "eye" of a webcam. Examining 37 higher education students from two Midwest institutions, the aim of this study was to determine if community college students and four-year university students differed in their behaviors when taking exams using a virtual proctor. This study also examined the two populations for differences in willingness to use this technology, with 88% of the total student population choosing to use virtual proctoring for their exam sessions. Of the 40 behaviors observed, eight of the top 10 overall behaviors were demonstrated by both populations of students. This research can further instructor knowledge about exam taking behaviors of students so when they are reviewing virtual proctored exam recordings, they are doing such as objectively as possible.

Currently, community college students comprise nearly half of the postsecondary students in the United States (Fong et al., 2017), particularly those in rural or other underserved populations (Wise, 2015). Community colleges have historically provided alternatives to four-year university campuses through access to vocational preparation courses and workforce development training programs for students with financial concerns or long commutes (Kasper, 2003). With financial constraints rising for higher education settings being reflected in community colleges as well, institutions of all types are moving towards eLearning in order to increase efficiency while still providing a quality education (Wolff, Wood-Kustanowitz, & Ashkenazi, 2014).

According to the National Center for Education Statistics (2016), in the fall of 2014, collectively for both two-year and four-year institutions, 28.46% of students completed a degree fully online. eLearning, also referred to in literature as online learning or web-based distance education (Baron & Crooks, 2005; Hannay & Newvine, 2006; Johnson, 2015; Li & Irby, 2008; Westra, 2016), has become an acceptable means of delivering quality, accessible education to students in many different disciplines (Li & Irby, 2008). Students enroll in eLearning for the convenience, adjustability in their learning, flexibility in fulfilling their daily responsibilities, and to show potential employers a commitment to obtaining more knowledge or learning new skills (Westra, 2016; Wise, 2015; Wolff et al., 2014). In addition, eLearning affords some students an opportunity for an education which would otherwise not be available because of the need for child care or additional academe costs (e.g., commuting expenses, parking fees, purchasing of textbooks) (Shea & Bidjerano, 2014).

With the increase in eLearning opportunities, educators question how to maintain academic rigor when considering methods of completing online course exams (Watson & Sottile, 2010). Even with a multitude of assessment possibilities available for instructors to validate a student's knowledge, the traditional multiple-choice type exams are still being used across disciplines (Garg & Lee, 2015). Placing an increased emphasis on grades, students in all settings may opt to cheat to achieve higher exam scores (McCabe, Trevino, & Butterfield, 2001), with the perception often being that cheating online would be easier (Poutre, Hedlund, & Nau, 2015; Watson & Sottille, 2010). In their study that surveyed 273 college alumni, Yardley, Rodriguez, Bates, and Nelson (2009) found that 81.7% of their participants reported having engaged in some form of cheating during their undergraduate career. Whereas, King and Case (2014) found in their study involving 1,817 higher education students that 29% of students taking an online course in 2013 cheated on an exam.

Some institutions that are concerned with academic integrity in their eLearning courses often consider utilizing virtual proctoring software designed to protect against academic dishonesty behaviors of their students when taking online exams (Baron & Crooks, 2005; Karim, Kaminsky, & Behrend, 2014). Virtual proctoring, also referred to in the literature as remote proctoring or online exam proctoring (Karim et al., 2014; Marcus, Raul, & Ramirez-Velarde, 2008; Rios & Liu, 2017; Rose, 2009) is defined as a student being on his or her own computer, establishing a secure Internet connection and having a functional webcam (and microphone) that subsequently video records the student's behaviors remotely while the student completes the exam (Beaudry, 2013). The technology associated with monitoring of online examinations can provide a level of security for exam integrity similar to that which can be achieved with a human proctor in live proctoring locations (Rose, 2009). Virtual proctoring can be a valuable resource to higher education eLearning programs because of its functionality, low cost, and help in deterring students from engaging in acts of academic dishonesty by cheating (Bedford, Gregg, & Clinton, 2009).

In spite of the importance that universities are placing on the use of virtual proctoring, currently there is little research that describes student behaviors while taking exams in any learning environment other than studies on behavioral indications of test anxiety or students engaged in acts of academic dishonesty (e.g., cheating). The purpose of this study was to examine the behaviors of students at the community college and the four-year university level across a variety of courses in order to document the behaviors that students display while completing exams using a virtual proctor. Additionally, this study explored if there was a statistically significant difference between community college students and four-year university students in the number of documented behaviors or in their willingness to utilize virtual proctoring.

Literature review

As the number of students in higher education institutions continues to rise, first it is important to identify through a review of literature the profile of higher education learners. Next, it is relevant to review assessments of student learning followed by purposeful uses of virtual proctoring, considerations about academic integrity, human compared to virtual proctoring options, and student exam taking behaviors.

Higher education learners

Today's student taking higher education courses differs from a student in the previous millennium. Not only are technological advances integrated into the daily lives of students, the diversity of environments in which individuals learn has changed. The demographics of a higher education student are changing. In the 1970's, 72% of college students were between the ages of 18 and 24 (Hussar & Bailey, 2013). The population of college students today age 25–34 is being projected to increase by 20%, aged 35 and older up to a 25% growth, between 2010 and 2021 (Hussar & Bailey, 2013). Often, high school students are taking college courses through dual-enrollment programs (Kronholz, 2011) as well as college students today being more likely to work full time concurrently (Carnevale, Smith, Melton, & Price, 2015). When compared to eLearning students, 55% of four-year university students attended school exclusively full-time (Hussar & Bailey, 2013) and required less self-discipline and had less effective time management skills (Hachey, Wladis, & Conway, 2014). Additionally, students who attended a four-year institution also had a greater need for peer and instructor support for their learning and higher levels of extrinsic achievement and motivation (Johnson, 2015).

To best match the demographic profile of today's college students, many institutions are incorporating eLearning courses or fully online degrees into their program offerings. The number of students taking at least one eLearning course increased by 3.9% over the previous year (Allen & Seaman, 2016). Specifically, community colleges had the highest enrollment rates in online learning for all higher education institutions and they hosted about half of all online learning programs in the United States (Hachey et al., 2014; Ruth, Sammons, & Poulin, 2007). Ellefson (2015) conducted a meta-analysis to evaluate community college student perceptions of eLearning and found that interactions among course content, the instructor, and the students yielded the greatest potential for learning and of having obtained a quality (online) education. Greater flexibility in where and when to study, a flexible pace, faster program completion, and financial needs dominated the research reviewed (Aslanian & Clinefelter, 2013; DaCosta, Kinsell, Seok, & Tung, 2010; Ellefson, 2015; Smith, 2014; Strachota, 2003). Hannay and Newvine (2006) found that because adult, part-time, online students spent more time reading textbooks and studying they felt they learned more in their online courses. In eLearning courses, having an instructor and peer social presence (e.g., timely feedback, demonstrating care about students as individuals) were strong influences on student expectations, motivation, engagement, participation, collaboration, satisfaction, retention, and success (Ellefson, 2015; Kuo, Walker, Schroder, & Belland, 2014; Strachota, 2003). However, within the literature, there is little written of how assessments for online students in community colleges and four-year universities are conducted or the effects on students while taking these exams.

Assessments of student learning

In academia, assessment of knowledge, as well as understanding how and why it is used, is important. When assessments are utilized to gauge student learning and appraise an individual's knowledge, understanding, abilities, or skills, it can help create productive instruction that leads to more effective learning (Marriott & Lau, 2008). Assessment procedures, broadly, and examinations in particular, are institutionally-created mechanisms that serve to shape the learning process among students, having been designed primarily to provide information about student, teacher, school, and system performance (Havnes, 2004). For example, technology-enabled assessments can be used to reduce the instructor's time in administration and scoring of traditional assessments while enabling educators and students to engage more with the course content (Marriott & Lau, 2008). Institutions concerned about academic integrity in their eLearning courses can consider implementing virtual proctoring software designed to deter students from engaging in dishonest academic behaviors (Baron & Crooks, 2005; Karim et al., 2014).

Purposeful use of virtual proctoring

To maintain academic rigor and a quality educational experience in all learning spaces, many instructors feel that some form of exam proctoring is needed (Alessio, Malay, Maurer, Bailer, & Rubin, 2017; Harmon & Lambrinos, 2008; Hollister & Berenson, 2009). On-campus college environments often utilize human proctors (e.g., the instructor) or testing centers. Many eLearning programs offer students the option of traveling to a designated testing center location or using a virtual proctor to complete online exams.

Research by Bedford et al. (2009) on both faculty and students and their use of virtual proctoring concluded that this technology may be a valuable resource to higher education eLearning programs because of its functionality, low cost, and help in deterring students from engaging in acts of academic dishonesty by cheating. Several studies found that with biometric student authentication, video environmental scanning, and audio recording features, the technology associated with monitoring of the online examination can provide security of exam integrity comparative to what can be accomplished with a human proctor in live proctoring locations (Bedford et al., 2009; Harmon, Lambrinos, & Buffolino, 2010; Rose, 2009; Watson & Sottile, 2010). Recently, research has examined various aspects of virtual proctoring. Atoum, Chen, Liu, Hsu, and Liu (2017) evaluated the use of online exam proctoring systems and found that in order to improve the overall detection performance of virtual proctoring for the detection of some cheating behaviors, the software systems needed to rely upon the "ignition of multiple behavior cues" (p. 3). Using a wearcam to detect the iris, Tsukada, Shino, Devyer and Kanade (2011) found what a subject sees in relation to their behavior, assisted with comprehensive behavior profiling. In a self-reporting inventory about test-taking behaviors, Stenlund, Lyrén, and Eklöf (2018) found "from a performance perspective, the most successful test taker profile is that of a calm test taker" (p. 412). In other words, instructors may be looking for calm behaviors during test taking as a metric of academic honesty. However, without examining what behaviors students actually exhibit, instructors must be careful not to make assumptions about students' cheating based on the movements that they exhibit.

Virtual proctoring seeks to dissuade the perception that because students are separated by distance, it is difficult to monitor assessments and, therefore, cheating on exams is easier and more common among online learning students (Poutre et al., 2015; Watson & Sottile, 2010). Querying the benefit of a virtual proctor in preventing students from cheating, Moten, Fitterer, Brazier, Leonard, and Brown (2013) found that 43% of their student participants thought the use of a webcam would prevent cheating. Karim et al. (2014) found that remote proctoring did not directly affect test-taker reactions and performance, but it did decrease instances of cheating. Students being aware of the instructors reviewing their recorded exam session can also reinforce the importance of academic integrity. Wilkinson's (2009) research on undergraduate nursing students found that students are, at least sometimes, engaged in cheating due to their lack of knowledge of that institution's academic integrity policy or their having a lack of understanding on what constituted a cheating violation for the particular course. In the eLearning environment, utilizing virtual proctoring tools with students taking exams can provide the instructor reasonable assurance that academic integrity has been maintained during the online exam process (Cluskey, Ehlen, & Raiborn, 2011), meanwhile, upholding exam integrity, academic rigor and university standards of a quality education. Thus, technology innovations such as virtual proctoring are improving instructor confidence that online summative assessments can be as secure as those completed in the presence of a human proctor in a traditional classroom setting or university testing center location (James, 2016).

Traditionally instructors within a classroom or lecture hall on campus have proctored exams within the same physical space that the student is taking their exam. Also testing centers, where students travel to for taking their exam, have been used. However, scheduling inconveniences, travel time, and other potential costs associated with these options are in opposition to the reason's students have chosen to take eLearning courses (Shea & Bidjerano, 2014; Wise, 2015). Additional drawbacks to the use of human proctors are a single person monitoring multiple students concurrently; poor training; lack of motivation; becoming tired, distracted, or overwhelmed; and being more subjective or biased towards the student they are proctoring (Marcus et al., 2008; Rios & Liu, 2017). Therefore, the subjectivity and variability of human proctoring does not guarantee a cheating-free evaluation (Rose, 2009).

A second option for proctoring exams is the use of a virtual proctor. Research by Marcus et al. (2008) found the use of a virtual proctor to be at least as reliable as a human proctor. A virtual proctor focuses on one student and acts in a more objective, unbiased, and uninterrupted way than does a human proctor (Marcus et al., 2008). Respondus Monitor, a technological tool to provide proctoring services, requires that student's complete exams in front of a computer-mounted or manufacturer-installed webcam that provides the instructor with live streaming images of the student and their environment while taking the assessment ("Respondus Monitor", 2016). Use of software like Respondus LockDown Browser ("LockDown Broswer", 2016) prevents students from searching for answers on the Web while taking exams through a course management system. To ensure that the student completing the exam is, in fact, the enrolled student, instructors could ask students to capture an image of a government issued photo identification, or the university photo student ID. Recording a 360 degree scan of their environment, including the specific area adjacent to their computer, captures video and sound to provide a complete monitoring solution and ensures other electronic devices, other people, or other external resources are not used to assist the student in answering exam questions. The exam session is also recorded and stored for the instructor to review after the student completes their exam ("An Insider's View", 2017).

Examinee behaviors

There is no clear theoretical framework to draw from to understand student exam taking behaviors, in either virtual proctored or human proctored sessions. Predominantly the literature on proctoring and test-taking behaviors focuses on issues of cheating and exam security (Baron & Crooks, 2005; Cluskey et al., 2011; Moten et al., 2013) or behaviors related to test anxiety (Duraku, 2016; Gerwing, Rash, Gerwing, Bramble, & Landine, 2015), rather than on student test-taking actions or non-cheating related behaviors. Rios and Liu (2017) captured examinee test-taking behavior by correlating keystroke usage and response time data. Mirza and Staples (2010) studied nurse practitioner students with webcam invigilation and concluded that it was an uncomfortable experience (e.g., recurrent feelings of fear, nervousness, and apprehension, which could also be attributed to a state of anxiousness). However, in an exploratory study, Romero-Zaldivar, Pardo, Burgos, and Delgado Kloos (2012) were the first to suggest identifying behaviors of engineering students during virtually proctored exams. At this time, however, no research has been found that examines the behaviors that students exhibit while taking virtually proctored exams, which has important implications when it comes to the instructor reviewing the recorded exam sessions. As research indicated previously that calm behaviors were reflective of good test taking (Stenlund et al., 2018), understanding what students are actually doing while taking a test is necessary in order to normalize these behaviors and help instructors to identify cheating in terms of the behavior observed. Remembering that what we assume to be happening may not be what is really happening is crucial (Razer & Friedman, 2017).

Methods

This exploratory video study used archived recordings of higher education students taking eLearning exams to provide a window into behaviors that students displayed. Students used Respondus Monitor software as a virtual proctor when taking their exams within their eLearning course.

Participants and setting

The participants for this study ($n = 37$) were drawn from all students who were previously enrolled in a 2014–2017 undergraduate psychology course (14 courses total) taught by one of this study's researchers who had self-selected to use virtual proctoring for their exams. Each course included four or five virtually proctored exams. The study population consisted of students from two Midwestern United States higher education institutions: a large public four-year university ($n = 24$) and a community college ($n = 13$) (a two-year institution). The self-identified gender classifications were 34 (92%) females and three (8%) males, which was consistent with the approximate gender composition of all students enrolled in these courses.

An email was sent to all eligible students (community college students, $n = 70$; four-year university students, $n = 202$) requesting their participation in this research. Each student who responded affirmatively ($n = 37$) then provided written consent for inclusion of their recorded exams sessions following completion of the course. Student participants were advised, as a part of their consent, that partaking in this study would not compromise their academic standing at either institution. All courses were completed, with final grades submitted, prior to this study commencing. The Institution Review Board (IRB) process for both institutions was followed, with approval for this research secured from both institution's IRB.

Tools and instruments

At the start of each course, students were given the opportunity to choose either a human proctor or a virtual proctor for completing their course exams. Students who made the decision to use a human proctor and/or an approved testing center location were excluded from this research analysis. Both institutions in this study had a contract with Respondus, Inc. for use of Respondus Monitor as a virtual proctoring tool. All Respondus Monitor recordings of student's exam taking sessions during the semesters in 2014 to 2017 were embedded within the Blackboard LMS used by both higher education institution for course delivery. The exam recordings were available to both institutions, as Respondus Monitor clients. Students were educated about use of the Respondus Monitor software in the course syllabus and embedded Blackboard course materials; specifically, that it was for the purpose of online exam security and that they were being recorded. At the start of each exam, during the mandatory setup steps prior to the exam being activated, the student acknowledged the use and purpose of Respondus Monitor. The next setup steps included validating student authentication, a slow 360-degree environment scan, a webcam check, and finally an acknowledgement that the student understood the parameters of the web invigilated exam session, including the institutions' policies on academic integrity.

Data collection

The data used for this study was drawn from archived video recordings (25.43 hours) captured and stored by the virtual proctoring system during the psychology course exams. The video recordings from consented students had names removed and a participant identification number assigned to each set of videos to protect the identity of each student participant during analysis.

Analysis

For analysis, the number of total students in both settings who selected the use of virtual proctoring was determined and percentages of the population for each institution, and across both institutions, were calculated. The first course exam for each consented participant was viewed in entirety. Additionally, one randomly selected exam (of the remaining three or four available) for each participant was also viewed for analysis. The time to complete each exam was recorded.

Prior to this study, the authors developed and piloted an observational protocol that consisted of the use of an observational matrix. The matrix consisted of exam taking behavioral indicators found in the research (Weinberger, Schwartz, & Davidson, 1979) as well as behaviors noted through instructional experiences of this study's researchers, with emerging codes for behaviors added when needed. Blank spaces were available in the matrix to document unexpected behaviors displayed.

Based on the observational protocol, the matrix was used to document and quantify observed behaviors using the a priori and emerging codes. For example, a student who scratched his or her nose while looking to the right would have a tally added to the matrix for scratches some part of the head/face as well as eye gaze shifting to the right. Each behavior was totaled for each student and entered into a spreadsheet (see Table 1).

Table 1. 10 most frequently observed behaviors by college population.

Most Frequently Observed Behaviors of the Two-Year College Students	n	Most Frequently Observed Behaviors of the Four-Year University Students	n
Gaze Right	694	Gaze Right	287
Props Head	525	Lick/Bite Lip	213
Scratches Some Part of Head/Face	445	Lip Reads Questions	210
Rubs/Picks Lips	369	Props Head	196
Shifts/Squirms in Seat	368	Scratches Some Part of Head/Face	195
Pursed Lips	362	Rubs/Picks Lips	88
Eyebrows Furrowed	352	Shifts/Squirms in Seat	79
Lick/Bite Lip	268	Twists/Plays with Hair	71
Lip Reads Questions	207	Eyebrows Furrowed	67
Head Moves Left-Right	182	Clears Throat	62

The frequency counts of behaviors observed were entered in the Statistical Package for the Social Sciences (SPSS) for statistical analysis. The observed behavior counts from the coding matrix were statistically analyzed using descriptive statistics to determine the frequency of each behavior and to identify possible relationships between the behaviors of the community college and four-year university students. In addition, we conducted independent samples t-test analysis to examine differences in behaviors. Four behaviors were found to be statistically different between the community college and the four-year university students: clearing throat, lip licking or biting, lip reading questions, and scratching some part of the head/face (see Table 2).

The Pearson's chi-squared test is applied to categorical data to determine if a given distribution of the categories (e.g., institution attended) are independent with respect to some factor (e.g., behaviors observed on web invigilated exams) (Creswell, 2015). The chi-squared test concluded that the null hypothesis was rejected in this study (χ^2 = .000), meaning which higher education institution the students attended occurred with equal probability.

Findings

For this study, 37 students from both a two-year community college and a four-year university completed their course exams using the Respondus Monitor virtual proctor technology. Our findings from this study add to the research in several areas: 1) to identify similarities and differences in patterns of behavior between both groups of students including use of the virtual proctoring tool, 2) begin to establish a baseline of identified behaviors exhibited by the two populations of higher education students while taking virtually proctored exams, 3) posit underlying causes of these behaviors, and 4) add to literature on online cheating within higher education settings.

First, we found that the majority of all students utilized virtual proctoring and displayed similar behaviors. Regarding the willingness of community college students and four-year university students to utilize virtual proctoring instead of a human proctor, 88% (238 out of 272) of all the students in this study

Table 2. Behaviors showing a statistical difference in the means of the community college (two-year institution) and four-year university students.

			Independent Samples Test			
Behavior	t	df	Sig. (2-tailed)	Mean	Standard Deviation	Institution
Clears throat	−3.296	58	0.002	4.7692	7.81189	2-year
				0.0787	1.68027	4-year
Lip licking or biting	−4.659	58	0.000	16.3846	13.93759	2-year
				5.7021	4.10151	4-year
Lip reads questions	−3.526	58	0.001	16.1538	17.54445	2-year
				9.4681	6.68500	4-year
Scratches some part of head/face	−2.292	58	0.026	15.0000	10.74709	2-year
				9.4681	6.68500	4-year

selected the Respondus Monitor tool for virtual proctoring of each of their eLearning course exams. When separated by institution type, 80% (56 out of 70) of community college students and 90% (182 out of 202) of the university students elected to use Respondus Monitor for virtual proctoring of each of their course exams. In addition, the length of time a student took to complete their exam ranged from 10 minutes to 49 minutes, with the average length for the community college students being approximately 25 minutes ($M = 24.50$ minutes, $SD = 10.31$) and approximately 22 minutes for the four-year university students ($M = 22.13$ minutes, $SD = 8.41$) to complete their exams. Collectively, the length of time a student took to complete their exam was approximately 23 minutes ($M = 23.03$ minutes, $SD = 9.11$). During the exam set up, 100% of the students acknowledged understanding the use and purpose of Respondus Monitor as a form of securing exam integrity: 82% of the students showed a picture ID, and 84% completed the environment scan slowly, providing a clear visualization of the student's workspace being free from books, notes, other people, or electronic devices.

When documenting behaviors identified on video, most were associated with motor agitation or shifting gaze. Of the 40 behaviors included within the observational protocol, the students' gaze shifting in some direction occurred most often. Students propping their head or scratching some part of their head or face while taking their exam occurred frequently as did a gesture associated with the student's lips (e.g., lip licking or biting; rubbing of the lips; pursed lips). There were multiple occurrences of some form of motor agitation (e.g., stretching, actions suggestive of cracking the neck, or moving the head directionally) in addition to students reading the exam questions while taking their exams (either audibly or lip reading). Students taking a deep breath, sighing, or consuming food or beverages while taking their exams were of fewer occurrences. The behaviors of overt perspiration, chewing or smoking tobacco, and demonstrating a rigid posture as identified in the literature were not demonstrated by any of the students observed.

When comparing the frequency of behaviors observed between the community college and four-year university students, more similarities than differences were found (see Table 1 above). Both populations of college students were observed to demonstrate the following eight behaviors: eye gaze shifting to the right, propping their head with their hand, scratching some part of the head or face, lip licking or lip biting, rubbing or picking at the lips, shifting or squirming in their seat, eyebrows furrowed, and lip reading the exam questions. Statistically, only four behaviors were found to be significantly different between populations (see Table 2 above). Two of the top 10 frequently observed behaviors to occur by the community college students, but not by the four-year university students, were moving their head left to right and having pursed lips. Two other behaviors found to occur by the four-year university students, but not the community college students, were twisting or playing with the hair and clearing their throat.

Discussion

This study adds to the research on virtual proctoring by identifying and comparing behaviors exhibited by two populations of higher education students. First, the implementation of virtual proctoring in both institution's eLearning courses did not appear to produce a barrier for either population of students. While the characteristics of community college and four-year institution students have been shown to differ, the chi-squared test and the calculated percentages indicate that the populations are utilizing virtual proctoring at similar levels. Understanding that many community college students are employed full-time (Carnevale et al., 2015) or are the primary caretakers of children or adults (Wolff et al., 2014) while also taking college courses, we posited that having the option to take virtual proctored exams appears to best meet the needs of the majority of eLearning students, particularly those in community college. However, with both populations utilizing the virtual proctor the majority (88%) of the time, and 80% of eLearning community college students and 90% of the four-year university students utilizing virtual proctoring, there is still room for growth.

Not being considered a digital native (Westra, 2016) or having a different level of maturity (Wise, 2015) could explain why fewer community college students than four-year university students chose to use virtual proctoring for their exams. To help support students in making the choice to use virtual proctoring, instructors should build educational content into their eLearning courses that offers clear instructions how to implement the virtual proctoring software. Furthermore, directions to access technology support and increased instructor availability to answer questions about the virtual proctor implementation could help motivate even more students to utilize this technology.

Secondly, results of this study show that eight of the top 10 overall observed behaviors were demonstrated by both the community college students and the four-year university students. Overt perspiration and experiencing shortness of breath were documented by Weinberger et al. (1979) as physiological responses of test anxiety. Neither of these behaviors were observed during the 25.43 hours of exam recordings watched. However, we posit that the behaviors of motor agitation (e.g., head propping, squirming/shifting in their seat, scratching some part of the head/face, or lip licking, biting, or rubbing) are physiological anxiety responses demonstrated by many people diagnosed with an anxiety disorder (American Psychiatric Association [APA], 2013). Additionally, lip licking or biting and scratching some part of the head/face were two of four behaviors found to be significantly different between the means of community college and four-year university students. Future research is needed in this area to examine what behaviors students demonstrate as an anxiety coping strategy. Instructors could then incorporate in their eLearning courses effective coping techniques to help students' decrease their anxiety when preparing for and/or taking their online exams.

Finally, within this study we found no evidence of cheating. Although the research of Stenlund et al. (2018) found that calm behaviors were indicative of good test taking behaviors, our study found that the prominently displayed behaviors of propping the head, scratching head/face, and lip licking or biting were not linked to evidence of cheating based on the environment scans. In addition, the behavior observed most often in both populations of students involved the shifting of the student's gaze to the right. While an abnormal gaze does not directly constitute a cheating behavior in a classroom setting or human proctored testing location, a directional change in the student's gaze has been found to be a strong indicator of cheating (Atoum et al., 2017). An assumption could be made that the student had access to material to their right accounting for their gazing in that direction to see the material. However, the review of the 360-degree environment scan recorded by each student prior to the start of their exam revealed that no student had any print material or electronic devices to their right that may have drawn their gaze for potential assistance in answering their exam questions, leading us to believe that this movement was for other reasons. Therefore, unlike previous research (Atoum et al., 2017; Stenlund et al., 2018), instructors viewing video from virtually proctored exams cannot assume that a shifting gaze or agitated movements and behaviors indicate that academic improprieties are occurring. Our study provides a broader perspective than previous research on the behaviors that students exhibit when taking face-to-face tests by examining behaviors while using a virtual proctor. However, more research is needed to connect student mental processes to the behaviors demonstrated before generalizations can be made.

This exploratory research begins to document the behaviors which students in both community college and four-year university settings present while taking exams using a virtual proctor. By identifying the behaviors that are displayed by both groups of students, we were able to provide a baseline of common student behaviors that may support instructors in identifying behaviors indicative of test anxiety and coping mechanisms that may be suspicious and warrant further investigation. Addressing this topic can alleviate an instructor's reluctance to utilize virtual proctoring and improve student comfort, as well as enhance academic integrity protocols.

Implication for future research and practice for community colleges

The purpose of this study was to document behaviors displayed by eLearning students using a virtual proctor and to establish a baseline for future research. As more community colleges and four-year universities offer eLearning courses, the need to integrate virtual proctoring for reasons of exam security and academic integrity is well documented in the literature (Baron & Crooks, 2005; Harmon

& Lambrinos, 2008; Hollister & Berenson, 2009; Karim et al., 2014). As other research on behaviors observed during actual virtually proctored exam sessions is not available, this study begins to document the behaviors that are displayed with the intent that future studies will build upon this to better understand both physiologically as well as psychologically what these observed behaviors mean. In addition, more research is needed to compare behaviors while test taking with human versus virtual proctors. Finally, this research could offer insight into the behaviors that instructors could look for during virtually proctored exam sessions that could suggest instances of a lapse of academic integrity, in addition to disproving, or validating, instructors' assumptions about the meaning of student behaviors when watching the recordings of virtually proctored exams.

References

Alessio, H. M., Malay, N., Maurer, K., Bailer, A. J., & Rubin, B. (2017). Examining the effect of proctoring on online test scores. *Online Learning*, 21(1), 146–161. doi:10.24059/olj.v21i1.885

Allen, L. E., & Seaman, J. (2016). *Online report card: Tracking online education in the United States.* Retrieved from http://onlineLearningsurvey.com/reports/onlinereportcard.pdf

American Psychiatric Association (APA). (2013). *Diagnostic and statistical manual of mental disorders (DSM-5®).* Washington, DC: American Psychiatric Association.

Aslanian, C. B., & Clinefelter, D. L. (2013). *Online college students 2013: Comprehensive data on demands and preferences.* Retrieved from http://www.learninghouse.com/wpcontent/uploads/2013/06/Online-College-Students-2013_Final.pdf

Atoum, Y., Chen, L., Liu, A. X., Hsu, S. D., & Liu, X. (2017). Automated online exam proctoring. *IEEE Transactions on Multimedia*, 19(7), 1609–1624. doi:10.1109/TMM.2017.2656064

Baron, J., & Crooks, S. M. (2005). Academic integrity in web based distance education. *TechTrends*, 49(2), 40–45. doi:10.1007/bf02773970

Beaudry, R. (2013, October 15). *What is a remote proctor?* Retrieved from https://bvirtualinc.com/what-is-a-remote-proctor

Bedford, W., Gregg, J., & Clinton, S. (2009). Implementing technology to prevent online cheating: A case study at a small southern regional university (SSRU). *MERLOT Journal of Online Learning and Teaching*, 5(2), 230–238.

Carnevale, A. P., Smith, N., Melton, M., & Price, E. W. (2015). *Learning while earning: The new normal.* Retrieved from https://cew.georgetown.edu/cew-reports/workinglearners/#full-report

Cluskey, G. R., Jr., Ehlen, C. R., & Raiborn, M. H. (2011). Thwarting online exam cheating without proctor supervision. *Journal of Academic and Business Ethics*, 4, 1–7.

Creswell, J. W. (2015). *Educational research: Planning, conducting, and evaluating quantitative and qualitative research* (5th ed.). Upper Saddle River, NJ: Pearson Education, Inc.

DaCosta, B., Kinsell, C., Seok, S., & Tung, C. (2010). Comparison of instructors' and students' perceptions of the effectiveness of online courses. *Quarterly Review of Distance Education*, 11(1), 25–36.

Duraku, Z. H. (2016). Factors influencing test anxiety among university students. *The European Journal of Social and Behavioural Sciences*, 18, 2325–2334.

Ellefson, G. J. (2015). *Student perceptions of online education at community colleges: A review of the literature* (Doctoral dissertation). Available from ProQuest Dissertations & Theses Global. (1700208801)

Fong, C. J., Davis, C. W., Kim, Y., Kim, Y. W., Marriott, L., & Kim, S. (2017). Psychosocial factors and community college student success: A meta-analytic investigation. *Review of Educational Research*, 87(2), 388–479. doi:10.3102/0034654316653479

Garg, N., & Lee, E. (2015, June). Mixed-format exams in higher education: Assessment of internal consistency reliability. In *1st International Conference on Higher Education Advances (HEAD'15)* (pp. 10–17), Editorial Universitat Politècnica de València. doi:10.3389/fpsyg.2015.00010

Gerwing, T. G., Rash, J. A., Gerwing, A. M., Bramble, B., & Landine, J. (2015). Perceptions and incidence of test anxiety. *The Canadian Journal for the Scholarship of Teaching and Learning*, 6(3), 1–14. doi:10.5206/cjsotl-rcacea.2015.3.3

Hachey, A. C., Wladis, C. W., & Conway, K. M. (2014). Do prior online course outcomes provide more information than GPA alone in predicting subsequent online course grades and retention? An observational study at an urban community college. *Computers & Education*, 72, 59–67. doi:10.1016/j.compedu.2013.10.012

Hannay, M., & Newvine, T. (2006). Perceptions of distance learning: A comparison of online and traditional learning. *Journal of Online Learning and Teaching*, 2(1), 1–11.

Harmon, O. R., & Lambrinos, J. (2008). Are online exams an invitation to cheat? *The Journal of Economic Education*, 39(2), 116–125. doi:10.3200/JECE.39.2.116-125

Harmon, O. R., Lambrinos, J., & Buffolino, J. (2010). Assessment design and cheating risk in online instruction. *Online Journal of Distance Learning Administration*, 13, 3. Retrieved from https://www.learntechlib.org/p/52616/

Havnes, A. (2004). Examination and learning: An activity-theoretical analysis of the relationship between assessment and educational practice. *Assessment & Evaluation in Higher Education*, 29(2), 159–176. doi:10.1080/0260293042000188456

Hollister, K., & Berenson, M. (2009). Proctored versus unproctored online exams: Studying the impact of exam environment on student performance. *Decision Sciences Journal of Innovative Education, 7*(1), 271–294. doi:10.1111/dsji.2009.7.issue-1

Hussar, W. J., & Bailey, T. M. (2013, January). *Projections of education statistics to 2021* (40th). Retrieved from https://nces.ed.gov/pubs2013/2013008.pdf

An insider's view of online proctoring. (2017, February 23). *University Business.* Retrievedfrom https://www.universitybusiness.com/article/insider-s-view-online-proctoring

James, R. (2016). Tertiary student attitudes to invigilated, online summative examinations. *International Journal of Educational Technology in Higher Education, 13,* 1–13. doi:10.1186/s41239-016-0015-0

Johnson, G. M. (2015). On-campus and fully-online university students: Comparing demographics, digital technology use and learning characteristics. *Journal of University Teaching & Learning Practice, 12*(1), 1–13.

Karim, M., Kaminsky, S., & Behrend, T. (2014). Cheating, reactions, and performance in remotely proctored testing: An exploratory experimental study. *Journal of Business & Psychology, 29*(4), 555–572. doi:10.1007/s10869-014-9343-z

Kasper, H. T. (2003). The changing role of community college. *Occupational Outlook Quarterly, 46*(4), 14–21.

King, D. L., & Case, C. J. (2014). E-cheating: Incidence and trends among college students. *Issues in Information Systems, 15*(1), 20–27.

Kronholz, J. (2011). High schoolers in college. *Education Next, 11*(3), 26–31. Retrieved from http://educationnext.org/high-schoolers-in-college/

Kuo, Y. C., Walker, A. E., Schroder, K. E. E., & Belland, B. R. (2014). Interaction, internet self-efficacy, and self-regulated learning as predictors of student satisfaction in online education courses. *The Internet and Higher Education, 20,* 35–50. doi:10.1016/j.iheduc.2013.10.001

Li, C.-S., & Irby, B. (2008). An overview of online education: Attractiveness, benefits, challenges, concerns and recommendations. *College Student Journal, 42*(2), 449–458.

LockDown Browser. (2016). Retrieved from https://www.respondus.com/products/lockdown-browser/

Marcus, A., Raul, J., & Ramirez-Velarde, R. (2008). *Addressing secure assessments for Internet-based distance learning: Still an unresolvable issue?* Retrieved from http://www.ufrgs.br/niee/eventos/RIBIE/2008/pdf/adressing_secure.pdf

Marriott, P., & Lau, A. (2008). The use of on-line summative assessment in an undergraduate financial accounting course. *Journal of Accounting Education, 26*(2), 73–90. doi:10.1016/j.jaccedu.2008.02.001

McCabe, D. L., Trevino, L. K., & Butterfield, K. D. (2001). Cheating in academic institutions: A decade of research. *Ethics and Behavior, 11*(3), 219–232. doi:10.1207/S15327019EB1103_2

Mirza, N., & Staples, E. (2010). Webcam as a new invigilation method: Students' comfort and potential for cheating. *Journal of Nursing Education, 49*(2), 116–119.

Moten, J., Fitterer, A., Brazier, E., Leonard, J., & Brown, A. (2013). Examining online college cyber cheating methods and prevention measures. *The Electronic Journal of e-Learning, 11*(2), 139–146.

National Center for Education Statistics. (2016). *Number and percentage of students enrolled in degree-granting postsecondary institutions, by distance education participation, location of student, level of enrollment, and control and level of institution: Fall 2013 and fall 2014* [Data set]. Retrieved from https://nces.ed.gov/programs/digest/d15/tables/dt15_311.15.asp

Poutre, B., Hedlund, D., & Nau, W. (2015). *Combining testing software, online proctoring and lockdown browsers to assure a secure assessment environment for students in hybrid or online programs.* Poster session presented at the 2015 University Assessment Symposium, Creighton University, Omaha, NE. Retrieved from https://dspace.creighton.edu/xmlui/handle/10504/74446

Razer, M., & Friedman, V. J. (2017). Reframing. In *From exclusion to excellence* (pp. 41–57). Rotterdam, Netherlands: Sense Publishers.

Respondus Monitor. (2016). Retrieved from https://www.respondus.com/products/monitor/

Rios, J. A., & Liu, O. L. (2017). Online proctored versus unproctored low-stakes internet test administration: Is there differential test-taking behavior and performance? *American Journal of Distance Education, 31*(4), 226–241.

Romero-Zaldivar, V. A., Pardo, A., Burgos, D., & Delgado Kloos, C. (2012). Monitoring student progress using virtual appliances: A case study. *Computers & Education, 58*(4), 1058–1067. doi:10.1016/j.compedu.2011.12.003

Rose, C. (2009). Virtual proctoring in distance education: An open-source solution. *American Journal of Business Education, 2*(2), 81–88. Retrieved from http://cluteinstitute.com/ojs/index.php/AJBE/article/view/4039

Ruth, S. R., Sammons, M., & Poulin, L. (2007). E-Learning at a crossroads-what price quality? *Educause Quarterly, 30* (2), 32–39.

Shea, P., & Bidjerano, T. (2014). Does online learning impede degree completion? A national study of community college students. *Computers & Education, 75,* 103–111. doi:10.1016/j.compedu.2014.02.009

Smith, D. F. (2014, May 1). *Who is the average online college student?* [Infographic]. Retrieved from https://edtechmagazine.com/higher/article/2014/05/who-average-online-college-student-infographic

Stenlund, T., Lyrén, P. E., & Eklöf, H. (2018). The successful test taker: Exploring test-taking behavior profiles through cluster analysis. *European Journal of Psychology of Education, 33*(2), 403–417. doi:10.1007/s10212-017-0332-2

Strachota, E. (2003). *Student satisfaction in online courses: An analysis of the impact of learner-instructor, learner-learner and learner-technology interaction* (Doctoral dissertation). Available from ProQuest Dissertations & Theses Global. (305284514)

Tsukada, A., Shino, M., Devyver, M., & Kanade, T. (2011, November). Illumination-free gaze estimation method for first-person vision wearable device. In *Computer Vision Workshops (ICCV Workshops), 2011 IEEE International Conference on Computer Vision* (pp. 2084–2091), Barcelona, Spain.

Watson, G., & Sottile, J. (2010). Cheating in the digital age: Do students cheat more in online courses? *Online Journal of Distance Learning Administration, 13*(1). Retrieved from http://www.westga.edu/%7Edistance/ojdla/spring131/watson131.html

Weinberger, D. A., Schwartz, G. E., & Davidson, R. J. (1979). Low-anxious, high-anxious, and repressive coping styles: Psychometric patterns and behavioral and physiological responses to stress. *Journal of Abnormal Psychology, 88*(4), 369–380.

Westra, K. L. (2016). *Faculty and student perceptions of effective online learning environments* (Doctoral dissertation). Available from ProQuest Dissertations and Theses database. (1795087610)

Wilkinson, J. (2009). Staff and student perceptions of plagiarism and cheating. *International Journal of Teaching and Learning in Higher Education, 20*(9), 98–105. Retrieved from http://www.isetl.org/ijtlhe/

Wise, A. (2015). *Factors that successful and unsuccessful community college students perceive as fostering and hindering their success in online learning* (Doctoral dissertation). Auburn University, Auburn, AL.

Wolff, B. G., Wood-Kustanowitz, A. M., & Ashkenazi, J. M. (2014). Student performance at a community college: Mode of delivery, employment, and academic skills as predictors of success. *Journal of Online Learning and Teaching, 10*(2), 166–178.

Yardley, J., Rodríguez, M. D., Bates, S. C., & Nelson, J. (2009). True confessions? Alumni's retrospective reports on undergraduate cheating behaviors. *Ethics & Behavior, 19*(1), 1–14. doi:10.1080/10508420802487096

Faculty of Color Unmask Color-Blind Ideology in the Community College Faculty Search Process

Luke J. Lara

ABSTRACT
This qualitative study explored the systemic barriers to hiring faculty of color in the community college. A phenomenological design was used to examine the community college full-time faculty search process from the perspective of 10 full-time faculty of color who actively participate in racial justice advocacy. The participants represented five community college districts throughout California and have participated on multiple full-time faculty search committees. This study utilized critical race theory as a guiding framework. An analysis of the participants' interviews identified that color-blind ideology is pervasive, despite institutional commitment to diversity and nondiscriminatory laws. The leadership and agency of faculty of color strategically challenged the dominant ideology to advocate the hiring faculty of color. Actionable recommendations are presented to combat color-blind ideology in hiring policies and practices at the national, state, and local levels.

Community colleges are in urgent need of faculty of color. Studies have shown that students from all races benefit from faculty of color (Fairlie, Hoffmann, & Oreopoulos, 2014; Hurtado, 2005; Madyun, Williams, McGee, & Milner, 2013; Milem, 2001; Riley, Bustamante, & Edmonson, 2015; Umbach, 2006; Villegas & Irvine, 2010). As enrollment of students of color increases in community colleges, scholars have called for proportional increases in faculty of color (Fujii, 2014; Fujimoto, 2012; Turner, González, & Wood, 2008). Yet, the urgent call to action has not translated to successful hiring of faculty of color. For example, recent data showed that 24.1% of all instructional staff identified as non-White out of 400,000 faculty employed in community colleges nationally (American Association of Community Colleges [AACC], 2016; National Center for Education Statistics, 2016). Moreover, 70% of the Hispanic and African American instructional staff worked in a part-time capacity (AACC, 2016). In contrast, half of the 6,200,000 community college student population identified as non-White (Ginder, Kelly-Reid, & Mann, 2017).

With greater access to higher education through community colleges, student populations have become increasingly more diverse: 48% White, 23% Hispanic, 13% African American, 6% Asian/Pacific Islander, 4% Other/unknown, 3% two or more races, 1% Native American, and 2% International Students (AACC, 2017). In fact, Nevarez and Wood (2010) pointed out that the percentage of White students in community college in 1986 *decreased* from 77% to 59% by 2006, representing an 18% overall increase of students of color during that 20-year span. Over the same period, faculty of color (e.g., African American, Latinx,[1] Native American, Asian American) only increased by 10% (from 9% to 19.1%). These data indicated a disparity in proportional representation of faculty of color, as compared to students of color in community colleges nationwide.

The process to hire a faculty member involves many components and stages, from developing a position to recruiting, interviewing, hiring, and then retaining the hired person (Turner, 2002). In an effort to increase the racial diversity of faculty in higher education, scholars have recommended practical and promising strategies derived over the last 40 years. These strategies include making diversity a core value of the institution, engaging in targeted recruitment, training search committees on affirmative action and nondiscrimination practices, modifying interviewing techniques, and developing retention programs (Evelyn, 2001; Smith & Moreno, 2006; Smith, Turner, Osei-Kofi, & Richards, 2004; Taylor, Apprey, Hill, McGrann, & Wang, 2010; Turner, 2002). Given that only a quarter of faculty in community colleges identify as non-White (AACC, 2016), these recommendations alone have been insufficient in increasing faculty of color representation.

Policy context can often shape the extent and scope of hiring faculty of color. Despite highly publicized legal challenges, the legal standing for diversity in hiring is fairly solid. The policy context for diversity and hiring focuses on affirmative action, which is a program to redress historically discriminatory practices toward marginalized groups (Evans & Chun, 2007). However, Cohen and Brawer (2008) solemnly reflected that despite affirmative action, "faculty hiring practices show little sign of change" (p. 457), in regard to hiring more faculty of color. In addition, color-blind ideology has been identified as a major obstacle to hiring faculty of color (Kayes, 2002; Turner et al., 2008). Delgado and Stefancic (2017) described the term color-blind as a "conception of equality, expressed in rules that insist only on treatment that is the same across the board" (p. 8), which is exemplified in affirmative action policies and other similar laws. That is, while affirmative action policies and Equal Employment Opportunity (EEO) laws seem to be nondiscriminatory (i.e., race-neutral), they often sustain systemic racism and maintain the status quo, instead of increasing diversity or addressing issues of equity (Crenshaw, Gotanda, Peller, & Thomas, 1995). Thus, to understand a racial phenomenon, it is imperative that the faculty search process be examined through a critical race theory (CRT) lens.

The purpose of this study is to identify structural barriers and opportunities for change by learning from the experiential knowledge of faculty of color who have served on full-time faculty search committees. The following section reviews relevant literature to provide a foundation of knowledge in faculty hiring practices and color-blind ideology within these practices. Next, the theoretical framework of CRT is examined and situated in the study. The methods section provides an overview of the study's phenomenological approach, procedures, participants, and data analysis. The findings section illuminates how color-blind ideology is operationalized in the faculty search process and the strategies faculty of color participants employ to advocate hiring more faculty of color. Finally, the implications and conclusions sections provide concrete policy, action-oriented, and future research recommendations for disrupting color-blind ideology and increasing racial diversity in community college faculty hires.

Literature review

The study of color-blind ideology and use of CRT as an analytical tool represent a small part of the literature on faculty hiring in the community college. In fact, two recent studies examined community college hiring practices through a CRT lens and provided a foundation for this current study (Fujii, 2014; Fujimoto, 2012). Most of the studies on hiring practices have focused on specific components of the search process, which progresses from identification of position need to job announcement to the interview and to eventual hire and retention, and there is little variation in the steps from institution to institution (Flannigan, Jones, & Moore, 2004; Green & Ciez-Volz, 2010; Murray, 1999; Twombly, 2005). Community college faculty candidates are primarily screened on their application, resume, credentials, and answers to interview questions (Flannigan et al., 2004). The following subsections outline what research has revealed as the key opportunities and challenges in hiring of faculty of color from the overall conceptualization of diversity and color-blind ideology to the various key components of the search process.

Diversity and color-blind ideology

In the realm of hiring, the term diversity is often a proxy for racial or gender diversity and the application and understanding of the term diversity in the workplace is typically broad and problematic (Baker, Schmaling, Fountain, Blume, & Boose, 2014; Bauman, Trawalter, & Unzueta, 2014; Unzueta, Knowles, & Ho, 2012). The conceptualization, discussion, and evaluation of diversity within the context of the search process is further complicated by the juxtaposition of diversity promoting laws (e.g., affirmative action) and non-discrimination laws (e.g., EEO laws), which are race-neutral (i.e., color-blind). For this reason, this study employs CRT to center race and racism in the examination of hiring practices by focusing on the experiential knowledge of faculty of color who have served on search committees.

The distance between hiring for racial diversity and attaining a racially diverse faculty is monumental (Flannigan et al., 2004; Fujii, 2014; Smith et al., 2004; Turner, 2002). Several studies have indicated that bias is prevalent in hiring practices (Bendick & Nunes, 2012; Kayes, 2002; Lee, Thau, & Pillutla, 2015). Sociologists Bonilla-Silva and Forman (2000) contended that racism – not simply bias – still exists and is rooted in color-blind ideology. Based on his research, Bonilla-Silva (2018) described central elements of color-blind ideology, which include abstract liberalism (e.g., race is not a factor in self-determination) and avoidance (e.g., use of coded language to discuss race). Color-blind ideology is a tool that is used to reproduce a system of white supremacy (Owen, 2007). This system privileges whiteness without needing to address race at all. This study interrogates how color-blind ideology is operationalized through the policies, structures, and practices within a hiring culture that maintains the status quo.

Recruitment

One of the major problematic components of hiring for racially diverse faculty is the recruitment phase. Research has debunked the myth that there are not enough faculty of color to apply and fill faculty positions (Jeffcoat & Piland, 2012; Smith, 2000; Smith & Moreno, 2006; Smith et al., 2004). In fact, in a recent study it was found that four-year institutions had a higher percentage of African American and Latinx professors as compared to two-year institutions (Smith, Tovar, & García, 2012). Thus, if there truly were not enough candidates of color, the four-year institutions would also reflect lower hiring outcomes for faculty of color. To ensure that community colleges attract a racially diverse pool of candidates, Turner (2002) recommended that hiring departments engage and establish relationships with professional academic networks and local graduate programs, which may have subgroups that are affiliated with race or gender.

Studies focusing on recruitment for faculty in the community college have suggested specific recommendations to address increasing faculty of color hires through faculty mentoring programs, rigorous recruitment strategies, clearly written job announcements, and targeted advertisements (Flannigan et al., 2004; Fujii, 2014; Murray, 1999; Twombly, 2005). In particular, Fujii (2014) argued that position announcements should clearly state the differences between minimum and desirable qualifications; qualifications listed in the job posting should be related to the actual job responsibilities; and positions should be advertised for at least six weeks. Fujii's recommendations highlight how systemic racism and structural barriers are embedded in the recruitment component alone, from the language that is used in job descriptions to how long a job announcement is advertised.

Search committee composition and training

Another critical component within the hiring structure is the search committee. Having a representatively diverse search committee is essential to increasing the number of faculty of color hires (Evans & Chun, 2007; Fujii, 2014; Smith et al., 2004; Turner, 2002). Turner (2002) indicated that "people of color, whether administrators or faculty, should have a presence on the committee" (p. 20). Fujii (2014) suggested that one third or more of the search committee should consist of faculty of color because, "It is difficult to have voice as the 'sole' or 'only' representative" (p. 913).

Multiple perspectives and experiences represented on a hiring committee help mitigate the tendency to hire someone for so-called fit, which is codified language in color-blind ideology (Bendick & Nunes, 2012; Fujimoto, 2012; Green & Ciez-Volz, 2010; Guerra, 2012; Kayes, 2002; Lee et al., 2015; Murray, 1999; Twombly, 2005). Lee et al. (2015) found "that decision makers perceive members of different social groups to be a better or lesser fit (i.e., possessing different levels of the required characteristics)" (p. 792), based on preconceived notions of social group stereotypes. For example, if a majority of the search committee membership is White, and the group has not agreed upon the value of diversity within the context of the search process, then a stereotype of who is a good fit can infiltrate the deliberations and skew the outcome toward unfair criteria. Kayes (2002) described fit as a barrier to achieving diversity in hiring and suggested that even people who are accepting of diversity often lack the tools or know how to advocate for "necessary changes in hiring practices, systems, policies, and procedures" (p. 66). Therefore, it is not only important to have a representatively diverse committee, it is also critical to have committee members that value diversity and that are properly trained in federal and state laws that govern interview policies and procedures (Twombly, 2005).

Interview questions

Murray (1999) advocated for behavioral descriptive interviewing as the best method to determine areas of knowledge, attitudes, and skills. This method of interviewing seeks to understand the interviewee's past behavior in similar situations, because it is a better predictor of future behavior than asking about hypothetical situations. In order to develop appropriate and effective questions, Murray, and Flannigan et al. (2004) emphasized that training of the search committee should consist of an understanding by each committee member as to what the job description entails, the connection between the institutional values and the position, and a consensus on how to assess candidates in the interview process (e.g., using a rubric).

The focus of interview questions created for a job search can also impact the outcome of the search. Murray (1999) contended that behavioral questions should inquire about positive experiences, seeking success and not failure. For example, probing past behavior and focusing questions on diverse student populations can maximize opportunities for faculty of color candidates to share how they have effectively taught students of color. CRT holds experiential knowledge as a key component to validating the lived experience of people of color (Delgado & Stefancic, 2017). In this case, the interview question's focus on teaching diverse student populations could potentially validate the candidate as a person of color and as a professional with inherent expertise.

Teaching demonstration

Researchers have pointed to the major emphasis on teaching, rather than research, as a clear distinction between the role of faculty in community colleges versus faculty at universities (Cohen & Brawer, 2008; Twombly & Townsend, 2008). Green and Ciez-Volz (2010) shared that the faculty of the community college need to be able to educate "learners with vastly different backgrounds, abilities, and levels of academic preparedness" (p. 81). Some literature speaks to necessary faculty qualifications and experiences, but there is little discussion of the effectiveness of teaching demonstrations or how to evaluate teaching in the interview process, especially at the community college (Alexander, Karvonen, Ulrich, Davis, & Wade, 2012; Flannigan et al., 2004; Green & Ciez-Volz, 2010; Twombly, 2005; Vega, Yglesias, & Murray, 2010). Flannigan et al. (2004) provided a detailed history of hiring practices, within a context of community college culture, growth, and general trends over the last 50 years. They found that it has only been recently that community colleges have included a teaching demonstration, mostly brief, if at all in the formal hiring process. While teaching may be the prime responsibility for community college faculty, it is certainly an area that needs further attention in the context of the hiring process. Green and Ciez-Volz (2010) provided broad guidance on how to assess teaching including establishing an understanding of learner-centered teaching as a foundation to develop clear evaluation criteria with rubrics.

In conclusion, studies affirmed that the faculty search process has many components, each is critical to ensuring the hire of faculty of color, and the process is vulnerable to racism (Fujii, 2014; Fujimoto, 2012). This study builds upon the previous CRT research of overt and subtle forms of racism in the search process by focusing on color-blind ideology in community college hiring practices. The present research illuminates a predominantly secretive process as to how faculty search committees value, conceptualize, discuss, and evaluate ideas of race within the context of the search process.

Theoretical framework

Because of the elevating primacy of race and perspective of faculty of color, critical race theory (CRT) was a useful theoretical lens to employ. CRT emerged in the 1970s, amidst the frustration of continued racial injustice after the civil rights movement of the 1960s (Crenshaw et al., 1995). Legal scholars, activists, and lawyers of color such as Derrick Bell, Alan Freeman, and Richard Delgado pioneered the CRT movement in response to continued structural racism in the legal realm (Delgado & Stefancic, 2017). Since then, CRT has expanded and been applied to other fields including education to examine educational processes, systems, and its agents, within the context of race and racism (Fujii, 2014; Ladson-Billings, 1998; Solórzano, Ceja, & Yosso, 2000; Tate, 1997; Yosso, Parker, Solórzano, & Lynn, 2004). CRT in education challenges "traditional claims of the educational system and its institutions to objectivity, meritocracy, color and gender blindness, race and gender neutrality, and equal opportunity" (Solórzano, 1998, p. 122). Critical race theorists contend that the displacement of the centrality of racialized identity through race-neutral practices perpetuates the oppression of people of color (Crenshaw et al., 1995).

CRT has five central tenants: (a) an assertion that racism exists, (b) a premise that the dominant ideology must be challenged, (c) a need to be committed to racial and social justice, (d) an affirmation that experiential knowledge of people of color is valued, and (e) a foundation that critical analysis must be transdisciplinary and within a historical and contemporary context (Delgado & Stefancic, 2017; Yosso et al., 2004). These tenants provide a guiding framework from the development of the research questions to the analysis of data and formulation of recommendations. This study expands upon the CRT approach by Fujii (2014) by focusing on echoing and validating the voices of faculty of color, who are the people actually affected by color-blind ideology and systemic racism.

Method

This qualitative study employed a phenomenological method to gathering and analyzing the shared human experience. That is, phenomenology is characterized by the exploration of "how human beings make sense of experience and transform experience into the consciousness, both individually and as shared meaning" (Patton, 2015, p. 115). This approach along with CRT provided a unique lens to examine hiring practices in the community college by exploring the collective experiential knowledge of faculty of color who have served on search committees.

The following subsections describe the design, procedures, and data analyses of the study. First, a description of the interview questions is provided. Second, the recruitment and profile of interview participants will be described. Third, the data collection procedure is summarized. Finally, the data analyses process is explained.

Interview instrument

The interview questions were developed to conduct between 60 and 90 minute, semi-structured interviews. Questions were open-ended, which allowed the flow of the conversation to be flexible and to be guided by the participant (Creswell, 2013). Each question was mapped to at least one of CRT's guiding tenets, assuring that questions were grounded and centered in the phenomena being studied. The following were the main questions asked in the interview: How did you learn about race and racism? What aspects of the full-time faculty search process represent barriers to hiring faculty of color? Can you share some of your experiences on full-time faculty search committees? What are strategies that you have used on search committees to advocate for hiring faculty of color? If you could change anything about the search process, what do you think should happen to facilitate hiring more faculty of color?

Recruitment and profile of participants

Full-time community college faculty were selected because they play a significant role in hiring practices concerning full-time faculty. Through criterion and snowball sampling recruitment strategies (Patton, 1990), participants were recruited via email. There were four criteria for participation in the study: (a) self-identification as a person of color; (b) current or former faculty status at a community college; (c) self-identification as an active advocate for hiring faculty of color; and (d) prior participation on at least one full-time faculty search committee. Up to 15 faculty participants were sought for this study or until saturation (e.g., no new information) was achieved (Creswell, 2013). Diversity in relation to race, gender, and discipline were pursued to gain a wide variation of perspectives on the shared phenomenon.

Table 1 provides information about the 10 study participants. All participants selected their own pseudonyms. Participants also self-selected their racial and gender identifiers. There were six females and four male participants. The participants also represented a variety of faculty discipline areas including Arts and Humanities; Social and Behavioral Sciences; Science, Technology, Engineering, and Math; and non-classroom focused areas. Nine of the study participants had participated on four or more full-time faculty search committees. Finally, the participants were from five different California community colleges, mostly representing southern California.

Table 1. Demographic data for study participants.

Name	Gender	Race	Years as faculty
Carmen	Female	Mixed race	20
Cliff	Male	African American or Black	15
Dena	Female	Middle Eastern	5
Gladys	Female	Latina, Hispanic, or Chicana	15
Jett	Female	Southeast Asian	15
Juan	Male	Latino, Hispanic, or Chicano	20
Kai	Male	Mixed race	20
Rashawn	Male	African American or Black	10
Soraya	Female	Mixed race	15
Violeta	Female	Latina, Hispanic, or Chicana	25

Data collection procedure

The data collection consisted of in-depth, semi-structured interviews, which is consistent with phenomenological inquiry (Creswell, 2013). All interviews were conducted in person or via an online video meeting platform, audio-recorded, and then transcribed verbatim over a four-month period. Participants were provided with an optional demographic questionnaire to complete prior to the interview. They were also given the opportunity to correct and modify transcribed interviews. The average length of the interviews was 76.5 minutes. The interviews generated a total of 206 single-spaced pages of verbatim transcripts.

Data analyses

This study followed a modified Stevick-Colaizzi-Keen method of data analysis of phenomenological data, as outlined by Moustakas (1994). These guidelines apply the fundamental characteristics of phenomenological research (epoché, phenomenological reduction, imaginative variation, and syntheses) in a systematic manner to reveal the essence of the phenomena being studied. All electronic data (e.g., interview transcripts, memos, demographic questionnaire data) were input into the qualitative analytic software program called NVivo. Interview transcriptions were reviewed multiple times, along with the audio recording to ground the analyses in the data. Following the modified Stevick-Colaizzi-Keen method, meaning units and themes emerged and were examined through a CRT lens. For each interview, the process ended with a composite textural-structure description "of the experience representing the group as a whole" (Moustakas, 1994, p. 122).

Findings

The participants' experiences overwhelmingly identified the pervasiveness of color-blind ideology within the search process. Equally as important, the participants also shared their strategies to counteract and resist color-blind ideology. CRT argues that "racism is ordinary ... the usual way society does business ... [it is the] everyday experience of most people of color in this country" (Delgado & Stefancic, 2017, p. 8). The faculty of color tell the story of how they have worked to transform the search process and disrupt the status quo: systemic racism.

Unmasking color-blind Ideology in the search process

Participants provided multiple examples of how color-blind ideology is operationalized and painted a picture of a search process that privileges White candidates over candidates of color. All participants reported that terms such as race and diversity were hardly invoked, inconsistently used, misunderstood, or devalued in the search process. Yet, participants shared numerous examples of how search committee members used coded-language (e.g., avoided race terms) to indirectly discuss a candidate's race.

Several of the participants discussed the problematic role of abstract notions of race within the concept of diversity in the search process. For example, Carmen argued, "'Diversity' is a loaded term ... we have been robbed of the ability to say, 'people of color.' ... The term diversity is [just] thrown around." She clarified, "Diversity is an important concept, but at the same time, it is a barrier to discussing what we're really talking about and that is racial diversity." Cliff acknowledged that race and racism were not discussed in the context of the search process at his institution because they focus on bias elimination. He proclaimed, "White America is ahistorical. White America begins with, 'I am not a racist.'" This pretense does not allow conversations about the value of race, or the history of racism, and the impact of these two on the search process. Thus, race and racism seem to be treated as nonfactors in the search process.

The policies initially in place to prevent racial bias may actively perpetuate color-blind ideology. Juan shared, "The EEO rules and regulations don't allow us to specifically look for women or faculty of color to hire." All participants inferred that EEO rules validate a color-blind ideology, eliminating the need to discuss race or racism.

In the absence of an explicit discussion on race and racism, participants identified discussions that on the surface appeared to be about something else, yet they picked up on the undertones and coded language used to avoid overt messages about race (Bonilla-Silva, 2018; Bonilla-Silva & Forman, 2000). Often, these conversations resulted in eliminating candidates of color from the search process.

Gladys described a situation where a search committee member engaged in coded language about race when deliberating about a candidate:

> [My colleague proclaimed], "Oh, but he's so arrogant. Do you want to have him as a colleague?" And I'm like right, he's arrogant because he's young. I don't think it's because he's a Latino. But because he's a young Latino male, it's seen as arrogant. He's a stellar, top-notch instructor. Is he arrogant? Well, he knows his shit. Yes. [The search member pressed me], "But you would have to share offices with him." It's not like they were saying "race," but at the end of the day it's like those little characteristics. Okay, so he's viewed as arrogant. But when somebody else that's White says things like that then they're not arrogant, [this committee member would probably say], "They really know their stuff."

The attribution of characteristics to the Latino candidate by a committee member shifted the conversation about his skills in a negative manner. The avoidance of racist language made it seem like this conversation was not about race, but about behaviors and alleged fit.

In another example, Rashawn recalled that he picked up on the nonverbal cues that White search committee members expressed during one particular search: "There's not even an inch of curiosity or interest in this [candidate of color] who seems to be qualified based on what we set as a committee. To me, that was very telling." He and other committee members of color noticed the nonverbal cues of the White committee members such as, facial expressions, eye movements, and how they looked at one another in silence. The absence of curiosity and lack of interest spoke volumes in coded language and was used as a tactic to eliminate candidates of color based on names and presumed race.

Jett shared that she hears, "This person is not a good fit," all the time in faculty search committee deliberations. She understood this statement was code for, "We don't want this person because they're not like us." Others shared stories of how the intersection of racism and sexism hindered the hiring of women of color. These conversations became about "fit," where this served as coded language about the candidate's race and gender. For instance, Carmen shared about a female candidate of color that had been interviewed and was positively supported by some members of the committee, because she was value-added as a woman of color. However, other members of the committee resisted this candidate by attempting to preemptively brand her as an "administrator" (e.g., not interested in staying in a faculty position). Codified language was used to eliminate a candidate based on an assumption that, if hired, she would have ambitions to become an administrator. In deliberations, White faculty questioned her commitment to teaching and her minimal teaching experience (e.g., less teaching experience than other candidates). With this double-sided approach, the line of questioning that the committee engaged in sank the candidate's prospects. Carmen concluded that this pretense was really about race and its intersectionality with gender, and that her colleagues were being racist and sexist.

Given the dominance of color-blind ideology, Cliff shared that discussions about racism among professionals in higher education rarely gets "farther than textbook" level. He explained that the dilemma is that "everybody knows that racism is bad, yet nobody [wants to] admit that they are a racist." Racism remains pervasive. He continued, "We have a lot of very sophisticated conversations," but no individual or institutional accountability. A conversation about "racism without racists" in the context of hiring does not go far, and certainly does not help generate sincere "discussion of what we mean by the best fit for our students." Cliff recognized we may not be engaging in enough conversation around this topic, "because we do so little training with the hiring committees." Training is important, because there are so many tasks that the search committee must complete.

Several participants shared that insufficient time to thoroughly devote to the tasks of the search committee contributed to maintaining the status quo. As a result, participants reported there is minimal revision to and input of job descriptions, interview questions, and evaluation criteria (e.g., past search materials are often recycled with little modification). Violeta noted, "We do little changes here and there, but it's not something completely different than you know, twenty years ago." As a committee member, Juan explained, "I get to choose which question I ask [the candidate in the interview]. That's as much say as I have in the entire development of the questions, the entire development of the job description." Jett, on the other hand, shared, "When I was the chair [I had input]. When I was a member [of another search committee], I didn't have [any]." She elaborated that as a regular committee member, "I did not get to give any input, in the job description. Only maybe the screening criteria, and I wouldn't even say it's input." The minimalist and passive approach to creating or modifying the job description, interview questions, and evaluation criteria served to maintain the status quo.

All the participants shared clear and fundamental examples of how color-blind ideology is operationalized in the community college faculty search process. Given the pervasiveness of color-blind ideology, the participants' perseverance to dismantle systemic racism is highlighted in the next section.

Disrupting color-blind ideology in the search process

The faculty of color participants proactively enacted agency, leadership, and creative efforts to disrupt color-blind ideology. CRT challenges that the dominant discourse and the claims of race-neutrality, which hide the real self-interest in maintaining racial power structures (Tate, 1997). That is, the system of higher education benefits from color-blind ideology, further marginalizing people of color. To disrupt this narrative and affect change, all of the participants discussed the importance of bringing race into the conversation and understanding the value of faculty of color because of their own racialized experiences throughout the search process.

Soraya reflected that open and honest discussion about hiring faculty of color should happen "on a regular basis, so that when it's time for a search committee, it's just naturally a part of the process and not seen as something coming out of left field." Juan expressed, "We should be able to say, 'If there's a lack of Black professors on this campus, then we should do something to look for Black professors on this campus.' We shouldn't be afraid to do that." He suggested that search committee training include discussions about the effects of color-blind ideology in the search process beyond merely individual implicit bias:

> I think the most important understanding is that the hiring committee understands the [existing] disparities, the idea that a White applicant is favored in a hiring *process* [emphasis added] more so than an applicant of color. And the hiring committee needs to understand that, as much as we may not want to be, if we don't consciously try to address it, then we may be unconsciously perpetuating it [systemically].

However, he expressed he did not know how this could happen with the EEO laws and how they are currently interpreted. His uncertainty underscores the tension between the goal of diversity and the unintended consequences of EEO laws.

The majority of the participants were optimistic about confronting this challenge and engaging in open and direct conversations about race and racism. Specifically, about how to validate the candidate's racialized life experiences in the search process as a positive consideration. For example, Soraya shared that by seeking a candidates' understanding, experiential knowledge, and application of culturally relevant curriculum, then the committee can appreciate how the candidate can relate to and validate students' experiences. Research has proven that students of color benefit from culturally relevant curriculum and teaching: faculty of color are likely the candidates to deliver culturally relevant pedagogy, content, and empathy for students in the community college and contribute to increased student outcomes (Fairlie et al., 2014; Hurtado, 2005; Madyun et al., 2013; Milem, 2001; Riley et al., 2015; Umbach, 2006; Villegas & Irvine, 2010).

Gladys warned that there needs to be meaningful conversations about the positive value of race in the context of the candidate's skillset, other experiences, in relation to the needs of the institution and the student population, otherwise it "becomes the thing that they just check off." Jett proposed that this conversation could take place if we reframed search committee trainings to focus on "our own biases and in the way that we do things that could be harmful to faculty of color." She questioned, "What are the criteria that we are placing, and are they really reflective of what our students need?" Training should focus on creating criteria "to hire someone that will be able to capture the characteristics, the traits, the practices, and the experiences in their application that says, 'This person can help our students succeed.'" Given that both students and candidates have racialized experiences, this reframing would allow the conversation of race and its value in the search process.

While all the participants encouraged open and frank discussions, they shared examples of how they enact personal agency (i.e., capacity) in and outside of the search process to advocate for hiring faculty of color, including joining a search committee, contributing to the development of interview questions, using an equity-framework to evaluate candidates, and mentoring people of color. For instance, volunteering to be on a search committee is a major strategy for hiring faculty of color. Violeta's commitment to "make a difference" compelled her to be part of the search committee process. Joining a search committee is time consuming, and participation is usually dictated by people's schedules, so her commitment to social justice overrides these other concerns.

Participants shared their strategies to influence the process despite some of the limitations experienced in contributing to the development of interview questions, as was discussed in the last section. Cliff explained, "[The] strategy I've used is just really asserting different kinds of questions. Just looking for certain things" in the interview and teaching demonstration such as, "their ability to respond to students from different backgrounds." Soraya has suggested asking equity related questions in the interview. Dena has applied an equity framework to look for evidence of equity work in the search process as a strategy to increase hiring more faculty of color:

> When I screen their application, I look to see what kind of equity work they have been involved in. I really do spend a lot of time on that portion of it. I look to see how long they have been doing this kind of work, and the kind of language they use to describe their work in equity-related instances. Whether it's building a curriculum ... for example, if somebody says, "I developed a curriculum on African American literature, because X, Y, and Z." I'm like, "Okay. Seems like you're doing equity work and you will fit well in the culture of this campus." That's one thing I look for in their application screening.

Given that race and racism can be abstract, employing an equity framework may give candidates of color an opportunity to have their lived experiences valued in the search process.

On search committees, Violeta shared, "I make sure that I do point out why it's important to bring diversity into our hiring pool ... why it's important to give preference to diverse applicants." She described a situation where she engaged in direct and open discussion about the value and meaning of racial identity in the search process:

> On our last hiring process, I was actually the one trying to convince the rest of the committee of why this Latino applicant was a much stronger applicant than the rest of the applicants that other people liked better. I was trying to let them know that being able to connect with our students by having that racial identity, common racial identity, was going to be an asset.

By engaging in direct conversation about why the candidate's race should be valued in the search process, she explicitly validated the candidate's racialized experiences and potential contributions if the candidate were to be hired.

Kai, along with several other participants, has directly addressed coded language during deliberation. Kai said, "My role on committees is to shift [the conversation] away from damaging folks with a comment." He gave an example of a White committee member commenting on a candidate of color: "Well, they seemed like overconfident and somewhat arrogant." Kai explained, "My job is to ask, 'Well, what do you mean by that? And what did they do to show that?' To kind of explore that so there's some fair vetting going on, or even to expose unfairness." He admitted, "That's not always taken well." However, by interrogating questionable discussion, coded language can be unpacked and explored.

Outside the search process, Gladys, Carmen, and Kai discussed their roles as mentors as effective strategies to hiring faculty of color. For example, Gladys is motivated to be a mentor because faculty of color have to confront many negative stereotypes before, during, and after the search process. She coaches and mentors faculty of color through the search process to ensure a successful outcome, and she argued, "we need more mentoring programs for candidates of color."

Participants expressed the importance of having a critical mass and a collective voice. Jett reflected that it is more difficult for others to dismiss the concerns of faculty of color with, "Oh, it's just so and so again, the angry person of color." She stressed that it is important to be strategic, "We can't have a small number of people do it all. We tax them, and we burden them and then they get burned out."

Several participants expressed that to facilitate a paradigm shift, faculty of color need to assume key leadership roles. Kai shared, "[We need] to get more people involved in the making of the process, more faculty of color who've gone through the wringer and have sat on both sides, and to now [reflect] back and say, 'You know, we've been doing it like this for a long time.'" Juan emphasized the importance of diverse perspectives influencing policy making: "With more Chicano, more Black, more women, more queer professors moving into state-wide Academic Senate positions, maybe we can start to change that conversation." The voices of faculty of color tend to be silenced if there is no representation on local and state level governance committees. Having more faculty of color participate in the search process, on the committees, and in leadership positions, should facilitate transformation.

Discussion

There is a dearth of literature on faculty hiring in the community college, especially from a CRT lens. Two specific studies using CRT provided inspiration for this current study: Fujii (2014) examined the communication of diversity goals and values from leadership in hiring processes and Fujimoto (2012) explored ethical decision-making in the context of hiring diverse faculty. Both of these studies employed CRT and a case-study approach. This study corroborates several of the findings in both Fujii's and Fujimoto's studies, and it contributes to the body of knowledge, by providing vital insight to the barriers and strategies to hiring faculty of color that are manifested from color-blind ideology from the perspective of faculty of color.

The participants overwhelmingly identified the pervasiveness of systemic racism as operationalized through color-blind ideology in the search process. Concepts like race and racism were rarely discussed, examined, and collectively interpreted within the search process. These terms are vague and present a critical challenge (Bauman et al., 2014) because they are absent, abstract, or decontextualized (Bonilla-Silva, 2018; Chow & Knowles, 2016). However, color-blind ideology was embedded in processes and policies governing the search process. There are many structures (e.g., time-bound processes) and policies (e.g., EEO laws) that serve to maintain the status quo throughout the search process. For example, the participants expressed that there were few opportunities to engage in meaningful conversations about these concepts within the search process with other search committee members, because of the lack of time and nondiscrimination EEO policies, which prevent discussions of race. The lack of time also contributed to insufficient search committee training and minimal opportunities to give input on the job descriptions.

Given these obstacles, concepts of race or racial diversity are prone to be inadequately developed within the search process. For example, when there is discussion about race, it is often done in coded language, such as when a committee member discusses a candidate in regard to fit and, as a result, an overt and explicit discussion of race is avoided. Examples of covert and implicit forms of racism in the search process were shared by all participants.

Despite the challenge of color-blind ideology, the participants actively worked to dismantle systemic racism. All the participants suggested that there needs to be a clearer focus on and appreciation of racial diversity by calling it out directly. Challenging the dominant discourse is a key tenant of CRT (Crenshaw et al., 1995). In this case, explicitly calling out racial diversity directly includes having open, direct, and intentional conversations about race and racism throughout the institution, within the search process, and specifically in trainings. CRT holds that it is critical to identify and examine structures and policies in order to eradicate systemic racism (Delgado & Stefancic, 2017). To end the cycle of systemic racism, these terms need to be discussed regularly, commonly understood, and integrated throughout the search process.

The role of agency, strategic leadership, and advocacy emerged as strong themes. Despite being a minority population, the optimism of the participants gave them strength to continually challenge color-blind ideology. These findings specifically connect to CRT, which advocates unwavering commitment to racial justice through activism (Yosso et al., 2004). This study affirms and expands upon the research that found communities of color engage in activism and to collectively support and validate one another (Kezar, Eckel, Contreras-McGavin, & Quaye, 2008). The participants of this study firmly believed the importance of advocating for hiring more faculty of color. Race should be valued in the hiring process, not as an outcome, but as a critical and essential characteristic.

Implications

This study offers several recommendations for policy and practice for various stakeholders in the community college arena, and for future research.

Implications for policy

Alleged race-neutrality is a tool for racism and we must revise the laws and policies that are supposedly race-neutral. They must be critically assessed through a CRT lens, which would prioritize repairing the adverse impact of these laws and policies on communities of color. State level decisions that disallowed affirmative action in state hiring should be repealed (see for example California Proposition 209 in Alvarez & Bedolla, 2004). Nondiscrimination laws, such as affirmative action, should also be challenged and modernized to reflect a broader definition of how race can be viewed as an asset in employment processes. As an open access institution with a highly racially diverse student population, community colleges must lead the way through education, advocacy, action, and reflection in order to disrupt the status quo.

Implications for practice

Faculty of color in this study engaged in on-the-ground practices but these individual efforts should be scaled up or taken up at the institutional level. Community colleges must engage in bold conversations and sustained dialogue about this topic to effect strategic change at the national, state, and local levels. Leadership from administration, the president, governing boards, and faculty leaders have been found to be key in setting the tone for hiring results, especially for hiring faculty of color (Fujii, 2014; Kayes, 2002; Kezar et al., 2008; Smith et al., 2004; Turner, 2002). Fujii (2014) stated that "diversity's value on the college campus should not have to be communicated when hiring; rather, it ought to be a message communicated at the institution throughout the year" (p. 912). A commitment to diversity would be reinforced, on multiple levels, from within and outside the institution. Hiring only represents the entry point to the institution and should be part of a holistic and comprehensive strategic plan to value, nurture, and sustain diversity (e.g., mentoring programs and continuing education).

Nationally, professional associations and organizations also have a tremendous opportunity to effect change through dialogue and action. For example, the American Association of Community Colleges (AACC), should explicitly outline best practices to promote and increase hiring faculty of color. Accrediting bodies for higher education institutions should also review and modify standards regarding human resources, especially criteria for selection of faculty, to include race-conscious principles. Additionally, these groups should define terms such as diversity, inclusion, and equity to centrally locate and value race. Racial diversity is the implied outcome that institutions desire, yet race tends to be displaced among myriad identities that constitute diversity. Color-blind ideology exists because it denies that race is a significant historical and contemporary factor that determines inequity in the United States (Ladson-Billings & Tate, 1995). By elevating racial diversity and being race-conscious, this should create external pressure on community colleges to recognize the impact of systemic racism within their institutions.

State and local governing boards must work with faculty of color to create and implement policies that explicitly sets racial diversity and equity in hiring practices as a top priority of the institution. This would provide college presidents the support to lead bold conversations about race and racism in relation to the hiring process. These bodies should instruct community colleges to review current hiring procedures for vulnerabilities to color-blind ideology.

Since faculty have a considerable role in the hiring of other faculty, Statewide Academic Senate groups should adopt resolutions on infusing race-conscious principles in hiring and acknowledging the role of race and racism in hiring practices both on the individual and systemic levels. This group should also encourage, support, and engage local Academic Senate groups in these same conversations and actions. This method will likely ensure a system-wide approach and discussion to build a common language, understanding, and implementation.

At the local level, institutions should establish a group of faculty, staff, administrators, and students that must consistently review local and national data regarding racial hiring outcomes and racial equity outcomes for students. This group must generate and facilitate discussion of the following questions: Why is race an asset? How can we achieve racial diversity within the boundaries of current state and federal laws? What are we seeking for in our hiring practices? How are our race-neutral policies and practices hindering us from hiring more faculty of color? What does it mean to be race-conscious? The mission of this group should be to seek racial equity in hiring practices across the institution and to dismantle systemic barriers. This group should report directly to the chief executive officer of the institution or chancellor of the district. In addition, this group should review previous search outcomes. Were they successful in hiring faculty of color? If yes, then what worked? If no, then the group must drill down and examine the circumstances to determine where systemic barriers existed in the process.

Implications for future research

A fruitful avenue for future research is to build upon the narrative of faculty of color and include interviews with faculty, administrators, staff, and students of color regarding the perceptions of color-blind policies in hiring practices so that multiple stakeholders' understanding of color-blind ideology is examined. Also, future research should study faculty of color's experiences beyond California to understand community college faculty search processes in other state contexts. In addition, a case study could be conducted to understand the impact of policy context (i.e., federal and state non-discrimination laws). For example, how do faculty of color navigate the hiring process in California versus New York.

CRT should be used in research to understand hiring practices for part-time faculty in regard to hiring faculty of color. This is important because most community colleges heavily rely on part-time faculty

(Charlier & Williams, 2011). Recent studies have indicated that up to 69% of instructional staff in public two-year colleges are part-time faculty (Kezar & Maxey, 2013). For this reason, CRT would be instrumental in uncovering and naming the informal processes that tend to occur in part-time hiring.

Finally, it would be helpful to understand where there are differences from discipline to discipline in regard to hiring outcomes. For instance, examining hiring processes in sociology and counseling disciplines, where concepts of race are likely defined and germane, as compared to math and science disciplines, where concepts of race tend to be abstract or absent. Understanding the differences could help facilitate targeted training for search committees and identify structural barriers within specific disciplines.

Conclusion

Given we are (a) in an era of increased institutional accountability on student outcomes beyond access, (b) half of the students are students of color, and (c) various studies have indicated that faculty of color have positive effects on student of color outcomes, it is imperative that colleges invest in faculty of color (Robinson, Byrd, Louis, & Bonner, 2013). The investment in faculty of color begins with an inquiry into the hiring process through a CRT framework, where systemic racism (i.e., color-blind ideology) is critically examined. Understanding the community college hiring process requires an understanding of the implications of color-blind ideology, which is rooted in a historical context and shaped by contemporary systems of inequality. As faculty of color, the participants in the study engaged in individual and collective acts of racial justice by challenging their colleagues on search committees, advocating for faculty of color in the hiring process, seeking formal leadership positions to change policy, and mentoring others. Their experiential knowledge provides insight to how color-blind ideology is operationalized and how it can be disrupted.

The study's findings do not point to one obstacle or one target to blame for the dismal hiring outcomes of faculty of color. Institutional actors (e.g., local governing boards, administrators, faculty, staff, students), along with outside agencies (e.g., professional associations, legislators, state governance boards), are stakeholders in the outcomes of hiring practices. They all need to engage in sustained dialogue about race and racism. Institutional action will lead to changing practices that will result in greater success for all students, especially students of color. This wide-ranging ripple effect will happen if institutions chose to implement race-conscious practices and invest in faculty of color.

Note

1. Latinx is used as non-binary inclusive terms representing the intersectionality of gender, race, ethnicity, language, and other social identities (Salinas & Lozano, 2017). Each participant defined themselves and used the gendered version of their racial identity. However, when this study discusses the group as a whole, a gender inclusive term is used.

ORCID

Luke J. Lara http://orcid.org/0000-0003-0787-0191

References

Alexander, A., Karvonen, M., Ulrich, J., Davis, T., & Wade, A. (2012). Community college faculty competencies. *Community College Journal of Research and Practice*, 36(11), 849–862. doi:10.1080/10668926.2010.515511.
Alvarez, R. M., & Bedolla, L. G. (2004). The revolution against affirmative action in California: Racism, economics, and Proposition 209. *State Politics & Policy Quarterly*, 4(1), 1–17. doi:10.1177/153244000400400101.
American Association of Community Colleges. (2016). *Data points: Diversity in instructional staff*. Vol. 4. Retrieved from http://www.aacc.nche.edu/Publications/datapoints/Documents/DP_Staff.pdf

American Association of Community Colleges. (2017). *Fast facts 2017*. Retrieved from https://www.aacc.nche.edu/wp-content/uploads/2017/09/AACCFactSheet2017.pdf

Baker, D. L., Schmaling, K., Fountain, K. C., Blume, A. W., & Boose, R. (2014). Defining diversity: A mixed-method analysis of terminology in faculty applications. *Social Science Journal, 53*(1), 60–66. doi:10.1016/j.soscij.2015.01.004.

Bauman, C. W., Trawalter, S., & Unzueta, M. M. (2014). Diverse according to whom? Racial group membership and concerns about discrimination shape diversity judgments. *Personality & Social Psychology Bulletin, 40*(10), 1354–1372. doi:10.1177/0146167214543881.

Bendick, M., & Nunes, A. P. (2012). Developing the research basis for controlling bias in hiring. *Journal of Social Issues, 68*(2), 238–262. doi:10.1111/j.1540-4560.2012.01747.x.

Bonilla-Silva, E. (2018). *Racism without racists: Color-blind racism and the persistence of racial inequality in America* (5th ed.). Lanham, MD: Rowman & Littlefield.

Bonilla-Silva, E., & Forman, T. A. (2000). "I am not a racist but. .": Mapping White college students' racial ideology in the USA. *Discourse & Society, 11*(1), 50–85. doi:10.1177/0957926500011001003.

Charlier, H. D., & Williams, M. R. (2011). The reliance on and demand for adjunct faculty members in America's rural, suburban, and urban community colleges. *Community College Review, 39*(2), 160–180. doi:10.1177/0091552111405839.

Chow, R. M., & Knowles, E. D. (2016). Taking race off the table: Agenda setting and support for color-blind public policy. *Personality and Social Psychology Bulletin, 42*(1), 25–39. doi:10.1177/0146167215611637

Cohen, A. M., & Brawer, F. B. (2008). *The American community college* (5th ed.). San Francisco, CA: Jossey-Bass.

Crenshaw, K., Gotanda, N., Peller, G., & Thomas, K. (Eds.). (1995). *Critical race theory: The key writings that formed the movement*. New York, NY: New Press.

Creswell, J. W. (2013). *Qualitative inquiry & research design: Choosing among five approaches* (3rd ed. ed.). Thousand Oaks, CA: Sage.

Delgado, R., & Stefancic, J. (2017). *Critical race theory: An introduction* (3rd ed.). New York: New York University Press.

Evans, A., & Chun, E. B. (2007). Special issue: Are the walls really down? Behavioral and organizational barriers to faculty and staff diversity. *ASHE Higher Education Report, 33*(1), 1–139. doi:10.1002/aehe.3301

Evelyn, J. (2001). The hiring boom at 2-year colleges. *Chronicle of Higher Education, 47*(40). Retrieved from http://chronicle.com/article/The-Hiring-Boom-at-2-Year/3125

Fairlie, R. W., Hoffmann, F., & Oreopoulos, P. (2014). A community college instructor like me: Race and ethnicity interactions in the classroom. *American Economic Review, 104*(8), 2567–2591. doi:10.1257/aer.104.8.2567

Flannigan, S., Jones, B. R., & Moore, W. (2004). An exploration of faculty hiring practices in community colleges. *Community College Journal of Research and Practice, 28*(10), 823–836. doi:10.1080/10668920390276894

Fujii, S. J. (2014). Diversity, communication, and leadership in the community college faculty search process. *Community College Journal of Research and Practice, 38*(10), 903–916. doi:10.1080/10668926.2012.725387

Fujimoto, E. O. (2012). Hiring diverse faculty members in community colleges: A case study in ethical decision making. *Community College Review, 40*(3), 255–274. doi:10.1177/0091552112450069

Ginder, S. A., Kelly-Reid, J. E., & Mann, F. B. (2017). *Enrollment and employees in postsecondary institutions, Fall 2016; and financial statistics and academic libraries, fiscal year 2016: First look (Provisional Data) (NCES 2018-002)*. U.S. Department of Education. Washington, DC: National Center for Education Statistics. Retrieved from http://nces.ed.gov/pubsearch

Green, D. W., & Ciez-Volz, K. (2010). Now hiring: The faculty of the future. *New Directions for Community Colleges, (2010)*(152), 81–92. doi:10.1002/cc.430

Guerra, P. L. (2012). Valuing diversity: A well-intended but empty promise. *Multicultural Education, 19*(3), 44–47.

Hurtado, S. (2005). The next generation of diversity and intergroup relations research. *Journal of Social Issues, 61*(3), 595–610. doi:10.1111/j.1540-4560.2005.00422.x

Jeffcoat, K., & Piland, W. E. (2012). Anatomy of a community college faculty diversity program. *Community College Journal of Research and Practice, 36*(6), 397–410. doi:10.1080/10668920902813477

Kayes, P. E. (2002). New paradigms for diversifying faculty and staff in higher education: Uncovering cultural biases in the search and hiring process. *Multicultural Education, 14*(2), 65–69.

Kezar, A. J., Eckel, P., Contreras-McGavin, M., & Quaye, S. J. (2008). Creating a web of support: An important leadership strategy for advancing campus diversity. *Higher Education, 55*(1), 69–92. doi:10.1007/s10734-007-9068-2

Kezar, A. J., & Maxey, D. (2013). The changing academic workforce. *Trusteeship, 21*(3), 15–21. Retrieved from: https://www.agb.org/trusteeship/2013/5/changing-academic-workforce

Ladson-Billings, G. (1998). Just what is critical race theory and what's it doing in a nice field like education? *International Journal of Qualitative Studies in Education, 11*(1), 7–24. doi:10.1080/095183998236863

Ladson-Billings, G., & Tate, W. F. (1995). Toward a critical race theory of education. *Teachers College Record, 97*(1), 47–68. doi:10.3102/0013189X033007003

Lee, S. Y., Thau, S., & Pillutla, M. M. (2015). Discrimination in selection decisions: Integrating stereotype fit and interdependence theories. *Academy of Management Journal, 58*(3), 789–812. doi:10.5465/amj.2013.0571

Madyun, N., Williams, S. M., McGee, E. O., & Milner, H. R. (2013). On the importance of African-American faculty in higher education: Implications and recommendations. *Journal of Educational Foundations, 27*(3/4), 65-84.

Milem, J. F. (2001). Increasing diversity benefits: How campus climate and teaching methods affect student outcomes. In G. M. Orfield Retrieved from ERIC database. (ED456202) Ed., *Diversity challenged: Evidence on the impact of affirmative action* (pp. 233-249). Cambridge, MA: Harvard Education Publishing Group.

Moustakas, C. (1994). *Phenomenological research methods.* Thousand Oaks, CA: Sage.

Murray, J. P. (1999). Interviewing to hire competent community college faculty. *Community College Review, 27*(1), 41-56. doi:10.1177/009155219902700104

National Center for Education Statistics. (2016). *Table 315.10. number of faculty in degree-granting postsecondary institutions, by employment status, sex, control, and level of institution: Selected years, fall 1970 through fall 2015.* Retrieved from https://nces.ed.gov/programs/digest/d16/tables/dt16_315.10.asp

Nevarez, C., & Wood, J. L. (2010). *Community college leadership and administration: Theory, practice, and change.* New York, NY: Peter Lang.

Owen, D. S. (2007). Towards a critical theory of whiteness. *Philosophy & Social Criticism, 33*(2), 203-222. doi:10.1177/0191453707074139

Patton, M. Q. (1990). *Qualitative evaluation and research methods* (2nd ed. ed.). Newbury Park, CA: Sage.

Patton, M. Q. (2015). *Qualitative research & evaluation methods* (4th ed. ed.). Thousand Oaks, CA: Sage.

Riley, R. L., Bustamante, R. M., & Edmonson, S. L. (2015). Intercultural competence and student engagement of U.S. community college students: A mixed method study. *Community College Journal of Research and Practice, 40*(1), 1-15. doi:10.1080/10668926.2014.961588

Robinson, P. A., Byrd, D., Louis, D. A., & Bonner, F. A. (2013). Enhancing faculty diversity at community colleges: A practical solution for advancing the completion agenda. *FOCUS on Colleges, Universities & Schools, 7*(1), 1-11.

Salinas, C., & Lozano, A. (2017). Mapping and recontextualizing the evolution of the term Latinx: An environmental scanning in higher education. *Journal of Latinos and Education*, 1-14. doi:10.1080/15348431.2017.1390464

Smith, D. G. (2000). How to diversify the faculty. *Academe, 86*(5), 48-52. Retrieved from http://www.jstor.org/stable/40251921

Smith, D. G., & Moreno, J. (2006). Hiring the next generation of professors: Will myths remain excuses? *Chronicle of Higher Education, 53*(6), 64.

Smith, D. G., Tovar, E., & García, H. A. (2012). Where are they? A multilens examination of the distribution of full-time faculty by institutional type, race/ ethnicity,gender, and citizenship. *New Directions for Institutional Research, (2012)*(155), 5-26. doi:10.1002/ir.20019

Smith, D. G., Turner, C. S. V., Osei-Kofi, N., & Richards, S. (2004). Interrupting the usual: Successful strategies for hiring diverse faculty. *Journal of Higher Education, 75*(2), 133-160. doi:10.1353/jhe.2004.0006

Solórzano, D. G. (1998). Critical race theory, race and gender microaggressions, and the experience of Chicana and Chicano scholars. *International Journal of Qualitative Studies in Education, 11*(1), 121-136. doi:10.1080/095183998236926

Solórzano, D. G., Ceja, M., & Yosso, T. J. (2000). Critical race theory, racial microaggressions, and campus racial climate: The experiences of African American college students. *Journal of Negro Education, 69*(1), 60-73.

Tate, W. F. (1997). Critical race theory and education: History, theory, and implications. *Review of Research in Education, 22*, 195-247. doi:10.3102/0091732X022001195

Taylor, O., Apprey, C. B., Hill, G., McGrann, L., & Wang, J. (2010). Diversifying the faculty. *Peer Review, 12*(3), 15-18.

Turner, C. S. V. (2002). *Diversifying the faculty: A guidebook for search committees.* Washington, DC: Association of American Colleges and Universities. Retrieved from ERIC database. (ED465359).

Turner, C. S. V., González, J. C., & Wood, J. L. (2008). Faculty of color in academe: What 20 years of literature tells us. *Journal of Diversity in Higher Education, 1*(3), 139-168. doi:10.1037/a0012837

Twombly, S. B. (2005). Values, policies, and practices affecting the hiring process for full-time arts and sciences faculty in community colleges. *Journal of Higher Education, 76*(4), 423-447. doi:10.1353/jhe.2005.0032

Twombly, S. B., & Townsend, B. K. (2008). Community college faculty: What we know and need to know. *Community College Review, 36*(1), 5-24. doi:10.1177/0091552108319538

Umbach, P. D. (2006). The contribution of faculty of color to undergraduate education. *Research in Higher Education, 47*(3), 317-345. doi:10.1007/s11162-005-9391-3

Unzueta, M. M., Knowles, E. D., & Ho, G. C. (2012). Diversity is what you want it to be: How social-dominance motives affect construals of diversity. *Psychological Science, 23*(3), 303-309. doi:10.1177/0956797611426727

Vega, W., Yglesias, K., & Murray, J. P. (2010). Recruiting and mentoring minority faculty members. *New Directions for Community Colleges, (2010)*(152), 49-55. doi:10.1002/cc.427

Villegas, A. M., & Irvine, J. J. (2010). Diversifying the teaching force: An examination of major arguments. *Urban Review, 42*, 175-192. doi:10.1007/s11256-010-0150-1

Yosso, T. J., Parker, L., Solórzano, D. G., & Lynn, M. (2004). From Jim Crow to affirmative action and back again: A critical race discussion of racialized rationales and access to higher education. *Review of Research in Education, 28* (2014), 1-25. doi:10.3102/0091732X028001001

Case Studies of Women of Color Leading Community Colleges in Texas: Navigating the Leadership Pipeline through Mentoring and Culture

Maria Yareli Delgado and Taryn Ozuna Allen

ABSTRACT
This qualitative, multi-site, case study examined the personal and professional experiences of women of color who currently hold higher-level administrative positions at a Texas community college district and the role that Bicultural Socialization Theory played in their pathway to the leadership pipeline. Using interviews, campus observations, document analysis, and analytic memos, this study found who are the mentors (i.e., cultural translators, cultural mediators, and role models) who supported women of color achieve high-level administrative positions. The findings revealed that women of color navigated home and work culture due to their ability to balance multiple responsibilities required at home and the responsibilities required by their leadership roles. The findings indicated that women of color were successful because they had the ability to drawn upon their minority culture towards a successful bicultural pathway. The implications and recommendations for practice and future research are included.

Community colleges in the United States enroll over 10 million students each year (National Center for Education Statistics [NCES], 2018. In the state of Texas, the location of this study, community colleges enroll approximately 706,900 students (Texas Higher Education Coordinating Board [THECB], 2017), which are increasingly students of color. Despite the ongoing diversification among students enrolled in Texas community college, recent reports indicated that people who hold higher-ranking administrative positions (i.e., academic deans, vice presidents, and presidents) at community colleges do not reflect the diversity of the student body at these institutions. For example, men (70%) most often hold college presidencies compared to (30%) female presidents (American Council on Education [ACE], 2017). Among the 30% of female presidents, 25% female presidents are White, compared to only 5% Women of Color presidents (ACE, 2017). The underrepresentation of Women of Color in top administrative roles fails to reflect the current demographic trends among Texas community college students (THECB, 2017).

In addition to managing the pressures of being underrepresented in executive administration, Women of Color often serve as mentors, role models, and advisors to students of color (Gonzáles-Figueroa & Young, 2005; Nixon, 2017). As a result, Women of Color administrators, must oversee multiple responsibilities, navigate their home and work culture, and cultivate key individuals such as cultural translators (individuals from own minority or People of Color culture), cultural mediators (individuals of the White culture), and role models (individuals from a People of Color culture) (De Anda, 1984) in order to achieve success in their career pathway. These key individuals (i.e., cultural translators, cultural mediators, and role models), as described by De Anda (1984) teach leaders how to function in two worlds (e.g., mainstream culture and home culture). Yet, little is known about how Texas Women of Color community college administrators utilize bicultural socialization, which indicates that individuals from non-White groups have to learn to function in two environments, the environment of their own culture and that of the main society culture (De Anda, 1984).

Therefore, the purpose of this qualitative, multi-site case study was to understand the personal and professional experiences of Women of Color who currently hold higher-level administrative positions at a Texas community college. Using bicultural socialization (De Anda, 1984) as the guiding framework, this study sought to address the following research questions: Who are the mentors (i.e., cultural translators, cultural mediators, and role models) that support Women of Color achieve high-level administrative positions? How do Women of Color navigate their home and work cultures to earn higher-level administrative positions in Texas community colleges?

Literature review

The literature presented in this section begins with a brief background on the history and purpose of community colleges and its leadership. Next, we discuss the role of women in leadership, particularly the underrepresentation of women in leadership literature. Finally, the section concludes by shedding light on some of the challenges Women of Color uniquely experience in their leadership roles.

Overview of community colleges and its leadership

Established in the early 20th century with the goal of providing vocational training, community colleges have led the way to economic and social mobility for millions of students (Cohen & Brawer, 2003). These higher education institutions have an open-door policy and programs to ensure all members of the community have an opportunity to access college (Bailey, Jaggars, & Jenkins, 2015; Cohen & Brawer, 2003).

Research shows community colleges are navigating new challenges in regards to leadership turnover and development (American Association of Community Colleges [AACC], 2016; Avolio & Gardner, 2005; Eddy, 2013). For instance, community colleges are contending with the exodus of current employees (AACC, 2016). Eddy (2013) found community colleges are confronted with the need to find replacements for their future retirees. Further, community college leaders are constantly met with new technologies and market opportunities (Avolio & Gardner, 2005). Other challenges include funding and the fluctuation of student enrollment that occurs at community colleges (Floyd, Maslin-Ostrowski, & Hrabak, 2010). However, the most significant challenge for college administrators is achieving diversity and inclusion. Since, some community colleges use these two terms in a simultaneous manner (Zamani-Gallaher, 2018), additional research is needed to understand how Women of Color and their cultural backgrounds can serve as assets to community college leadership roles.

Women in leadership

Leadership has been traditionally studied from a perspective of White male administrators (Eagly & Karau, 2002), leaving women historically underrepresented in leadership positions and literature (American Association of Community Colleges, 2016). Even when research began to focus on women issues, it was largely ignored until 1970 (Chemers, 1997). However, due to the increasing number of women in leadership roles and academia, studies focusing on women in leadership started to be an interest area for research (Northouse, 2013). Researchers contribute to the lack of women representation in leadership roles and studies focusing on women issues to gender-specific responsibilities. For example, Johnson (2016) suggested that women have the tendency to accept lower salaries for employment positions at a higher rate than men.

Moreover, when examining leadership at community colleges, the literature reveals women leaders encounter a variety of obstacles in their path to success. Such obstacles begin when women leaders began building their leadership style as a result of the expectations of the community college and the norms established by male roles such as leading from the front instead of leading from the back (Tedrow & Rhoads, 1999), creating a lack of authenticity and cumulative disadvantage when confronted with the choice of professional promotion (Eddy, 2013). Tedrow and Rhoads (1999) found that women at community colleges who try to succeed in these types of environments (i.e., norms established by male roles) face significant psychological and communicational challenges. Domestic errands and the expectations about children responsibilities cause challenges for women aspiring to obtain higher leadership positions (Townsend & Twombly, 2007).

Eddy (2008) wrote that women aspiring to be college presidents often waited for their husbands to retire prior to seeking that presidency job, resulting in a lengthy process. Another challenge is the tendency that women have when they depict themselves as facilitators instead of leaders (Eagly & Karau, 2002), creating a negative perception for women at the time they are promoted to positions of authority (Rudman & Glick, 2001). Additionally, women receive less formal training than the training received by men (Knoke & Ishio, 1998), due to the prejudice against women leaders (Northouse, 2013). Deaux and Kite (1993) indicated that prejudice against women can be explained by the stereotypes among women and men. Such stereotypes of women leaders (e.g., concern for others, sensitivity, warmth, and helpfulness) are perceived as less valuable than those typically associated with men (e.g., confidence, assertiveness, and independence rationality) (Deaux & Kite, 1993). As a result of these obstacles and the limited inclusion of women's perspectives in leadership research, additional scholarship is needed to further understand women's experiences, especially if they identify as Women of Color.

Women of color in leadership

When the literature is delineated into ethnic categories, the disparities confronting Women of Color are even more compelling, because Women of Color often experience racial or ethnic prejudice (Bell & Nkomo, 2001; Griffin & Reddick, 2011). Moreover, research reveals Women of Color experience dual challenge of racism and sexism (Davis, 2009) and challenges with career advancement (Chang, Longman, & Franco, 2014). Sagaria (2002) found that Women of Color experience disadvantages in the hiring search, since hiring committees typically favor White men and some White women.

For instance, in the case of African American women their ethnicity plays a bigger role than being a woman, because as African American they have to deal with challenges that White women do not have to confront (Patitu & Hinton, 2003). Crawford and Smith (2005) found that in most university campuses, African American females with aspirations to become administrators encounter a lack of cultural sensitivity on their campuses, which directly impacts their long-term career.

Hispanic women experience challenges that include gender role expectations, societal expectations, and must negotiate the assumption that they are submissive and should have passive roles in administration (Gonzáles -Figueroa & Young, 2005). Moreover, Hispanic women have to learn to negotiate the White culture values with a more family oriented ethnic identity (Long & Martinez, 1994). In the case of Asian American women administrators they have challenges such as sexual and racial harassment, along with the accent discrimination (Cho, 1996). However, the main challenge for Asian American administrators is not fitting the typical stereotypes of Asian women such as docile, passive, and silent (Ideta & Cooper, 1999).

Women of Color administrators at community colleges are not exempt from obstacles related to equity in the workplace, as evidenced by the lack of representation in leadership roles (ACE, 2017). Moreover, administrators of color face barriers such as isolation, loneliness, and racially motivated victimization (Crawford & Smith, 2005). Given the intersectionality of these disadvantages and challenges, additional scholarly work is needed to understand the pathway and experiences of Women of Color who successfully achieved leadership roles in community colleges.

Theoretical framework

Bicultural socialization theory suggests that individuals from minority groups (i.e., non-White group) have to learn to function in two environments, the environment of their own culture and that of the main society culture (De Anda, 1984). De Anda (1984) depicted six factors that are important for understanding bicultural socialization, such factors include; (a) degree of overlap of commonalty between the two cultures with regard the norms, values, beliefs, perceptions, (b) the availability of cultural translators, cultural mediators, and models, (c) the amount and type (positive or negative) of corrective feedback provided by each culture regarding attempts to produce normative behavior, (d) the conceptual style and problem-solving approach of the minority individual and their network with the prevalent or valued styles of the majority culture, (e) the individual's degree of bilingualism, and (f) the degree of dissimilarity in physical appearance from the majority culture, such as skin color and facial features.

In the present study, the concept of bicultural socialization is used to understand the similarities among and differences between the mainstream culture and the minority culture; that is, to explore how Women of Color community college administrators navigated their home culture and work culture. Since, bicultural experiences occur because there are similarities between the two cultures and not because the two cultures are totally different (De Anda, 1984).

De Anda (1984) incorporated the concept of shared values and shared norms that can be used to describe, how people can make it possible to understand and predict two cultural environments and adjust behavior according to the norms of each culture. The fusion of two worlds or two cultures through their shared values and norms helps researchers to explain how individuals can interact in two different cultural environments, and it is possible for these individuals to adjust their behavior according to the norms of each culture (Braxton, Sullivan, & Johnson, 1997). Also, individuals may fuse the two cultures through their shared values and norms, which can lead to more productive behavior. Through the use of bicultural socialization (De Anda, 1984), this study sought to identify and understand the individuals, resources, and events from home and work cultures that enabled Women of Color to achieve leadership roles in Texas community colleges.

Methods

This study employed a qualitative, multiple case study design (Creswell, 2013). Case studies investigate real-life cases or events over time (Yin, 2009). The use of case studies was essential in this study; this methodology allowed for an in-depth learning about the pathway that Women of Color used in order to traverse the community college system to earn high ranking administrative positions. The purpose of these case studies was to examine the role that bicultural socialization played among Women of Color administrators' ability to navigate their home and work culture to achieve success.

Site selection and participant recruitment

This study took place on campuses within a community college district in North Texas. The district was founded in 1965 and managed by the Board of Trustees, which is composed of seven members who are elected in six-year terms. The district is a centralized district, which means that there is one governing body, but each campus has its individual leadership model. For instance, the district has six Presidents, six Vice Presidents of Academic Affairs, and five Vice Presidents of Student Services.

The sites were selected using purposeful sampling. Purposeful sampling is defined as selecting particular settings, persons or events because this will purposefully inform and provide an understanding of the study's research problem (Stake, 1995; Yin, 2009). Five campuses were selected because they met the following criteria: (1) have administrators who identified as female and African American, Asian American, Native American or Hispanic who (2) hold higher-ranking administrative positions (i.e., Presidents, Vice Presidents of Instruction, Vice President of Student Services, Academic Deans), and (3) have been in the position for more than one year. Ultimately, four sites were included in this study.

Participant recruitment and selection

After receiving Institutional Review Board (IRB) approval, purposeful sampling (Maxwell, 2005) was used to recruit participants. Once the authors obtained the e-mail addresses of the 16 female Presidents, Vice Presidents of Instruction, Vice President of Student Services, and Academic Deans, they sent a recruitment e-mail to allow participants to self select into the study. Six participants were selected, because they successfully attained a high-ranking leadership administrative position (i.e., vice president or dean). Therefore, they were already identified as "successful" because of their leadership role. In order to protect the identity of participants, pseudonyms were assigned. Table 1 provides additional information on the participants for this study.

Data collection

Data collection began in fall 2016 and concluded in spring 2017. This study utilized the following data sources: interviews, observation notes, documents, and analytic memos (Yin, 2014). Bicultural socialization (De Anda, 1984) was the theory selected for this study and along with the interview protocol and research questions were vital for the data collection and analysis of this study.

Interviews

To ensure participants fully understood of the study, the authors covered the informed consent document with them and answered any questions prior to beginning the interviews. One-on-one, semi-structured interviews were used to understand the experiences lived by the person being interviewed (Seidman, 2013). Each participant was interviewed twice. Each interview ranged from 15 to 60 minutes. During the first interview, participants were asked to share their life experiences and provided a deeper understanding of the experiences of the individuals or issues that supported their success. In the second interview, participants shared additional details on how they navigated their home culture and work culture, how these two cultures influenced one another, and specifically, how home culture influenced the participants' pathways to achieve success in their leadership roles.

Campus observations

The use of participant observations in a study is important because it provided proximity of real time actions, cover case's context, and provides insight into interpersonal behavior and motives (Yin, 2014). In the case of this study, three campus observations of 60 minutes were proposed to participants (e.g. official meeting or any events that participants suggest). The purpose of the observations was to look for vocabulary, tone, or vernacular participants used when they talked to people of the White culture and the culture of color.

Table 1. Participants Background and Pseudonyms.

Name	Race/Ethnicity	Position	Years of Experience	Highest Degree Earned
Laura	Hispanic	Vice President	7+	Doctorate
Florence	Asian American	Dean	7+	Doctorate
Ava	African American	Dean	2+	Masters
Elizabeth	Hispanic	Vice President	7+	Doctorate
Barbara	African American	Vice President	5+	Doctorate
Linda	African American	Dean	5+	Masters

Document analysis

The use of documents (e.g., letters, agendas, administrative documents) is helpful to validate information from other sources, such as interviews or observations (Yin, 2014). Documents corroborated participants' names, titles, or positions in the hierarchy of organization (Yin, 2014). For the purpose of this study the following documents were collected: (1) six organization charts, (2) two curriculum vitae or resume, (3) two leadership philosophies, and (4) 14 meeting agendas.

Analytic memos

The use of memoing was used to collect evidence that can be particular to a specific idea that might have captured the attention of the researcher through the data collection process (Yin, 2014). The authors wrote memos after each interview and throughout the data collection and analysis process. The memos helped to reflect and annotate common themes and subthemes that aligned with the research questions and theoretical framework.

Data analysis

For the data analysis, the authors organized the transcribed interviews, documents, and campus observations in order to reduce data into relevant text passages (codes) and condensed the codes into themes and sub-themes (Creswell, 2013; Lincoln & Guba, 1985). Within-case analysis and cross-case synthesis (Merriam, 1988) were ideal to analyze the data collected from the six case studies. The within-case analysis approach provided first detailed description of each participant and themes within that specific case. For instance, the paperwork for each case was separated in an electronic folder (i.e., interview transcripts, analytic memos, campus observations' notes, and documents). Then the information was examined individually and looked for insightful passages within each case. Once all the significant passages were noted, then the second step was to conduct an analysis across cases (Merriam, 1988). The cross-case synthesis approach developed the findings for the study by first treating each individual case as a separate case study, and then aggregating across the series of individual studies (Yin, 2014).

Trustworthiness

In order to promote trustworthiness, we conducted member checks, debriefed with experts, and triangulated multiple data sources (Seidman, 2013). For this case study, each participant was interviewed individually. Participants had the opportunity to review the transcripts of the interviews in order for them to check for accuracy on their responses. In addition, we debriefed with peers who are experts on community colleges, Women of Color in leadership, and bicultural socialization. These debrief sessions provided an opportunity to check biases and identify new areas of research (Lincoln & Guba, 1985). Using multiple data sources also helps ensure trustworthy data (Yin, 2014). Thus, this study collected multiple data sources, including one-on-one interviews, campus observations and field notes, document analysis, and analytic memos (Yin, 2014).

Findings

The purpose of this study was to examine the experiences of Women of Color in the leadership pipeline. The findings presented in this study include how Women of Color described their personal and professional experiences in their pathway to high-ranking administrative positions. Participants shared about the importance of developing an extensive mentoring networking (i.e., cultural mediators, cultural translators, and role models). Women of Color participants also talked about how they navigated their home and work culture through their ability to balance home and work responsibilities and their understanding of their culture of color to strive for success.

Mentorship

Participants provided examples of the positive influence that mentors had in their success path towards higher-ranking administrative positions. They explained securing the support of encouraging individuals or cultural mediators, mentors, and role models as an essential strategy for their success in their leadership roles.

Cultural mediators

Participants in this study specifically discussed how cultural mediators or individuals from the mainstream group (De Anda, 1984) were vital in their success, because they provided job opportunities for higher-ranking leadership positions and showed appreciation and understanding of participants' culture. Laura said that her former supervisors, "they all hired me and if they hadn't given me a job I would not have been able to have achieved what I have now." Similarly, Florence and Barbara stated that the cultural mediators supported their careers by offering them jobs. Barbara stated, "If he had not given me that chance, I feel like I still would not be here today." Florence added, "People who has helped me the most were Caucasians." These individuals offered employment opportunities, but they also demonstrated an appreciation of her culture and understanding the strengths that encompass her culture. She concluded, "Therefore, [cultural mediators] helped me to come to where I am today."

Cultural translators

Participants talked about the role that cultural translators or individuals from their own minority culture (De Anda, 1984) played in their pathway to higher-ranking administrative positions. These individuals were essential for their success, because they provided the cultural connection, helping participants to stay optimistic during difficult times. They shared stories about feeling fortunate for having individuals of their own culture in their professional settings, because they guided them towards the pathway to success and encouraged them to strive for their professional goals. Barbara stated,

> You come out of a certain culture environment, you may not be as cultured in the workplace, so you want to be able to mimic people who have made it as far as they have made it. Look at what they're doing, and then try to imitate that.

Laura approached her mentorship role with aspiring leaders with the aim to promote successful bicultural navigation. She talked about the importance of showing young professionals that they have choices about living a bicultural world. Ava had a similar experience regarding cultural translators offering advice of how to navigate the mainstream culture and her culture of color.

She shared an experience when she was feeling sick and had to attend a meeting. Since she was sick, she did not look as joyful as she always looked, but she was attentive at the meeting and took notes. After the meeting was over, she was approached by her immediate supervisor a White women, who told her that some people at the meeting were very concerned about her and apparently they wanted to know if she was unhappy. Ava was confused with the question, but told her supervisor that she had a headache. Ava stated,

> If an Anglo counterpart were to come in here and not smile, would that conversation have been the same? I go back to my office, and my [cultural translator told me], understand this. If you were not smiling, people do not know what to do. I was like, are you saying I can't not feel well? I can't have a bad day? She's was like, yes you can, as long as you keep it here in this office and no one see it.

As a result, Ava continues to practice the habit of smiling because she has noticed that if minorities are hired for higher ranking positions they have to portray that they are happy. She added, "I practice smiling because apparently it is very important that it appear that I am overjoyed every day." Ava recognizes that the strategy of constantly having to be on guard regarding how the mainstream culture perceives her is what has helped her to be successful in her job.

Role models

Participants shared the importance of role models or individuals of the minority culture (De Anda, 1984) in their success as Women of Color administrators. They expressed that the presence of role models was positive for them successfully traversing the leadership pipeline because they serve as providers of opportunities, support, and showed them a path of how to act in a professional setting. Laura stated, "they [minority culture] played a wonderful role, people in my culture [and] both the Latinos, the African Americans, and Asian Americans." In the case of Barbara, role models socialized her into leadership positions. More specifically, role models provided the foundation for what she should do, how she should act, and how she should respond in a professional setting. Barbara stated,

> In many cases [role models showed me], how I should dress. Fashion is not my thing. Trying to put together the fashionable, professional dress so that it didn't look, for lack of a better term, ethnic, or way out of the norm.

Elizabeth connected with different cultures such as African Americans because of the similarities that prevail with the being first generations. She added, "You can always learn from each other and encourage each other to cross that barrier." Ava had a similar experience with minorities, who are not African Americans. She said that the presence of role models has been positive because they [people of color] "see us [African Americans] as one." She added, "We are a minority group and we need to be supportive of one another." Such support is essential for their professional goal achievement.

Navigating home and work culture

Women of Color participants shared the strategies that they used in order to navigate their home and work culture. For example they shared stories about the importance of balancing the responsibilities at home and those responsibilities that come with their role as administrators. They also expressed that understanding their culture was essential for their success in the mainstream culture.

Balancing multiple responsibilities

Participants described the difficulty they encountered balancing their home and work responsibilities. Laura stated "for males is ok to work for long hours but for females is not". Laura, discussed how she and other women have struggled about deciding to get married, have children, or have a career. She said that if a woman of color wanted to have all three, they needed to be prepared for the challenges that come along. Barbara encountered similar difficulties when she began her career, she stated "as an administrator in trying to navigate that with my family responsibilities or my community responsibilities." She further added, "it was a lot of navigation to make sure that we all those balls that were floating in the air with them [children] and their activities." It was challenging to meet family expectations and responsibilities and those activities she had to perform as part of her administrator role.

Drawing upon culture towards a successful pathway

Participants accredited their success in the leadership roles due to their ability to have a solid understanding of their cultural background. Participants shared stories about the fact that family values and cultural background made them stronger leaders. Linda and Ava shared stories about how their knowledge of the history of their slave ancestors gave them the strength to strive for success in their leadership roles. Linda said that coming from a culture that used to "eating at the back, coming in the back door, to eating at the same establishment that my Anglo counterparts could easily just walk in and have a seat," has given her the resilience and tenacity to move forward in her goals as an administrator. Ava similarly shared her experience adding, "My culture as a whole has played a huge role in me achieving success because is allowed me to come to terms that this is the place that I live in, and yes, I can be successful," regardless of having a linage of ancestors who used to be slaves. Elizabeth mentioned that she comes from a family of strong Latina women who are in charge of their family. She stated,

> I think I grew up around that and knowing – they were powerful women, even though they might stay in the house and didn't work. I took their confidence and their strength and applied it just to me as a core inside.

Laura added that her mother embedded faith and the importance of a good value system. As part of a good value system she addressed that sometimes when women move up the ladder there are expectations of them changing the cultural value system. She further stated, "young professionals [need] to understand they don't have to change all about who they are" in order to fit the cultural values that it is expected while pursuing that higher-ranking leadership position.

Florence uses her expertise in Indian classical music as a way to succeed in her role as leader. She stated, "I was a professional singer in Bollywood, in India, and I also did a lot of the theater and drama, and all those types of things in India." She further stated, "when people here know that I am more than a scientist it helps me in my professional success because they can look at me as not just a science person but also as an art person." People at her campus understand that she has more skills to offer than her math and science skills.

Discussion and implications

In this study, we used bicultural socialization theory (De Anda, 1984) as a lens to investigate the leadership pathway for Women of Color administrators at community colleges. Bicultural socialization suggests that individuals of color have to learn to function in two environments, the environment of their own culture and the environment of the mainstream culture (i.e., White culture). The present study found that participants achieved success due to the extensive mentoring network they built, which includes cultural mediators, translators, and role models. This study further found that successful Women of Color administrators had to balance multiple responsibilities required by both environments, and they also leveraged their home culture to navigate the mainstream culture and achieve success in the leadership pipeline.

The present study found that Women of Color were successful in achieving high-ranking administrative positions because of the support they received from cultural mediators or individuals from the mainstream group (De Anda, 1984). Cultural mediators served as providers of information, guides or informal agents of socialization to individuals of the minority culture. These findings differ from bicultural socialization, since De Anda (1984) proposed that cultural mediators offer insight into the norms and behaviors of the mainstream culture, and the findings from this study suggest cultural mediators may only serve as gatekeepers to job opportunities. The participants in this study shared that cultural mediators offered their support through their education and created avenues for success by opening the door to high-ranking administrative positions. Future research should examine the difference among cultural mediators at a four-year and the mediators at the community college system. Additionally, scholars might investigate the experiences of Women of Color administrators' at other community college districts to explore the emergence of cultural mediators in their leadership pathway.

The findings of this study showed that cultural translators provided explicit steps for achieving leadership roles and also offered cultural support by instructing participants how to develop the ability to operate in a bicultural environment. For instance, the cultural translators shared how Women of Color administrators should perform their duties. This study is in line with other studies on cultural performance or ability to adjust behavior according to the norms of each culture (Braxton et al., 1997), because cultural translators serve as promoters of dual socialization by sharing their own experiences and facilitating the understanding of the values and perceptions of the mainstream culture (De Anda, 1984). Future research could examine the perspectives of cultural translators who mentor Women of Color administrators to understand how they approach mentorship and career advising. Further, additional research can explore the emotional and psychological responses Women of Color experience when expected to "perform" according to the mainstream culture. Findings from future studies could provide insight into best strategies for mentoring Women of Color emerging leaders.

This study found that role models served as providers of opportunities, support, as well as individuals that these Women of Color could emulate and follow their success pathway, since these role models were individuals of color. Literature highlights mentoring as a factor for achievement among individuals pursuing higher administrative positions, because these mentors provide support, training, and guidance (Dindoffer, Reid, & Freed, 2011). Giddis (2003) also concluded that the availability of mentors was important for the success of women in higher education. Moreton (2001), and Dunbar and Kinnersley (2011) further emphasized the view of the positive role that mentors have in the success of women's career advancement and promotion. However this study sheds light to the positive influence of role models (individuals of color) for the success of Women of Color in the leadership pipeline.

This study found that Women of Color ability to navigate their home and work culture was essential for their success in their administrative roles. Their ability to balance multiple responsibilities that were centered on their personal and professional lives aligns with Northouse (2013) suggestion that their responsibilities are often the result of gendered norms and cultural background values. The fact that domestic and child–rearing responsibilities generate challenges for women aspiring to climb the leadership ladder and obtain higher-ranking administrative positions supported by the participants in this study. However, little is known about the types of resources that community colleges have in place to support Women of Color who are pursuing high-rank administrative role and pursuing a family (i.e., family leave, child care). To address these family responsibilities and support efforts to diversify the leadership pipeline, community colleges can evaluate current resources and implement family support programs such as free or reduced childcare, workshops that target Women of Color and their family needs, maternity concierge services, and peer support programs. These programs could benefit students and administrators.

Finally, participants drew upon their culture knowledge, assets, and strengths in order to achieve success in their leadership positions. They attributed their professional success to a solid understanding of their cultural background. Participants used their ancestors' background (i.e., slavery, faith, family values) as inspiration and strength force to continue striving for their goals in difficult situations. The use of family values and cultural background made the participants stronger leaders at their institutions. Similarly, the literature (Montas-Hunter, 2012; Sagaria, 2002) found that Women of Color (i.e., Hispanics and African Americans) needed to have a shared value system with the mainstream group in order to survive the academe, therefore, requiring high levels of ethnic identity and acculturation. Future research could investigate the unique experiences of each ethnic group to understand how they specifically rely upon their culture to achieve success. Additionally, scholars may conduct ethnographic studies to fully understand how community colleges strive to create a culturally inclusive campus for staff and administrators.

Conclusion

The lack of representation of Women of Color in leadership positions at community colleges is problematic, since these institutions serve diverse students, yet they encounter challenges in leadership turnover and employee development (American Association of Community Colleges, 2016), finding themselves with the challenge of finding qualified candidates to replace their retirees (Eddy, 2013). Therefore, it was important to design a study that focuses on understanding how Women of Color use mentoring networks in order to achieve higher-ranking administrative positions. Moreover, it is imperative to learn how Women of Color' cultural background can be used as an asset for their success in their leadership roles at community colleges.

This study shed light on the experiences of Women of Color and their particular pathways to achieve success in acquiring high-ranking administrative positions. The study found the importance for Women of Color to develop an extensive mentorship system such as the availability of cultural mediators, cultural translators, and role models. Further, the Women of Color participants shared strategies for success such as being able to balance multiple responsibilities at work and the responsibilities that are required at home. The study underlined the importance for Women of Color to draw upon their culture as a source of strength and empowerment in the leadership pipeline. Successful Women of Color were able to leverage their cultural assets to navigate the dominant culture towards a successful pathway in their leadership careers as administrators. Concluding that Women of Color needed to understand their culture in order to be successful in the White culture, more exactly it shed light to the importance of being bicultural.

In conclusion this study illustrated the pathways for Women of Color who are pursued higher-ranking administrative positions. It provided information on how to create a mentoring network in order to navigate the leadership pipeline. Moreover, this study informed Women of Color about the importance of using their cultural background as an asset for their success and not as a barrier. The findings of this study can be used at the community colleges interested in developing Women of Color leaders and furthering a pipeline to executive level positions. It is very important to emphasize that for the success of Women of Color at community colleges it is essential to use bicultural socialization by navigating the environment of their non-White culture and that environment of the mainstream society culture.

References

American Association of Community Colleges. (2016). Diversity in instruction staff. *Data Points. AACC analysis of Integrated Postsecondary Education Data System (IPEDS) 2013 fall full- and part-time staff by occupational category, race/ethnicity and gender*. Retrieved from https://www.aacc.nche.edu/wp-content/uploads/2017/09/DP_Staff.pdf

American Council on Education. (2017). *American college presidents' study*. Retrieved from http://www.aceacps.org/women-presidents/

Avolio, B. J., & Gardner, W. L. (2005). Authentic leadership development: Getting to the root of positive forms of leadership. *The Leadership Quarterly, 16*(3), 315–338. doi:10.1016/j.leaqua.2005.03.001

Bailey, T. R., Jaggars, S. S., & Jenkins, D. (2015). *Redesigning America's community colleges*. Cambridge, MA: Harvard University Press.

Bell, E., & Nkomo, S. (2001). *Our separate ways: Black and white women and the struggle for professional identity*. Boston, MA: Harvard Business School Press.

Braxton, J. M., Sullivan, A. V. S., & Johnson, R. M. (1997). Appraising Tinto's theory of college student departure. In J. C. Smart (Ed.), *Higher Education: A handbook of theory and research* (Vol. 12, pp. 107–164). New York, NY: Agathon Press.

Chang, H., Longman, K. A., & Franco, M. A. (2014). Leadership development through mentoring in higher education: A collaborative autoethnography of leaders of color. *Mentoring & Tutoring: Partnership in Learning, 22*(4), 373–389. doi:10.1080/13611267.2014.945734

Chemers, M. M. (1997). *An integrative theory of leadership*. Mahwah, NJ: Lawrence Erlbaum.

Cho, S. (1996, March). Confronting the myths: Asian Pacific American faculty in higher education. *Ninth annual APAHE conference proceedings* (pp. 31–56). San Francisco: Asian Pacific Americans in Higher Education.

Cohen, A. M., & Brawer, F. B. (2003). *The American community college*. San Francisco, CA: John Wiley & Sons.

Crawford, K., & Smith, D. (2005). The we and the us mentoring African American women. *Journal of Black Studies, 36*(1), 52–67. doi:10.1177/0021934704265910

Creswell, J. W. (2013). *Qualitative inquiry and research design: Choosing among five approaches*. Thousand Oaks, CA: Sage.

Davis, A. T. (2009). Empowering African American women in higher education through mentoring. *Journal of the National Society of Allied Heath, 6*(7), 53–58.

De Anda, D. (1984). Bicultural socialization: Factors affecting the minority experience. *Social Work, 29*(2), 101–107. doi:10.1093/sw/29.2.101

Deaux, K., & Kite, M. (1993). Gender stereotypes. In F. L. Denmakr & M. Plaudi (Eds.), *Psychology of women: A handbook of theory and issues* (pp. 107–139). Westport, CT: Greenwood.

Dindoffer, T., Reid, B., & Freed, S. (2011). Women administrators in Christian universities: Making family and career co-central. *Journal of Research on Christian Education, 20*(3), 281–308. doi:10.1080/10656219.2011.624447

Dunbar, D. R., & Kinnersley, R. T. (2011). Mentoring female administrators toward leadership success. *Delta Kappa Gamma Bulletin, 77*(3), 17–24.

Eagly, A. H., & Karau, S. J. (2002). Role congruity theory of prejudice toward female leaders. *Psychological Review, 109* (3), 573–598. doi:10.1037/0033-295X.109.3.573

Eddy, P. L. (2008). Reflections of women leading community colleges. *The Community College Enterprise, 14*(1), 49–66. Retrieved from https://login.ezproxy.uta.edu/login?url=https://search-proquest-com.ezproxy.uta.edu/docview/218800576?accountid=7117

Eddy, P. L. (2013). Developing leaders: The role of competencies in rural community colleges. *Community College Review, 41*(1), 20–43. doi:10.1177/0091552112471557

Floyd, D. L., Maslin-Ostrowski, P., & Hrabak, M. R. (2010). Beyond the headlines: Wounding and the community college presidency. *New Directions for Community Colleges, (2010*(149), 65–72. Retrieved from http://search.ebscohost.com.ezproxy.uta.edu/login.aspx?direct=true&db=a9h&AN=48860710&site=ehost-live

Giddis, R. (2003). *The mentoring experience for women leaders in Florida's community colleges* (Unpublished doctoral dissertation). University of Florida, Gainesville. (UMI 3105610)

Gonzáles-Figueroa, E., & Young, A. M. (2005). Ethnic identity and mentoring among Latinas in professional roles. *Cultural Diversity and Ethnic Minority Psychology, 11*(3), 213. doi:10.1037/1099-9809.11.3.213

Griffin, K. A., & Reddick, R. J. (2011). Surveillance and sacrifice: Gender differences in the mentoring patterns of Black professors in predominately White research universities. *American Educational Research Journal, 48*(5), 1032–1057. doi:10.3102/0002831211405025

Ideta, L. M., & Cooper, J. E. (1999). Asian women leaders of higher education: Stories of strength and self-discovery. In L. Christian-Smith & K. Kellor (Eds.), *Everyday knowledge and uncommon truths: Women of the academy* (pp. 129–146). Boulder, CO: Westview Press.

Johnson, J. (2016). Gender differences in negotiation: Implications for salary negotiations. *UCLA Women's Law Journal, 23*(2), 131–151. Retrieved from http://search.ebscohost.com.ezproxy.uta.edu/login.aspx?direct=true&db=a9h&AN=122325504&site=ehost-live

Knoke, D., & Ishio, Y. (1998). The gender gap in company job training. *Work and Occupations, 25*(2), 141–167. doi:10.1177/0730888498025002002

Lincoln, Y. S., & Guba, E. G. (1985). *Naturalistic inquiry*. Newbury Park, CA: Sage.

Long, V. O., & Martinez, E. A. (1994). Masculinity, femininity, and Hispanic professional women's self-esteem and self-acceptance. *Journal of Counseling & Development, 73*(2), 183–186. doi:10.1002/j.1556-6676.1994.tb01733.x

Maxwell, J. A. (2005). *Qualitative research design: An interactive approach* (2nd ed.). Thousand Oaks, CA: Sage.

Merriam, S. (1988). *Case study research in education: A qualitative approach*. San Francisco, CA: Jossey-Bass.

Montas-Hunter, S. S. (2012). Self-efficacy and Latina leaders in higher education. *Journal of Hispanic Higher Education, 11*(4), 315–335. doi:10.1177/1538192712441709

Moreton, A. (2001). *Career paths of female chief academic officers in the Council for Christian Colleges and Universities* (Unpublished doctoral dissertation). University of North Texas, Denton.

Nixon, M. L. (2017). Experiences of women of color university chief diversity officers. *Journal of Diversity in Higher Education, 10*(4), 301–317. doi:10.1037/dhe0000043

Northouse, P. G. (2013). *Leadership: Theory and practice* (6th ed.). Thousand Oaks, CA: Sage.

Patitu, C. L., & Hinton, K. G. (2003). The experiences of African American women faculty and administrators in higher education: Has anything changed? *New Directions for Student Services, 2003*(104), 79–93. doi:10.1002/(ISSN)1536-0695

Rudman, L. A., & Glick, P. (2001). Prescriptive gender stereotypes and backlash toward agentic women. *Journal of Social Issues, 57*(4), 743. Retrieved from http://search.ebscohost.com.ezproxy.uta.edu/login.aspx?direct=true&db=a9h&AN=5487088&site=ehost-live

Sagaria, M. A. D. (2002). An exploratory model of filtering in administrative searches: Toward counter-hegemonic discourses. *Journal of Higher Education, 73*(6), 677–710. Retrieved from https://login.ezproxy.uta.edu/login?url=http://search.proquest.com.ezproxy.uta.edu/docview/61906576?accountid=7117

Seidman, I. (2013). *Interviewing as qualitative research: A guide for researchers in education and the social sciences*. New York, NY: Teachers College Press.

Stake, R. (1995). *The art of case study research*. Thousand Oaks, CA: Sage.

Tedrow, B., & Rhoads, R. A. (1999). A qualitative study of women's experiences in community college leadership positions. *Community College Review, 27*(3), 1–18. doi:10.1177/009155219902700301

Texas Higher Education Coordinating Board. (2017). *Accountability report. Community colleges complete report.* Retrieved from http://www.txhigheredaccountability.org/acctpublic/#twoYearAll

Townsend, B. K., & Twombly, S. B. (2007). Accidental Equity: The status of women in the community college. *Equity & Excellence in Education, 40*(3), 208–217. doi:10.1080/10665680701334777

U.S. Department of Education. Institute of Education Sciences, National Center for Education Statistics. (2018). *The condition of education. Undergraduate enrollment.* [Data file]. Retrieved from https://nces.ed.gov/programs/coe/indicator_cha.asp

Yin, R. (2014). *Case study research: Design and methods* (5th ed.). Thousand Oaks, CA: Sage Publications.

Yin, R. K. (2009). *Case study research: Design and method* (4th ed.). Thousand Oaks, CA: Sage.

Zamani-Gallaher, E. M. (2018). Practical leadership in community colleges: Navigating today's challenges. *Community College Review, 46*(1), 104–106. doi:10.1177/0091552117743568

"Where are My People At?": A Community Cultural Wealth Analysis of How Lesbian, Gay, and Bisexual Community College Students of Color Access Community and Support

Melvin A. Whitehead

ABSTRACT
Previous studies about lesbian, gay, bisexual, transgender, queer, and similarly-identified (LGBTQ+) college students have overwhelmingly centered White students and students attending four-year institutions. However, the literature suggests that community colleges – which tend to enroll higher percentages of students from minoritized racial and ethnic groups – may provide fewer LGBTQ+-specific resources to students than four-year institutions. Using community cultural wealth as a conceptual framework, this case study explored the experiences of lesbian, gay, and bisexual Students of Color attending a community college in accessing community and support. Specifically, I sought to understand how these experiences connected to participants' use of cultural capital. For this study, I conducted interviews with seven self-identified lesbian, gay, and bisexual Students of Color. Data analysis was guided by attention to the forms of cultural capital participants used in accessing community and support. Findings from the study describe how participants used social capital and navigational capital to access community, support, and needed resources. I conclude with specific recommendations for community college practices.

Compared to those attending four-year institutions, relatively little is known about the experiences of community college Students of Color who are lesbian, gay, bisexual, transgender, queer, and/or similarly-identified (LGBTQ+). Much of the literature examining the campus experiences of Students of Color at community colleges exclude mention of intersecting LGBTQ+ identities or heterosexist and cissexist oppression. Additionally, much of the research concerning LGBTQ+ college students centers those who are White and attending four-year institutions, and describes "theoretical and developmental models that were developed using traditional-aged, racially homogenous...students" (Zamani-Gallaher & Choudhuri, 2016, p. 48). Among LGBTQ+ People of Color at any institutional type, Rankin, Weber, Blumenfeld, and Frazer (2010) found that this population may experience higher rates of discrimination than their White queer- and trans-spectrum peers.

What is known about LGBTQ+ Students of Color is largely based on studies conducted at four-year institutions. However, there are substantial differences between two- and four-year institutions that warrant empirical study about those attending two-year institutions, particularly community colleges. Most community colleges are non-residential (Mullin, 2012), which can contribute to what Ivory (2012) referred to as "commuter campus syndrome" – the tendency of students at commuter campuses to go to class and leave shortly thereafter – a pattern that limits opportunities to engage with identity-based groups and generate a sense of community. Community colleges also enroll higher percentages of students from racially minoritized groups (National Center for Education Statistics, 2016; Zamani-Gallaher & Choudhuri, 2011), use adjunct faculty in higher numbers

(Cohen, Brawer, & Kisker, 2014), and enroll higher numbers of students who live at home and commute to school (Mullin, 2012). All of these trends are relevant for contextualizing institutionalized support for LGBTQ+ Students of Color attending community colleges and the extent to which this population engages with on-campus resources. For these reasons, inquiry grounded in community cultural wealth and centered on LGBTQ+ Students of Color at community colleges is relevant and necessary for 1) deepening researchers' and practitioners' understanding of this population; 2) revealing how the intercentricity of their racial, ethnic, gender, and sexual identities shaping their experiences manifest in community college contexts; and 3) foregrounding the forms of capital this population uses to resist the discrimination and other oppressive structures reflected in the literature. Such an understanding of LGBTQ+ Students of Color enrolled in community colleges may be useful in informing the development of inclusive institutional policies and practices.

The purpose of this case study was to explore the experiences of self-identified LGBTQ+ Students of Color attending a community college, defined as a "not-for-profit institution regionally accredited to award the associate in arts or the associate in science as its highest degree" (Cohen et al., 2014, p. 5). Specifically, this study sought to understand 1) LGBTQ+ Students' of Color experiences with accessing community and support, and 2) how these experiences were shaped by participants' use of cultural capital.

Literature review

In this section, I discuss the literature regarding LGBTQ+ students attending community colleges and LGBTQ+ Students of Color at any institutional type. Three strands of research emerged from the literature: campus climate; structural support; and identity and interpersonal relations.

Campus climate

Numerous studies have discussed the racist and/or chilly climates for Students of Color at historically White institutions, though most of them focus on four-year institutional settings (Maxwell & Shammas, 2014). The few studies examining racial and ethnic climates at community colleges – in addition to other studies about racially/ethnically minoritized student populations at community colleges – have suggested that campus environments at these institutions are racist and/or alienating for Students of Color (Mattice, 1994; Weissman, Bulakowski, & Jumisko, 1998). Scholars have found that Students of Color at community colleges have experienced loneliness and tokenization in their classrooms (Mattice, 1994) and have reported interactions with campus counselors who did not listen to their needs nor could connect to them across language and cultural differences (California Tomorrow, 2002). Black and Latina/o/x[1] community college students have reported enduring racist comments from student peers, racist invalidating attitudes and behavior from faculty members, and low expectations from others on campus (California Tomorrow, 2002; Carrasquillo, 2013; Gardenhire-Crooks, Collado, Martin, & Castro, 2010).

Campus climate literature pertaining to LGBTQ+ students in community colleges suggests similarly hostile environments (Franklin, 1998; Kiekel, 2012; Zamani-Gallaher & Choudhuri, 2016). In the first mention of lesbian, gay, and bisexual (LGB) students at two-year colleges in the literature, Franklin (1998) found that one-fourth of the respondents in a survey of students attending a two-year college admitted to making anti-gay remarks and 10% admitted to either threatening or committing physical violence to someone perceived to be gay or lesbian. Studies examining campus climates for LGBTQ+ students at community colleges since Franklin's (1998) study suggest that such climates have improved, though some forms of stigmatization remain (Garvey, Taylor, & Rankin, 2014; Kiekel, 2012; Zamani-Gallaher & Choudhuri, 2016). In these studies, students have reported perceiving the campus climate to be generally inclusive (Garvey et al., 2014; Kiekel, 2012), as evidenced by institutional documents (e.g., non-discrimination policies and other institutional statements and guidelines) that communicated the value of LGBTQ+ inclusivity; visible LGBTQ+

communities and support systems on campus; and respect from faculty, peers, and staff (Kiekel, 2012; Zamani-Gallaher & Choudhuri, 2016). However, LGBTQ+ community college students have also reported a lack of inclusivity of LGBTQ+-related issues and identities in curricula and faculty who were either indifferent to or openly unsupportive of LGBTQ+ issues (Garvey et al., 2014; Zamani-Gallaher & Choudhuri, 2016).

Structural support

In their efforts to address the disproportionately low retention, graduation, and transfer rates among Latina/o/x, Black, Native American, and low-income students (American Association of Community Colleges, 2012), many community colleges have developed programs, formed partnerships, and constructed their environments in ways that bolster support for these communities. These efforts include an integration of Native cultures into institutional purpose, curricula, and physical design (DeLong, Monette, & Ozaki, 2016); learning communities and curricular pathways targeting underserved Asian American and Pacific Islander communities (Murphy & Tomaneng, 2016); support groups, mentoring, and targeted academic and career development services for Black and Latina/o/x students (Atwater & Holmes, 2016; Tovar, 2015; White, 2010), partnerships with local Latina/o/x-serving organizations; and financial aid literacy workshops targeting Latina/o/x local high school students (Padrón, 2016).

Structural support for LGBTQ+ students at community colleges may be less prevalent. In the only empirical work concerning structural support for LGBTQ+ students at community colleges, Nguyen, Brazelton, Renn, and Woodford (2018) found four common LGBTQ+-specific resources offered across two- and four-year institutions: LGBTQ+ resource centers, LGBTQ+ counseling services, LGBTQ+ career services, and LGBTQ+ student organizations. These resources played important roles in providing LGBTQ+ students with various forms of support (psychological, academic, social, and vocational). However, findings from their study suggested that LGBTQ+-specific counseling services, resource centers, and student organizations may be less common at two-year institutions than at four-year institutions, and that LGBTQ+ community college students may have the most limited access to necessary support (Nguyen et al., 2018).

Identity and interpersonal relations

While the empirical literature about LGBTQ+ Students of Color attending community colleges is scarce, studies about LGBTQ+ Students of Color (at any institution type) and LGBTQ+ students attending community colleges (of any race) were useful for guiding the direction of this study. These studies suggest that adverse campus climates, barriers to structural support, and complexities in navigating identities and interpersonal relationships may figure prominently in the lived experiences of LGBTQ+ community college Students of Color. In this section, I provide an overview of the literature about LGBTQ+ Students of Color in higher education.

In addition to overt discrimination, harassment, and violence, the literature suggests that LGBTQ+ Students of Color are also harmed by less explicit forms of racial oppression, particularly as they relate to group membership. Gay-straight alliance (GSA) student organizations at many schools serve as spaces for students to come together and support one another around LGBTQ+ identities and issues. However, O'Mara (1997) argued that the suppression of racial and ethnic identities within GSAs may also alienate Students of Color. Similarly, some scholars have suggested that this single-identity focus within LGBTQ+ groups and spaces can lead to racial segregation and the normalization of whiteness (Nicolazzo, 2016), which, in turn, can deter Students of Color from participating and serve to maintain a White majority.

There is evidence suggesting that many LGBTQ+ Students of Color feel alienated and unvalued on their campuses (Strayhorn, 2012), feel the need to suppress their sexual identities within peer groups (Zamani-Gallaher & Choudhuri, 2016), and experience stigmatization in groups formed around a shared single identity (Nicolazzo, 2016; Peña-Talamantes, 2013). To maintain their in-group racial support and guard against the emotional consequences of performing their sexually minoritized selves, research suggests that some Black queer students perform heteronormatively around their Black heterosexual cisgender peers (Zamani-Gallaher & Choudhuri, 2016). While the literature about transgender Collegians of Color is scant, Black non-binary trans* students in Nicolazzo's (2016) study reported a lack of spaces on campus in which they felt free to discuss and navigate both their Black and trans* identities. Although peer groups should ideally be spaces where students can find safety and community, and be free to express their racial, ethnic, and sexual marginalized selves; students with multiple marginalized identities can experience these spaces as antipathetic or alienating.

Conceptual framework

Community cultural wealth (CCW) is a conceptual framework that was developed by Tara Yosso (2005) to describe the various knowledge, skills, and abilities that Communities of Color use to survive. CCW is a critique of "deficit thinking" (p. 75) – a model that places a premium value on the knowledges associated with White upper- and middle-class cultures (Yosso, 2005). Deficit thinking posits that Communities of Color – particularly those from low-wealth backgrounds – lack the social and cultural capital necessary for social mobility and frames Students of Color as disadvantaged due to their racial, ethnic, and class backgrounds (Yosso, 2005). CCW disrupts this centering of White upper- and middle-class cultures as an accepted standard and draws heavily upon the tenets of critical race theory, including emphases on: 1) the centrality of People of Color's experiential knowledge in matters of race and racism, 2) a commitment to social justice, and 3) the intercentricity of race and racism with other identities and forms of oppression (McCoy & Rodericks, 2015).

CCW is comprised of six forms of cultural capital: *aspirational, linguistic, familial, resistant, navigational, and social* (Yosso, 2005). *Aspirational capital* refers to Students' of Color abilities to retain their hopes for the future, even while encountering barriers (Yosso, 2005). *Linguistic capital* describes the intellectual and social skills a Student of Color develops through communication experiences in more than one language and/or linguistic style (Yosso, 2005). *Familial capital* describes cultural knowledge nurtured among family members that "carry a sense of community, history, memory, and cultural intuition" (Yosso, 2005, p. 79). *Resistant capital* refers to the knowledge and skills that Students of Color develop through engaging in oppositional behaviors that challenge inequality (e.g., resisting dominant societal messages about one's cultural groups; Yosso, 2005). *Navigational capital* refers to Students' of Color abilities to maneuver educational institutions, particularly those built without them in mind (Yosso, 2005). *Social capital* describes Students' of Color abilities to draw upon networks of people and community resources needed to access support (Yosso, 2005). In an elaborated conceptualization, Stanton-Salazar (1997, 2011) described social capital as key forms of social support that are embedded within one's network. Stanton-Salazar's (1997, 2011) framework for understanding social capital among low-wealth Students of Color foregrounds the roles of *institutional agents*, or high-status individuals within a student's network who have the capacity to connect that student to highly-valued institutional resources and opportunities. Findings from this study are framed by the CCW framework's social capital and navigational capital.

Methodology

This study was informed by a transformative paradigmatic stance (Mertens, 2005). The transformative paradigm is concerned with the lives and experiences of marginalized groups, the root causes of inequities and asymmetric power relationships, and connecting research to political and social action. (Mertens, 2005). This paradigm was an appropriate match for the study due to the latter's focus on the lives and experiences of a marginalized group (LGBTQ+ Students of Color), use of a critical theoretical framework that focuses inquiry on multiple forms of oppression, and aim of informing practice. A qualitative instrumental case study design (Stake, 1995) was used to gain insight into the research questions through an investigation of LGBTQ+ Students' of Color experiences within a specific institutional context. Case study designs produce rich, in-depth, context-dependent data (Patton, 2015), which can be useful in bolstering the transferability of the study's findings and informing practice at other institutions.

Sampling methods

The unit of analysis was a single community college, referred to in this manuscript as Blackmon Junior College (BJC; a pseudonym). Purposive sampling allowed for the selection of an information-rich case that could produce in-depth data concerning the focus of the study (Patton, 2015). The following criteria were used to select a case: an urban campus setting, a total enrollment of at least 10,000 students (of which Students of Color comprised at least 25%), a nonresidential campus, and the presence of a GSA. Although some scholars have challenged the myth of isolated queer life in rural areas, there is some research suggesting that urban areas may be more tolerant of those with non-normative sexualities (Greenberg, 1988). For this reason, an urban campus setting – particularly a large one with a GSA – facilitated the process of finding students willing to participate in this study.

Purposive sampling was used to identify seven participants. To participate in the study, students must have: 1) self-identified as a Person of Color, 2) self-identified as being LGBTQ+, and 3) been currently enrolled at the institution. To recruit students for interviews, I asked the advisors of the college's GSA to distribute flyers about the study across the institution's multiple campuses. Recruitment emails were also sent to the GSA advisors to distribute to students on the GSA's listserv. Lastly, a call for participation was posted on the institution's blog, which facilitated the recruitment of eligible students who were not affiliated with the GSA. All postings about the study included eligibility criteria for participation, as well as information about the financial incentive (a $25 Amazon gift card). All participants completed a demographic information survey to confirm their eligibility for the study. Prior to the start of each interview, each participant gave verbal consent after reading the informed consent document and being given the opportunity to ask clarifying questions about their participation.

Data collection methods

Seven students were interviewed over a two-month period (November 2017-January 2018). Interviews were conducted via video-conferencing and phone (depending on the medium with which the participant was most comfortable). Each interview lasted 35 to 90 minutes and centered on the student's experiences at and perceptions of the institution, as well as their experiences with communities and support. Table 1 shows the demographics represented in the sample. The names of

Table 1. Participant demographics.

	Full-time /Part-time	Campus	Length at institution	Identities	Age
Joseph	Full-time	Central	3.5 years	Gay man, Hispanic, Cuban	21
Angelina*	Full-time	Central	3 semesters	Hispanic, Bisexual Woman, First Generation American	19
Veronica	Full-time	Central	2.5 years	Black, Bisexual, Questioning (gender)	21
Ian	Full-time	Gilstrap	2 years	Vietnamese-American, Gay man	19
Cole	Full-time	Overstreet	1 semester	Black Lesbian, Woman	18
Ayla	Full-time	Online	2 years	Hawaiian, Chinese, Irish (identifies most strongly with Hawaiian heritage), Bisexual, female	24
Rell	Part-time	Childs	1.5 years	Black, African-American, Stud, Gender Fluid, Lesbian	19

*Interview data were culled from notes, rather than transcriptions, due to a failed audio recording

the participants and the campuses at which they attended classes are pseudonyms and the identities listed were given in the participants' own words. All interviews were audio-recorded with the participants' permission and handwritten notes were taken during each interview to capture participant responses in case of audio recording failure. The recording for one of the interviews did fail, so data from this interview were culled entirely from interview notes. Consequently, the data from this interview are less rich and descriptive. The participant for this interview is noted with an asterisk in Table 1.

Data analysis

Data analysis was guided by attention to the forms of cultural capital used by the participants in the study. All interviews were transcribed by a third party and reviewed for accuracy. The process of reviewing the audio transcript led to additional thoughts about the data, which were captured in additional notes. Memos – preliminary drafts of emerging themes across the interviews – were maintained throughout the process of collecting data and reviewing transcriptions. All memos were labelled with descriptive titles and dates and grouped with related notes. All data (interview transcripts, memos, and notes) were then imported into NVivo for initial and concept coding (Saldaña, 2016). Most codes were based upon memos, while others were entirely inductive (directly from the interview transcripts). After completing the initial coding for the interviews, descriptions for all codes were developed. Axial coding was then completed for all interview transcripts. During this stage, I developed categories and subcategories from the codes, detailed their properties and conditions, and described how they related to one another (Saldaña, 2016). After all coding was completed, axial codes were developed and collapsed into major themes. Each theme was then further defined by detailing its characteristics and conditions.

Positionality

I am a doctoral candidate studying College Student Affairs Administration at a historically White institution in the southeastern U.S. I identify as a Black queer transgender man from a mixed social class background. Although I have never attended a community college as a student, I worked at one for five years where I served as an advisor for the college's GSA. During my time as the GSA advisor, I repeatedly observed the initial surge of and gradual decline in participation among Students of Color each year – a pattern that always resulted in a majority White membership. These observations prompted me to wonder how LGBTQ+ Students of Color experienced the GSA and where and how they accessed support and community. My identities as queer, transgender, and as a Person of Color may have provided me with insider status with the participants in this study. Such insider status may have allowed me to access information that would otherwise be unavailable to me if I did not share these identities. For example, Black participants were particularly frank with me about their experiences with anti-Black racism and racial microaggressions. However, my lack of experience as a community college student and my unfamiliarity with their institution gave me an outsider status with the participants. During this study, I intentionally developed an interview protocol that would allow me to collect data that challenged my assumptions, lest my positionality lead me to overemphasize findings confirming my previous experiences and observations.

Trustworthiness

To build the trustworthiness of this study, findings were triangulated by examining data across multiple participants. Member checking (Guba & Lincoln, 1981) was also used. All participants were emailed a summary of preliminary findings and asked to confirm whether or not the summary accurately captured what they had shared. Two participants responded and indicated that it did. The reliability of this study was strengthened by the use of an "audit trail" of evidence linking all conclusions to specific data (Guba & Lincoln, 1981, p. 122).

Limitations

Several limitations were present within the research design. First, the sample of participants did not include anyone who identified as transgender. Interviewing transgender Students of Color may have provided additional data that would have been helpful for understanding the ways in which they experience community and support and use cultural capital to navigate the institution. Second, all the participants were between the ages of 18 and 24 – the typical age for undergraduate students – and most were enrolled full-time. These demographics are not representative of community college student populations, who tend to be older and are less likely to be enrolled full-time than students attending four-year institutions (Zamani-Gallaher & Choudhuri, 2011). Third, participants were not systematically asked to describe the environments at their respective campuses. During the study, it became evident that their experiences were, in some ways, shaped by differences in the individual regional campus environments. Therefore, an understanding of the role that campus location plays in shaping participants' experiences is limited.

Findings

This study sought to understand LGBTQ+ community college Students' of Color experiences with accessing community and support and how these experiences were shaped by participants' utilization of cultural capital. A lack of visible representation of students, staff, and faculty sharing salient identities (e.g., their racial/ethnic identities and/or sexual orientation) also emerged as a theme and underlay participants' use of cultural capital. While multiple forms of cultural capital were reflected in participants' responses, findings from this study are specifically framed by two forms of capital that were most prevalent: social capital and navigational capital.

Limited visible representation

The scarcity of visible representation of students, staff, and faculty who shared participants' salient social identities undergirded the necessity for participants to use social and navigational capital. This theme was present across all participants, and it had varying effects on them. Angelina, who had initially described the campus environment as "student-life centered," said that the lack of visible representation of people sharing her identities had a negative impact on her self-esteem. Cole shared that the lack of visible representation of others like her was a demotivator for campus involvement:

> Sometimes [the lack of representation] is a burden because it makes me feel like I'm just here…it makes me not want to get involved, it makes me feel like I just need to go to school, get my education, and then leave, like I don't feel the need to be involved in anything that [BJC] offers.

The limited visible representation of those who shared the participants' identities also served to limit their ability to find meaningful communities. Ian, who had not disclosed his gay identity to others on campus, had initially described the campus environment as welcoming. However, he also spoke about how the lack of visible representation of those with shared identities was a barrier to finding people with whom he could connect and left him feeling isolated:

> You don't really see anyone you can relate to, in a way. It's like, even though I said that this place is welcoming, in a way, it's like you want to find people who you can really connect with, people you can talk to about things you want to keep secret or it's just really personal to you. It was a little bit hard, that's for sure, but I've been able to manage so far.

Rell spoke about how the scarcity of Black studs and the lack of physical spaces for them to meet on campus shaped her experiences building community:

> I would say they're there, but there's no space for us to speak on [our experiences as Black studs] ... I would say it's somewhat rare every time you see someone that is a Black stud.... We don't speak to each other. It's usually like some strange masculinity eye contact off where we're just eyeing each other for no reason and it's because it's a rarity for us to see one another and I feel if [the GSA] had better advertising, they could all meet up, we could all just be cool and just talk.

Other participants were deterred from engaging in identity-based groups, specifically the GSA, because it was not perceived to be well-attended. Joseph expressed frustration about the large number of students at BJC and the low attendance at the GSA:

> I still am salty that there are so many students when I first got here and then recently when I went to the [Fall Fest], you can't find them, and then when you go to the [GSA] meeting, like five people [are there]. So it's like, where are my people at, where are you guys at?

All participants reported not feeling well-represented in the campus environment, which – to them – meant that they perceived very few people at the college who shared their salient identities. Despite this challenge, participants used social and navigational capital to access the salient communities and spaces they needed to survive.

Social capital

Participants' social capital was comprised of networks of resources and people that they used to access various forms of support (Yosso, 2005). Participants built social capital through engagement with on-campus student groups, off-campus organizations, campus resources, virtual communities and spaces, peers within their programs, and supportive staff and faculty members. On-campus social capital was necessary for accessing academic and emotional support, engendering a sense of belonging within the institution, and allowing participants to feel comfortable and free to be themselves. Ayla and Angelina discussed their deep engagement with one student club – the GSA – in which they had previously served in leadership roles. When speaking about the GSA, Ayla said: "The group itself is probably the most support I have ever had with any kind of physical [face-to-face group]." Angelina described the GSA as inclusive and accepting and indicated that the group provided a space to talk about LGBT issues. Speaking about the social support he received from his instructors, Joseph shared:

> I feel like I can honestly tell my teachers – and one of them I'm really close to – and I literally can tell her anything, I don't feel judged... I just walk in and they already treat me as if I'm gay...some people would think that's bad, but I think it's good because I don't feel like I have to like pretend. I just feel like it's already known, I don't even have to talk about it, and then it just made me feel comfortable

Participants also reported using social capital to access off-campus sources of support through virtual and face-to-face communities. These forms of support helped participants feel respected in one's racial/ethnic culture, helped participants feel that they were part of a larger community of people who shared their salient identities, and provided them with communities to which they could turn for advice, empowerment, representation, and emotional and mental health support. For some participants, social capital was linked to a need for social support specifically from individuals with their shared salient identities. Cole had previously received mental health support through an app for LGBTQ+ individuals living with depression:

> I had suffered from depression and suicidal thoughts after me and my prior girlfriend broke up and it would be like, I would make posts about that and they would help me – they had like advisors within the app who would personally contact you if they felt that you were a risk and that helped me a lot because they eventually ended up contacting me about twice a week.

Speaking to the importance of her engagement with other Black people on Twitter, Rell shared:

> I feel affirmed by [Black Twitter] because – it's like we all grew up the same way, it's like by referring to the little things in life growing up because …most of us grew up in poverty and it's like we can joke about the things that we grew up on. The poverty became the culture… I know it sounds strange, but everyone had the same cheap plastic cups and they showed a cup on that and it's insane how viral that post went because we all recognize, oh okay, we all used the same extremely cheap Dollar Tree cups growing up and it's crazy how we can all relate to the little things.

All participants indicated accumulating social capital through access to emotional, academic, social, and mental health support through various sources. On-campus and off-campus sources of support met both similar and divergent needs; on-campus forms of support facilitated connections to the institution, while off-campus forms were useful in finding representation of those who shared salient identities and generating a sense of community and shared experiences. Ultimately, this form of cultural capital allowed participants to survive campus environments they perceived to be devoid of people sharing their salient identities.

Navigational capital

Navigational capital refers to "the ability to maneuver through social institutions" (Yosso, 2005, p. 80). In this study, participants used navigational capital to access support and physical safety, avoid encounters with homoantagonism, and aid decisions about disclosure about one's identities. Furthermore, the ways in which participants accrued navigational capital were nuanced and grew increasingly more refined over time in response to either stigmatizing experiences in their environments or the anticipation of such experiences. These stigmatizing experiences included microaggressions, discriminatory interactions, hostile body language, and verbal slurs. Ayla shared her experience with a campus counselor:

> I've spoken with a counselor once and it just felt like the moment I mentioned something LGBT-related she kind of withdrew, like she was less into the discussion we were having. I excused myself shortly after and I never really went back to another counselor, even though I would get stressed out between everything. I had to rely more on [John], my [GSA] advisor, to kind of vent things out towards or get a better perspective….He takes his time and deals with us.

Here, Ayla described how her negative experience with a counselor allowed her to seek support from a source known to be more helpful and affirming.

Navigational capital was also used to counteract the effects of low visible representation of those with shared salient identities and supplant the institution's lack of meaningful communities and adequate social support. Several participants reported searching for and accessing online communities and local community organizations. Ian shared:

> The only place that I usually go to feel like part of the community is online basically. So, I would normally just search for any LGBTQ movies just go to those links and watch them. Or I would go to YouTube and find these different YouTube communities or YouTubers that basically have publicly self-identified themselves under that LGBTQ and I would just watch their videos because it's just nice to see representation.

Navigational capital was also used to assess the extent to which existing spaces on campus, like the GSA, would be inclusive and affirming. Two participants noted the racial and gender demographics of individuals in the GSA's Facebook group. Based on what Veronica saw, they concluded that engagement with the GSA had the potential to be a tokenizing experience: "The [GSA] club itself – the Facebook page it has – is led by White males, so I was like, I've got nothing to do with that unless I actually go and then I'm the representation itself." Veronica later sought out a local LGBTQ+ community group that included "lots of non-White people."

Finally, navigational was also used to make decisions regarding disclosure of one's sexual orientation. Two participants reported holding back on sharing parts of themselves, even within communities that were important to them and provided emotional support. When asked about what topics Cole felt she could not share with her closest group of friends from school, she responded:

Maybe some of the things that I do out in public or some of the events that I go to. Like I don't think they'd really understand that a couple of months ago I did go to [an LGBT] pride event and it was in Atlanta. I don't think they would understand why I went or understand my reasoning behind going.

Participants' use of navigational capital was vital for their survival at the institution in that it enabled them to manage stress brought on by microaggressions, ensure physical safety for themselves and their friends, assess the likelihood of receiving support in specific spaces, and maneuver social situations with those without their shared salient identities. Overall, participants' use of this form of cultural capital suggested a construct of the campus environment as an intricate terrain with pockets of support (albeit at varying levels) and harm; participants used navigational capital to maximize encounters within environments known to be affirming and minimize encounters with the potential to be antagonistic.

Discussion

Using community cultural wealth to explore the experiences of lesbian, gay, bisexual, and gender non-conforming (GNC) Students of Color at a community college in accessing community and support revealed two significant points for discussion. First – like LGBTQ+ Students of Color attending four-year institutions (Nicolazzo, 2016; Strayhorn, 2012) – the participants in this study reported feeling alienated and experiencing multiple forms of marginalization. Participants' experiences with alienation and marginalization were connected to their perceptions that few people in the campus environment shared identities that were salient to them. Their perceptions, in turn, may have been a result of the limited resource, program, and student organization offerings targeting these salient identities. For example, participants expressed the need for resources and spaces for LGBTQ+ students, Black students, Black LGBTQ+ students, Latina/o/x students, and first generation-American students – none of which were offered by their institution. Findings from this study corroborate previous literature about the minimal representation of LGBTQ+ identities and issues in community college curricula and programming (Garvey et al., 2014; Zamani-Gallaher & Choudhuri, 2016) and suggest that this lack of visible representation may have especially profound effects on LGBTQ+ community college Students of Color. Further, these effects may be exacerbated through the lack of single identity-based support (e.g., based on one's race or status as a first-generation American), and support based on an intersection of one's multiple minoritized identities (e.g., as a Black lesbian).

Second, findings from this study extend the literature about LGB/GNC Students of Color by describing how – despite the scarcity of LGBTQ+-specific resources and the low visibility of those sharing their salient identities – participants used social and navigational capital to fill in these gaps. Participants built social capital by engaging with a variety of individuals, communities and spaces and used it to access various forms of support, as well as engender feelings of belonging, empowerment, and comfort. This study also highlights how LGB/GNC Students of Color respond to racism and homoantagonism in their campus environments through building navigational capital that enables them to access spaces that feel safe, affirmed, and not alone.

Implications and recommendations

The findings from this study offer several implications for community colleges in supporting LGBTQ+ Students of Color. First, community colleges should develop and cultivate the spaces that LGBTQ+ Students of Color need to feel supported and valued. In so doing, community colleges can better facilitate LGBTQ+ Students' of Color accrual of social capital. Participants in the study expressed the need for various social identity-based resources and spaces. Although BJC had a student group for LGBTQ+ students, some participants did not perceive the group to be racially diverse. Through offering such spaces on campus – or supporting students in creating and cultivating these spaces themselves via kinship networks (Nicolazzo, Pitcher, Renn, & Woodford, 2017) – community colleges can strengthen support for LGBTQ+ Students of Color through building their social capital.

Second, findings suggest the need for effective marketing of Safe Zone programs and the GSAs, which can be helpful for LGBTQ+ Students' of Color in refining their navigational capital. When asked about what the college could do to better support them, one participant suggested an ally training program, which indicated that they were not aware that such a program already existed at the institution. Another participant who *was* aware of the Safe Zone program indicated that the presence of the program helped her feel supported. Similarly, two participants were unaware of the GSA and expressed a need for such a group. Even though the GSA was posted on BJC's webpage of available student groups, findings suggest that this alone is insufficient for communicating the existence of the group to students, particularly to those attending classes at regional campuses. To create a supportive and affirming environment for LGBTQ+ Students of Color, community colleges can explore additional means of reaching this population. For example, institutions could create a separate web page listing resources for LGBTQ+ students – a suggestion offered by three participants – or explore offline ways of promoting these resources.

Finally, community colleges should center LGBTQ+ Students of Color in college programming and curricula to create environments in which LGBTQ+ Students of Color see themselves well-represented. Among the participants in this study, scarce visible representation of those sharing salient identities engendered low self-esteem and feelings of isolation and discouraged them from getting involved with the campus. Institutions can center LGBTQ+ Students of Color in programming through bringing LGBTQ+ Speakers of Color to campus for lectures and keynotes; highlighting the contributions of LGBTQ+ People of Color in course curricula; assessing environments for LGBTQ+ Students of Color in existing programs; and developing programming that provides them a space to process the intersection of salient identities.

Future directions and conclusion

Ultimately, findings from this study underscore the importance of centering students who are often at the margins and repeatedly overlooked in programming and resource offerings – specifically, students with multiple marginalized identities. Centering these populations in programming decisions and resource offerings can help cultivate the supportive campus environments they need to succeed. Future research should explore the experiences of transgender Students of Color attending community colleges, particularly those in cities and states with a recent history of anti-trans legislation. Data collected for this study suggested that transgender Students of Color at BJC may experience the campus environment in ways that are markedly different from the participants in this study. Such research can help practitioners gain a fuller understanding of how campus environments are shaping the experiences of trans students on their campuses, particularly trans Students of Color, who may be most vulnerable to sexual, verbal, and physical harassment while in college (James et al., 2016). Additionally, future research should further explore, through a campus ecology lens, how LGBTQ+ Students' of Color experiences with marginalization in campus and off-campus environments shape their accumulation of navigational capital. Specifically, the Minoritized Identities of Sexuality and Gender Students and Contexts Model (Vaccaro, Russell, & Koob, 2015) can be useful in illuminating how students' use of navigational capital vary (if at all) across institutional and home contexts.

Note

1. Queer communities have used the term "Latinx" to refer to Latin American communities in ways that resist the masculine-centricity embedded in "Latino" and binary assumptions about gender embedded in "Latino/a" and Latin@ (Salinas & Lozano, 2017). I use "Latina/o/x" to promote gender inclusivity.

Funding

This work was supported through a grant from the Southern Association for College Student Affairs.

References

American Association of Community Colleges. (2012). *Reclaiming the American dream: Community colleges and the nation's future*. A report from the 21st-century Commission on the Future of Community Colleges. Retrived from: http://files.eric.ed.gov/fulltext/ED535906.pdf doi:10.1094/PDIS-11-11-0999-PDN

Atwater, K., & Holmes, J. B. (2016). Hillsborough community college, Tampa, Florida. In A. Long (Ed.), *Overcoming educational racism in the community college: Creating pathways to success for minority and impoverished student populations*. [Kindle version]. Sterling, VA: Stylus.

California Tomorrow. (2002). *The high-quality learning conditions needed to support students of color and immigrants at California community colleges*. Sacramento, CA: Author.

Carrasquillo, C. A. (2013). *In their own words: High-achieving, low-income community college students talk about supports and obstacles to their success* (Unpublished doctoral dissertation). University of California, San Diego.

Cohen, A. M., Brawer, F. B., & Kisker, C. B. (2014). *The American community college* (6th ed.). San Francisco, CA: Jossey-Bass.

DeLong, L. M., Monette, G. E., & Ozaki, C. C. (2016). Nurturing student success in tribal colleges. In C. C. Ozaki & R. L. Spaid (Eds.), *Applying college change theories to student affairs practice* (pp. 65–74). No. 174. San Francisco, CA: New Direction for Community Colleges.

Franklin, K. (1998, August). *Psychosocial motivations of hate crimes perpetrators: Implications for educational intervention*. Paper presented at the 106th Annual Convention of the American Psychological Association, San Francisco, CA.

Gardenhire-Crooks, A., Collado, H., Martin, K., & Castro, A. (2010). Terms of engagement: Men of color discuss their experiences in community college. n.p.: MDRC.

Garvey, J. C., Taylor, J. L., & Rankin, S. (2014). An examination of campus climate for LGBTQ community college students. *Community College Journal of Research and Practice*, 39(6), 527–541. doi:10.1080/10668926.2013.861374

Greenberg, D. F. (1988). *The construction of homosexuality*. Chicago, IL: University of Chicago.

Guba, E. G., & Lincoln, Y. S. (1981). *Effective evaluation*. San Francisco, CA: Jossey-Bass.

Ivory, B. T. (2012). Little known, much needed: Addressing the cocurricular needs of LGBTQ students. *Community College Journal of Research and Practice*, 36(7), 482–493. doi:10.1080/10668926.2012.664086

James, S. E., Herman, J. L., Rankin, S., Keisling, M., Mottet, L., & Anafi, M. (2016). *The report of the 2015 U.S. transgender survey*. Washington, DC: National Center for Transgender Equality.

Kiekel, C. (2012). *Perceptions of climate and engagement for LGBTQ community college students* (Unpublished doctoral dissertation). California State University, Northridge. doi:10.1094/PDIS-11-11-0999-PDN

Mattice, N. J. (1994). *Campus climate survey*. Santa Clarita, CA: College of the Canyons.

Maxwell, W., & Shammas, D. (2014). Research on race and ethnic relations among community college students. In E. M. Zamani-Gallaher, J. Lester, D. D. Bragg, & L. S. Hagedorn (Eds.), *ASHE reader series on community colleges* (4th ed., pp. 347–357). Boston, MA: Pearson.

McCoy, D. L., & Rodericks, D. L. (2015). Critical race theory in higher education: 20 years of theoretical and research innovations. *ASHE Higher Education Report*, 41(3), 1–117. doi:10.1002/aehe.20021

Mertens, D. M. (2005). *Research and evaluation in education and psychology* (2nd ed.). Los Angeles, CA: Sage.

Mullin, C. M. (2012). *Why access matters: The community college student body (policy brief 2012-01pbl)*. Washington, DC: American Association of Community Colleges. Retrieved from: http://www.aacc.nche.edu/Publications/Briefs/Documents/PB_AccessMatters.pdf

Murphy, B., & Tomaneng, R. M. (2016). Negotiating multiple identities: De Anza College's IMPACT AAPI program. In A. Long (Ed.), *Overcoming educational racism in the community college: Creating pathways to success for minority and impoverished student populations*. [Kindle version]. Sterling, VA: Stylus.

National Center for Education Statistics. (2016). *Status and trends in the education of racial and ethnic groups 2016*. Retrieved from http://nces.ed.gov/pubs2016/2016007.pdf

Nguyen, D. J., Brazelton, G. B., Renn, K. A., & Woodford, M. R. (2018). Exploring the availability and influence of LGBTQ+ student services resources on student success at community colleges: A mixed methods analysis. *Community College Journal of Research and Practice*. doi:10.1080/10668926.2018.1444522

Nicolazzo, Z. (2016). 'It's a hard line to walk': Black non-binary trans* collegians' perspectives on passing, realness, and trans*-normativity. *International Journal of Qualitative Studies*, 29(9), 1173–1188. doi:10.1080/09518398.2016.1201612

Nicolazzo, Z., Pitcher, E. N., Renn, K. A., & Woodford, M. (2017). An exploration of trans* kinship as a strategy for student success. *International Journal of Qualitative Studies in Education*, 30(3), 305–319. doi:10.1080/09518398.2016.1254300

O'Mara, K. (1997). Historicising outsiders on campus: The reproduction of lesbian and gay insiders. *Journal of Gender Studies, 6*(1), 17–31. doi:10.1080/09589236.1997.9960666

Padrón, E. J. (2016). "I do belong": Cultivating Hispanic and low-income student success. In A. Long (Ed.), *Overcoming Educational Racism in the Community College: Creating Pathways to Success for Minority and Impoverished Student Populations*. [Kindle version]. Sterling, VA: Stylus.

Patton, M. Q. (2015). *Qualitative research & evaluation methods* (4th ed.). Los Angeles, CA: Sage.

Peña-Talamantes, A. E. (2013). Empowering the self, creating worlds: Lesbian and gay Latino/a college students' identity negotiation in figured worlds. *Journal of College Student Development, 54*(3), 267–282. doi:10.1353/csd.2013.0039

Rankin, S., Weber, G., Blumenfeld, W., & Frazer, S. (2010). *State of higher education for lesbian, gay, bisexual, & transgender people*. Charlotte, NC: Campus Pride.

Saldaña, J. (2016). *The coding manual for qualitative researchers* (3rd ed.). Los Angeles, CA: Sage.

Salinas, C., Jr., & Lozano, A. (2017). Mapping and recontextualizing the evolution of the term Latinx: An environmental scanning in higher education. *Journal of Latinos and Education*. doi:10.1080/15348431.2017.1390464

Stake, R. E. (1995). *The art of case study research*. Thousand Oaks, CA: Sage.

Stanton-Salazar, R. D. (1997). A social capital framework for understanding the socialization of racial minority children and youths. *Harvard Educational Review, 67*(1), 1–40. doi:10.17763/haer.67.1.140676g74018u73k

Stanton-Salazar, R. D. (2011). A social capital framework for the study of institutional agents and their role in the empowerment of low-status students and youth. *Youth & Society, 43*(3), 1066–1109. doi:10.1177/0044118X10382877

Strayhorn, T. L. (2012). *College students' sense of belonging: A key to educational success for all*. New York, NY: Routledge.

Tovar, E. (2015). The role of faculty counselors and support programs on Latino/a community college students' success and intent to persist. *Community College Review, 43*(1), 46–71. doi:10.1177/0091552114553788

Vaccaro, A., Russell, E. I. A., & Koob, R. M. (2015). Students with minoritized identities of sexuality and gender in campus contexts: An emergent model. In D.-L. Stewart, K. A. Renn, & G. B. Brazelton (Eds.), *Gender and sexual diversity in U. S. higher education: Contexts and opportunities for LGBTQ college students. New directions for student services, No. 152* (pp. 25–39). San Francisco, CA: Jossey-Bass.

Weissman, J., Bulakowski, C., & Jumisko, M. (1998). A study of white, black, and hispanic students' transition to a community college. *Community College Review, 26*(2), 19–42. doi:10.1177/009155219802600202

White, K. A. (2010). *The California community college experience, for real: A study of African American male student perceptions and experiences* (Unpublished doctoral dissertation). University of California-Davis, Davis.

Yosso, T. (2005). Whose culture has capital? A critical race theory discussion of community cultural wealth. *Race Ethnicity and Education, 8*(1), 69–91. doi:10.1080/1361332052000341006

Zamani-Gallaher, E. M., & Choudhuri, D. D. (2011). A primer on LGBTQ students at community colleges: Considerations for research and practice. In E. M. Cox & J. S. Watson (Eds.), *Marginalized students . New directions for community colleges, no. 155* (pp. 35–49). San Francisco, CA: Jossey-Bass.

Zamani-Gallaher, E. M., & Choudhuri, D. D. (2016). Tracing LGBTQ community college students' experiences. In C. C. Ozaki & R. L. Spaid (Eds.), *Applying college change theories to student affairs practice New directions for community colleges, No. 174* (pp. 47–63). San Francisco, CA: Jossey-Bass.

Evolving Narratives about College: Immigrant Community College Students' Perceptions of the Four-Year Degree in the Great Plains

Moises Padilla, Justin Chase Brown, and Elvira Abrica

ABSTRACT
A significant percentage of the enrollment growth in higher education can be attributed to the recruitment of more diverse students, including those from immigrant households. Although research on immigrant students is growing in light of changing U.S. demographic shifts, this literature is inchoate. This paper examines evolving perspectives of the value of a four-year degree among immigrants and children of immigrants. Thus, in this paper article we synthesize current dominant narratives of immigrant students about the utility and viability of a four-year degree (and the changing impact on community college enrollment) and how they have shifted over time. We observe a current pulse that questions the ideological attitude of college for all, with some noting that a four-year degree has less significance and payoff than in the past within today's changing economy. Moreover, we present our findings through an empirical study of immigrant community college students' perceptions of the viability and value of the four-year degree and the implications for research and practice.

The prevailing narrative in the United States has been one of college for all – where students are expected to go to a four-year college or university after completing high school (Fishman, Ekowo, & Ezeugo, 2017). This expectation is well-reasoned – the benefits of obtaining a bachelor's degree are many and include, for example, higher salary earnings, less reliance on public assistance programs, and increased levels of civic participation (Ma, Pender, & Welch, 2016). Amidst the focus on promoting access to four-year institutions and increasing rates of bachelor's degree completion nationally, there are growing concerns regarding the diminishing value of the bachelor's degree, career prospects after graduation, and soaring student and parent loan indebtedness (Goldrick-Rab & Kendall, 2014). For example, while most individuals surveyed (75%) see the value in getting a college degree, many (25%) also feel that higher education in its current state is falling short of the promise it offers (Fishman et al., 2017). Rhetorically, politicians emphasize the importance of increasing the number of bachelor's degrees, particularly in STEM, to maintain global competitiveness (National Science Board, 2018), but simultaneously reference community colleges as vocational schools that do little more than prepare blue collar workers (Kreighbaum, 2018).

The purpose of this study was to understand immigrant community college students' perceptions of the utility, viability, and value of the four-year degree. Narratives, beliefs, and perceptions about college – quality, value, and return on investment – all matter in shaping individual behaviors (McDonough, 1997). While there has been an emphasis on how immigrant students *decide between* four-year and two-year institutions upon graduation from high school (i.e., college choice process), there has been less consideration of how students who have already chosen to attend a community college conceptualize the prospect of attending a four-year institution and/or internalize broader narratives and tensions about the bachelor's degree. For many students, the choices of where to attend college is not necessarily sequential (Acevedo-Gil, 2017). That is, while the higher education landscape frames community colleges as tangential to four-year colleges, where four-year bachelor's degree granting institutions are an epicenter around which community colleges orbit, community colleges are increasingly *the* epicenter for immigrant student groups. Community college student status should not automatically be interpreted as a function of the inability to access a four-year degree, but as a function of students' agency that is reflective of broader, conflicting, and complex narratives about college.

In this article, we present empirical findings from a study of immigrant community college students' perceptions of the utility, viability, and value of the four-year degree. In using the terms, *'utility, viability, and value'*, we recognize immigrant community college students perceive the four-year degree as a viable means to a specified end. We juxtapose these findings with a synthesis of dominant narratives in academic literature regarding the utility and value of four-year degrees to illustrate a disconnect between extant framing of four-year institutions and immigrant community college students' perceptions. Two research questions guided our inquiry: (1) What is the current perspective of the utility and viability of a four-year college degree among immigrant community college students? and (2) How is the utility and viability of a four-year degree for immigrant community colleges students evolving? We purposefully situated our study in the context of the Great Plains region of the United States, including states such as North and South Dakota, Kansas, and Nebraska, as a way to illuminate immigrant community college students' evolving perceptions of the utility and viability of attending a four-year institution in a context not typically centered in either higher education or community college literatures. Attending to community college issues in specific regional contexts are urgently needed amidst national demographic and economic shifts by geographic area.

Literature review

To contextualize the importance of immigrant community college students' perceptions of four-year college degrees, we offer an overview of the broader narratives that have historically shaped student perceptions of college. We then highlight the specific dynamics (e.g., race, immigrant generational status, economic conditions) that underscore the evolving narratives about the utility of a four-year college degree. It is within these dynamics among immigrant community college student perspectives that findings unfold.

Historical influences and the perception of college

Throughout the history of higher education, the utility and viability of obtaining a college degree has shifted. During the colonial era, few colleges existed and only a select few had the opportunity and benefited from attending those institutions (Caple, 1998). During that time period, the purpose of attending college was to "to train young men for the ministry" (Caple, 1998, p. 10). It was not until the Morrill Act of 1862, where public lands were awarded to states to provide colleges for the benefit of mechanical arts and agriculture, where those afforded the opportunity to attend college was widened (Komives & Woodard, 2003). According to Caple (1998), the Morrill Land Grant Act of 1862 was unquestionably the most influential policy in shifting the attitude of the American people toward increasing college attendance. Yet, the numbers of individuals who perceived college as a viable option was small in numbers and reserved for the privileged elite (Caple, 1998). It was not until the G.I. Bill in the 1940s, and subsequently additional federal college financing options in the 1960s, where critical masses of students were offered the necessary resources to attend college, especially for historically marginalized groups (Komives & Woodard, 2003). During that time, college was finally perceived as a viable and accessible option to ascend the socioeconomic ladder and obtain stable employment (Komives & Woodard, 2003).

In recent years, the prevailing narrative many high school students receive, including those with immigrant backgrounds, is that they should attend college upon graduation because it will help them live a more financially stable life. For example, Ma et al. (2016) summarized the benefits of higher education and placed an emphasis on how higher levels of education leads adults to earn higher incomes, are more likely than others to be employed, and increases their likelihood of moving up the social economic ladder. Furthermore, many high school students are encouraged to pursue a college degree because it will help them in other aspects of their lives, such as leading healthier lifestyles, having higher levels of engagement in the community, and being involved in their children's activities (Ma et al., 2016; Perna, 2005). Such narratives have long fueled students' perceptions of and pursuit of four-year institutions (Engle & Tinto, 2008). However, as economic and social realities continue to present challenges to college access and success (Rudgers & Peterson, 2017), the articulation of the many promises of higher education – particularly for immigrant communities – seems increasingly out of touch with reality. Some see the privileged majority as the beneficiaries of such promises of higher education, while the marginalized are subjected to the opportunity costs as well as the social and economic risks of attendance with no such reward (Nichols, 2015).

Immigrant students and community colleges

According to Teranishi, Suárez-Orozco, and Suárez-Orozco (2011), "immigrant youth and children of immigrants make up a large share of the nation's population" (p. 153) and increasing their educational attainment should become a national priority. Despite the risks of attendance and achievement gaps, the evidence indicates that immigrant students generally have high expectations for higher education (Teranishi et al., 2011). Kim and Díaz (2013) highlighted how immigrant students' "demand for higher education exceeds the capacity of the current community college system" (p. 92) and Conway (2010) supported this claim by explaining immigrant students' high demand for higher education can be attributed to their desire to achieve economic success. Yet, although immigrant students generally have high expectations for higher education, these expectations do not always translate into increased enrollments. In fact, "immigrant students experience lower postsecondary enrollment rates compared to their native-born counterparts" (Kim & Díaz, 2013, p. 47). Furthermore, even though upward mobility in economic status from one generation to the next continues to grow for immigrant populations, growth is at a slower rate compared to previous years due to the "slowing economic growth and the widening gap between the haves and the have-nots" (Conway, 2010, p. 211). Consequently, the perception that one needs to obtain a four-year degree in order to move up the socioeconomic ladder is slowly dissipating (Conway, 2010) and positions community colleges as a viable option for immigrant students to reach economic success (Teranishi et al., 2011).

Research on immigrant students is becoming more abundant, yet a notable deficiency is on their *evolving* perspectives of the value of a four-year degree. Teranishi et al. (2011) reported how more immigrant students are attending community colleges in comparison to any other type of postsecondary institutions. Community colleges are a viable option distinctive from four-year institutions because community colleges traditionally offer an "open access admissions process, are affordable, and provide a wide variety of curricular functions including the development of basic skills such as reading, writing, and mathematics" (Kim & Díaz, 2013, p. 91). Moreover, limited research exists on immigrant students' experiences within community colleges (Conway, 2010). Thus, without an understanding of the evolving perspectives of the value of the four-year degree among immigrant students, or immigrant students' experiences within community colleges, we are unable to appreciate the breadth of challenges these students face let alone identify solutions. As we explore the perceptions of immigrant community college students, we begin by introducing the conceptual framework that informed our study of students' perceptions of the four-year degree.

Conceptual framework

To examine immigrant community college students' perceptions of the four-year degree and the extent to which it represents a shift in broader discourse and narratives about the utility of a college degree, we draw on sociologist Pierre Bourdieu's concepts of *habitus* and *field* (Bourdieu, 1990). Undeniably, concepts of social and cultural capital are among the most popular sociological exports to the field of education. Yet, the use of capital as a central conceptual framework in studies examining the resources and networks that contribute to student success engender some conceptual flaws. Namely, the capitals are only part of Bourdieu's larger theory of social reproduction. Bourdieu's theory also included the key concepts of habitus and field to explain how, within a given social context, some forms of capital are valued over others lending to a covert reproduction of social inequity (Bourdieu & Passeron, 1990).

Habitus is a concept that "calls us to think of action as engendered and regulated by fundamental dispositions that are internalized primarily through early socialization. Bourdieu speaks of the internalization or 'incorporation' of the fundamental social conditions of existence into dispositions" (Swartz, 1999, p. 104). Habitus serves as the social milieu or surrounding environmental influences that shape what students perceive as opportunities as well as how they fit in with those opportunities. Metaphorically, habitus is akin to the water in which fish swim, the characteristics of which shape (beyond ability and different than desire) a course or trajectory. Habitus is, then, the micro-level social context in which participants live and attend community colleges in the Great Plains.

Field, meanwhile, refers to the social spaces in which individuals act out struggles for various resources. Field would be the landscape of higher education – the broader structure of post-secondary institutions more generally. Using a sports analogy, field is like a sports field in that there are specific rules of the game that guide whether players' demonstrated efforts (a function of their various forms of training, effort, ability, desire) are successful or not. Participants' perceptions of four-year colleges are thought to be reflective of their milieu – one that is shaped by their surrounding environmental influences.

In this paper, we draw on the concepts of habitus and field to understand the "deep-structuring cultural matrix" (Swartz, 1999, p. 104) that shape participants' evolving perceptions, narratives, ideas, and beliefs about the value of a four-year degree. We discuss the ways in which, given the particular field of contested power that is higher education, such perceptions have important implications for broader discourse about the utility of a four-year degree and for individual outcomes.

This article is purposefully myopic in focusing on the concepts of habitus and field, to the exclusion of the admittedly inseparable concepts of capital, as a way to showcase the value of these concepts in explicating surrounding beliefs, narratives, and ideas that may go unnoticed and unattended to. In other words, a plethora of research has used capitals in isolation – and we use field and habitus in isolation – but do so intentionally to frame students' perceptions of the four-year degree. Previously, McDonough and colleagues (McDonough, 1997; McDonough & Calderone, 2006; McDonough, Lising, Walpole, & Perez, 1998; Perez & McDonough, 2008) have similarly utilized Bourdieu's work to showcase how the *perceptions, narratives, and ideas* students have about college are culturally and socially inscribed and, ultimately, influential in shaping students' college going behavior and access.

Positionality statement

A central part of the research process is engaging in reflection on the how individual positionalities inform the research at hand (Yao & Vital, 2016). Each of the authors occupy a role within the four-year university, which propelled our interest in understanding how community college students might view the institution we represent. I, the first author of the study, identify as Latino male and first-generation college student. Having been born outside of the U.S. and grown up in the rural Great Plains, it is particularly important to me to document the lived realities and educational opportunities among those who share my immigrant upbringing. The second author identifies as a white male born in the U.S., whose leadership role on campus compels his interest in understanding perceptions of the institution. The study's Principal Investigator, the third author identifies as a non-immigrant Chicana female, born and raised in southern California. As such, the third author brings to this study a sociological lens emphasizing how students' sociocultural contexts shape their knowledges and understandings about what institutions are "right" for them.

Methodology

This study is part of a larger qualitative research study focusing on the career decision-making of immigrants and children of immigrants attending community colleges in the Great Plains region. An interpretive qualitative approach was selected for this article because the researchers were interested in how the participants gave meaning to their construction of reality. This is the desirable qualitative approach when observing how individuals interpret their experiences, construct their reality, and give meaning to their experiences (Merriam & Tisdell, 2016). This study was derived from a broader study focused on examining the ways in which race, ethnicity, and/or proximity to an immigrant experience (i.e., immigrant generation) informed career decision-making within the community college context. The Great Plains region was an appropriate setting for the study in light of current demographic and economic changes that are occurring in the area – a large influx of refugee and migrant populations from traditionally and non-traditionally emigrant countries. A salient theme across all participants that emerged from the larger study – the analytic focus of this paper – was participants' perceptions, attitudes, and ideas about the value and utility of a four-year college degree. That is, while discussing their career and educational aspirations, participants shared a wealth of information about their perceptions of a four-year college degree which compelled further analysis and development.

Data collection

Individuals were enrolled in the study if they attended community college and identified as either a first-generation (foreign-born), one-and-a-half generation (foreign-born but emigrated to the U.S. as children), or second-generation (children born in the U.S. to at least one foreign-born parent) immigrant. Participants were recruited via snowball and purposive methods (Lichtman, 2010). A total of 31 semi-structured interviews with the students were conducted, each lasting approximately 60 minutes. All audio recordings of interviews were later transcribed verbatim. During the interviews, participants were asked about the significance of their social identities (e.g., racial/ethnic identification immigrant generation), academic factors (e.g., enrollment status, community college services), and other environmental factors (e.g., financial situation) in informing their community college experiences and career decision-making.

Participants

Out of the 31 study participants, 14 (45%) identified as Hispanic/Latino, 10 identified as Asian (32%), three identified as Black (10%), and four identified as Middle Eastern (13%). Twenty of the participants identified as female (65%). Fifteen identified as first-generation immigrant (48%), five as one-and-a-half generation immigrant (16%), and 11 as second-generation immigrant (35%). Ten participants were on a community college path to complete credit and then transfer to a four-year college (academic transfer) in order to complete a Bachelor's degree (36%), five were on a path to complete the Associate's degree and then transfer to a four-year college (18%), 10 were on a path to complete the Associate's degree and find employment in their chosen field (36%), one was on a path to complete a vocational or professional certificate and find employment (3%), and three were on another career path (10%). A demographic summary of the participants is available in Table 1.

Table 1. Participant demographics (N = 31).

Participant (Pseudonym)	Race/Ethnicity	Gender	Student Status	Major
1. Angela	Hispanic/Latino	Female	Full-time	Elementary Education
2. Esperanza	Hispanic/Latino	Genderqueer	Full-time	Spanish and English
3. Sarah	Hispanic/Latino	Female	Part-time	Criminal Justice
4. Carina	Hispanic/Latino	Female	Full-time	Human Services
5. Veronica	Hispanic/Latino	Female	Part-time	None – I plan to transfer
6. Julia	Asian American/ Biracial (Asian & Latino)	Female	Full-time	Nursing
7. Michelle	Hispanic/Latino	Female	Part-time	Culinary Arts
8. Joe	Hispanic/Latino	Male	Full-time	Auto Body Technology
9. John	Hispanic/Latino	Male	Part-time	Chemistry
10. Sam	Hispanic/Latino	Male	Full-time	Criminal Justice
11. Antonio	Hispanic/Latino	Male	Part-time	Information Technology
12. Frank	Hispanic/Latino	Male	Full-time	Information Technology
13. Mark	Hispanic/Latino	Male	Full-time	Information Technology
14. Oscar	Hispanic/Latino	Male	Part-time	Business
15. Angeline	Asian/Asian American	Female	Full-time	Academic Transfer
16. Pink	Asian/Asian American	Female	Part-time	Medical Assisting
17. Tara	Other (Nepali)	Female	Full-time	Nursing
18. Yanek	Asian/Asian American	Male	Full-time	-
19. MJ	Asian/Asian American	Female	Full-time	Accounting
20. Jenna	Asian/Asian American	Female	Full-time	Nursing
21. Bree	Asian/Asian American	Female	Part-time	Pre-health
22. Yvonne	Asian/Asian American	Female	Full-time	Geo Info Systems
23. tephanie	Asian/Asian American	Female	Full-time	Human Services
24. Tai	Asian/Asian American	Female	Part-time	English
25. Jason	African American/Black	Male	Full-time	Energy Generation Ops
26. Gina	Other (African)	Female	Full-time	Business
27. Lukfomi	African American/Black	Female	Part-time	Early Childhood Education
28. Abbad	Other (White)	Male	Full-time	Aided Design Drafting
29. Amal	Other (White)	Female	Full-time	Aided Design Drafting
30. Siam	Middle Eastern/North African	Female	Full-time	Biochemistry
31. Stacey	Middle Eastern/North African	Female	Full-time	Nursing

Data analysis

Given our analytic focus on immigrant students' perceptions of the four-year college, the research team engaged in an initial round of coding to identify thematic and conceptual categories in students' perceptions, writing analytic memos throughout this process to make sense of these categories. Following initial coding rounds, the team sought confirmatory as well as refuting evidence of the initial themes through a secondary round of coding. During the final stage of analysis, the team then examined nuances across demographic characteristics and the extent to which students' perceptions aligned with previously documented perceptions, per our literature review, and/or larger narratives or beliefs about four-year colleges. A combination of member checking and peer debriefing were employed to ensure trustworthiness of the findings (Creswell, 2012).

Findings

Our analysis yielded several important findings regarding participants' perceptions of two-year and four-year institutions. Namely, participants rhetorically positioned community colleges as being *above* four-year institutions, both in terms of their own educational pathway and in terms of an observed, broader societal shift. That is, they provided a number of reasons why the community college is – and should be for everyone else in their generation – the more desirable educational pathway. The degree to which participants described four-year institutions as outdated or archaic, while juxtaposing community colleges as viable, diverse, affordable, welcoming, and offering more direct pathways toward desirable and well-paying careers was telling and moving commentary that reflected the broader academic debates about the viability of both institutions. We highlight participants' reflections or narratives on the value and viability of a four-year degree, in contrast with that of a community college education, in terms of alignment with career goals, concerns about labor market returns, perceptions of differences between two-and four-year environments and affordability.

Academic and career alignment

In describing their career goals, participants shared how their interests had evolved from the end of high school to the start of college, indicating that the community college context allowed for refinement of their goals. For example, Stephanie, who identified as a second-generation daughter of immigrants and Asian woman, described how in high school she was interested in majoring in international business. Since her local community college did not have such a program, she planned to go to "school to be a transfer student." She explained that her high school counselor was instrumental in guiding her toward other options. She stated:

> As time went on, I ended up changing what I wanted to do. So instead of international business, I wanted to get a business management degree. I sat down with an advisor and we kind of mapped out where I would be to get a degree. After we mapped it out I ended up going to [local community college] to get an associate's degree.

Stephanie discovered that obtaining an associate's degree would align with her career goals. She was exposed to and agreeable to the idea presented by her high school counselor. Stephanie, like many of her peers, started at the community college with a broad impression of what she wanted to do and narrowed her career interests based on feedback from institutional agents, in this case a high school counselor. Her family, including immigrant parents, played a significant role in shaping her career aspirations. She said:

> I first wanted to be a fashion designer and then I wanted to be a doctor and then a lawyer. My parents were like, 'You should be a doctor.' I'm like, 'Okay I'll be a doctor.' Then my dad is like, 'Maybe you should be a lawyer.' I'm like, 'Okay I'll be a lawyer.' Then that changed when I got to high school and I took a criminal justice class for fun and I actually liked it. I went to the prison as a field trip and I got to talk to a police officer. I got to job shadow a forensic scientist teacher all throughout high school and I just wanted to go into that field. And seeing a lot of bad incidents happening on TV inspired me to work as a police officer.

Stephanie's educational journey in the community college was centrally informed by career goals; goals that were fundamentally shaped by those who were around her and the ideas that she was exposed to. Another participant, Sarah, who identified as a second-generation daughter of immigrants and Latina, described how her career choice was informed by direct personal experiences and explained how the community college would prepare her to take that first step in her career. She stated:

> I've had some experiences; some family members have been to prison and some friends and I think that's part of the reason [she's pursuing criminal justice]. They're still people, they make mistakes and once they come out it's back to normal... I know some of them [desired employment positions] do require bachelor's degrees, but I think I would start out being a correctional officer and then maybe start off exploring in some of the field where they only require an associate's degree.

Through the coursework available in the community college, the experience of visiting a prison, the influence of mainstream media, and personal experiences, Stephanie landed on the aspiration of being a police officer and Sarah is pursuing an associate of arts degree with hopes of becoming a correctional officer. Ultimately, the extent to which Stephanie's and Sarah's aspirations aligned with the community college setting were informed by the academic and social environment, consistent with the other participants in the study. This strong alignment, in turn, very much shaped participants' perspectives of the community college in a positive way and contextualized the sometimes more negative perceptions they had of four-year institutions and the utility of a bachelor's degree.

Primacy of immediate labor returns

Participants repeatedly and passionately described that the four-year model of education is increasingly becoming obsolete as community colleges increasingly provide a more direct path to employment and labor opportunities. That is, participants were primarily concerned with earning money and upward social mobility. The fastest way to do this, they felt, was through the avenues for careers created by the community college. For example, Gina, who identified as a one-and-a-half generation immigrant from Africa, described her perception of how the traditional model of higher education does not work for everyone. She expressed the following reflection:

> I love school, but I don't love traditional schooling… And a lot of those jobs you still don't acquire because the generation before us, they have those jobs in place, and not many are going to be retiring soon. So for you to get this degree and hope that you're going to get this high-level position that someone's been at for 20, 30 years and doesn't think that they're going to be going anywhere anytime soon, you're just kind of like stuck. Because if you have the degree but the job openings aren't there, what do you do? And that's why I think, I think this generation's awesome because they're really creating their own opportunities and building their own brands. Instead of waiting for someone to hire them, they're like, "I'll be my brand and you'll want to hire me." You know? So I just think that's cool.

Gina expressed how traditional schooling, where students are expected to go to school full-time, acquire knowledge, get their degree, and then get a job is an outdated model. For her, she believes there is a generation of students eager to start their own business ventures and create their own entrepreneurial opportunities. This is perhaps reflective of Gina's immigrant background in that, as an immigrant, she has high expectations for upward mobility and, like many immigrants, sees entrepreneurship as a means of achieving economic success (Fairlie & Lofstrom, 2013).

When asked follow-up questions about whether or not they see any difference in the prestige of a community college education versus a four-year bachelor's degree, participants reported that prestige is meaningless if they cannot make money after graduation. As Gina further expressed:

> I don't think that having a degree from a prestigious college would make a difference to me. I feel like I know, I feel like I'm learning the business side of almost any industry well enough to create my own stream of revenue. And I definitely want more than one stream of revenue as well, so it's just kind of working the ins and outs, but also our generation in this time has an advantage because there's other ways to make money than just having a regular nine to five job. There's also social media where you can make money, and take advantage of those occupations.

As Gina describes, for some students, career aspirations and the necessity of immediate labor returns evolve into an unexpected experience of building a personal brand and creating innovative partnerships to generate revenue streams. Frank, a Latino male and second generation son of immigrants whose parents migrated to the United States from Mexico, shared a similar thought process when it came to the value and viability of a four-year degree and how the current model of higher education does not work for everyone. He shared that:

> It's not sustainable anymore, really. There are certain degrees that you would have to have a four year degree, like I guess like your degree at [the local community college] for psychology wouldn't be as highly touted as from [the local four-year college], things like that. I guess in my specifically mind, I think it's more beneficial to me as an older person to go to [the local community college] rather than [the local four-year college]. I want to start my career sooner rather than later and usually the other people that are switching their careers and stuff like that, they have a family and they're at [the local community college] and they're going that route. They've already had a career before. They haven't been jobless for 50 years and then they're starting now. I just want to be able to get my foot in the door now rather than later instead of going another three years.

For Frank, obtaining the credential necessary for his specific area of study is more important than the experience of a four-year institution. Also, as an older student, attending the community college allows him to make progress towards the credential he desires while at the same time gain valuable experience through internships and work experience.

Comparisons of two-year and four-year environments

Participants – both those who had previously attended four-year institutions and those who had only had experience with community colleges – shared their perceptions of community colleges as more welcoming and diverse than four-year institutions. Consistently, participants indicated that they perceived community colleges as more welcoming to students with diverse backgrounds, including representation of broader age range, varied educational experiences and aspirations, and ethnic diversity. Amal, a first-generation immigrant originally from the Middle East, described her difficulties with learning English and how the community college allowed her to make progress. She stated:

> I go to take a test to discover my level [English proficiency]. They said I am in the five level. So, I took classes for five level and above. Last month I made the test again and now I'm in level eight. I made progress, three levels. I will try again maybe next year.

For Amal, the community college setting is welcoming to students like her and indicated how, as a result of her experience, more students who are friends with her enrolled at the community college. Similarly, Frank articulated that he valued both seeing variation in age and backgrounds among his peers as well as the ways in which the community college setting accommodates students from "different walks of life."

> There's people having to be able to do only night classes. They're well into their life and into their family and that'd be the only time that they have to spare and stuff. With the slower pacing, it's a lot of times for them because the teachers sympathize with them because they have families too. I understand also because you're doing full time and you might not have time for a class because family is the most important thing.

For Frank, community college was a desirable option for him based on many of the same factors articulated by Stephanie (e.g., family, institutional agents, etc.), but he also articulated how the community college works best for people who may not be of traditional college age or have families. Frank was interested in business and/or nursing as a career path and described his experience in a tightly-knit program where instructors made him feel wanted and cared for as a student. Frank had previously attended the state's land-grant institution where he experienced a different dynamic with instructors. Through various stop-outs (periods of enrollment followed by bouts of non-enrollment) at both two year and four-year colleges, he felt that the campus environment of the community college was much more diverse and welcoming of diverse students than the four-year context.

The context of affordability

The value of the community college versus the four-year college cannot be sufficiently examined without the context of affordability. Many participants perceived community college as a logical financial and academic pathway. In terms of pursuing academic transfer (starting at the community college with the intent to transferring to a four-year degree), the general coursework is perceived as being either equivalent at each institution or irrelevant. One participant, Esperanza, who identified as a first generation immigrant and gender queer, summarized the general discussion and her recommendation to other students considering the academic transfer route:

> I would recommend a lot of people that are either going to go to a university it's way cheaper to take the academic transfer. You find out the hard way. A lot of people do and I've met some people who are going to [four-year college] and they have to take general education classes and they're paying crazy amounts of money for a class that they could take for half the price. It's hard. You do want to go to university and be like, "I'm a university student." And feel really good about it but sometimes you can't. You can't afford to do that. I would recommend people to take the academic transfer if they ask me.

For Esperanza, there is no difference in quality or value of the education received. What is simply necessary for the credential and the least expensive and obstructive path is more logical. Participants also referred to how inexpensive the local community college was by comparison and that the local four-year college would accept all transfer credits. A student named M.J. said he wanted to "...save a little bit of money compared to going straight to the university." Overall, though, and quite unexpected was that participants seemed to describe this issue based on the sticker price of college credits without reference to financial aid eligibility.

Participants also viewed the cost (i.e., their price) of college as a necessary burden to obtain a credential in their desired field rather than, overall, something to be valued as an investment in their future. Siam, who identified as a second generation daughter of immigrants and Middle Eastern woman, spoke about general coursework was "...a waste of time and a waste of money." She spoke about not wanting to focus on general coursework but rather her major. Moreover, participants discussed the value of different programs and the choice process on studying vocations, such as that of a plumber, electrician, and an auto-mechanic, or the social sciences, such as sociology and psychology. They spoke about being discouraged from the social sciences compared to the immediacy of a vocational program and then being able to work your way up, such as being an auto-mechanic and moving up to be a head-mechanic and earning more money. Frank stated the following:

> I heard that plumbers make $2,000 because it's a trade and it's easy and not really a lot of people want to do it and there's high demand. I guess a lot of people that don't know or that don't really have a passion for a lot of things, I'd say that [local community college] trade is a, I probably would have done it myself too if I didn't really enjoy or if I wasn't good at the [Computer Information Technology] program. Because it's a very, you come out with, everybody needs a plumber or needs [an] electrician. You come out two years and make really good money for your family.

Furthermore, participants also discussed the general struggle of paying for college and being able to afford it. It became evident that sometimes students suffer alone without seeking help or financial aid, perhaps not knowing of its availability or if their immigration status might prevent them from being eligible. For example, Esperanza shared the following:

> I've seen a lot of people who don't feel as supported as I feel. A lot of times, the information doesn't get across as well as I think it should. I just recently met a girl that I was working with that she thought she had to pay for school by herself because she didn't know you could get financial aid. She didn't know that people can give you money to go to school. So, there's a lot of information that is not getting across to a lot of people. I think we could do a better job on getting this information to the people who need it and not only the people who need it the most, just everybody who needs it. Not everybody can get financial aid, but if you know about it, at least you know about it.

For Esperanza, familiarizing students with available financial aid options would increase the perceived levels of support students need to persist. Also, Esperanza's comments reveal how many students, including those from immigrant families, endure challenges when it comes to paying for college even though solutions to ameliorate those challenges exists.

Discussion

In this study we explored the current perspective of the utility and viability of a four-year college degree among immigrant community college students. Moreover, we explored how their perspectives were evolving about the utility and viability of a four-year degree. We found participants in this study shared their beliefs that a four-year model as becoming increasingly obsolete and that the community college was the most viable option toward reaching their goals. They talked about community colleges as a superior means of securing a viable career when compared to a four-year degree. Four-year degrees were portrayed as a relic of the past; participants cited a host of reasons ranging from affordability to being unwelcoming of diversity. There was much talk about all of the ways in which colleges are unaffordable and ineffective institutions that grant degrees that translate less and less into the careers students want. Of our 31 participants, only 10 said their goal was to transfer to a four-year institution.

There is a national imperative to increase the number of bachelor's degree holders, particularly in STEM (National Science Board, 2018). Our study provides evidence that students are not only aware of macro-level narratives regarding the viability and utility of four-year degrees, but they espouse such narratives in ways that translate into their decision-making. While students were fans of the community college, the field of higher education is not one in which community colleges are privileged in terms of funding, status, resources, or prestige. Future research might consider how, in a given field in which certain forms of capital are valued or not, immigrant students' forms of capital are activated or transmitted. Furthermore, future research might explore further implications for policy, research, and practice – how politics and/or trending views are shaping immigrant students' perspective on the four-year degree.

Bourdieu's (1990) concepts of habitus and field endures as a useful theoretical tool to understand and contextualize observed perceptions among students. Participants described themselves as *ending up* in community colleges largely through happenstance. They relied heavily on their surrounding academic and social environments to understand various career options and pathways to get closer to entering these careers. That is, their decisions both in entering the community college and once in the community college were principally informed by their habitus, comprised of their family, peers, media, and some institutional agents. For example, Gina's emphatic belief that she could become a famous YouTube personality can be understood as an aspiration that she arrived at from a variety of influences. Namely, her proximity to an immigrant experience imbued her with what sociologists refer to as an immigrant optimism, a belief in U.S. institutions as vehicles for upward social mobility. The profound influence of social media – what she described as a zeitgeist unique to *her generation* – highlights the ways in which a social milieu and series of influences inform one's decision-making. Future research might consider ways in which traditional ways of thinking of habitus may be shaped by social media influences.

Community college practitioners should consider how they explicitly support the needs of immigrant students who may have different beliefs and attitudes (i.e., habitus) about the nature of their educational trajectory than later generation students. While they might be an easily overlooked population for espousing optimistic attitudes, educators should use caution in subscribing to the notion that these students are not in need of support. It would behoove community college leaders and educators to understand that within the varied pathways of the community colleges, participants may make meaning of these pathways in different ways. Students' extant knowledge of the available routes and pathways – particularly in regional contexts like the Great Plains where there are unique dynamics of race, ethnicity, and immigrant generation – may inform their decision-making in ways not readily understood by majority populations in these contexts.

Conclusion

This study focused on immigrant community college students' evolving perceptions of the utility and viability of a four-year degree. The focus was intentionally placed on the perceptions of participants who had made their decision to enroll in a community college because these perceptions inform the broader narratives people believe and eventually adopt. Moreover, this study focused on immigrant community college students' perceptions because they inform policy and practice. Our findings highlight the reality that rhetoric around college is confusing and conflicting, particularly as it pertains to community colleges in the landscape of higher education. Recommendations to conduct further research, especially when it comes to policy and practice, were offered. However, one thing is clear: the hierarchical role and power differential between four-year and two-year colleges. The students' narratives in this paper, though, challenge this broader discourse, emphasizing the advantage of community college to meet their needs. Yet, it is simultaneously important to recognize how these perceptions are informed by a particular social milieu in upholding these beliefs. And for all the great things participants said about the community college context, their perceptions may or may not translate into upward mobility.

Disclosure of potential conflicts of interest

No potential conflict of interest to disclose.

Funding

This work was supported by the 2017 Center for the Study of Community Colleges grant

ORCID

Elvira Abrica http://orcid.org/0000-0001-6140-5325

References

Acevedo-Gil, N. (2017). College-conocimiento: Toward an interdisciplinary college choice framework for Latinx students. *Race Ethnicity and Education*, 20(6), 829–850. doi:10.1080/13613324.2017.1343294

Bourdieu, P. (1990). *The logic of practice*. Stanford, California: Stanford University Press.

Bourdieu, P., & Passeron, J. C. (1990). *Reproduction in education, society and culture* (Vol. 4). Thousand Oaks, CA: Sage.

Caple, R. B. (1998). *To mark the beginning: A social history of college student affairs*. Lanham, MD: University Press of America.

Conway, K. M. (2010). Educational aspirations in an urban community college: Differences between immigrant and native student groups. *Community College Review*, 37(3), 209–242. doi:10.1177/0091552109354626

Creswell, J. W. (2012). *Qualitative inquiry & research design: Choosing among five approaches* (4th ed.). Thousand Oaks, CA: Sage.

Engle, J., & Tinto, V. (2008). *Moving beyond access: College success for low-income, first-generation students*. Washington, DC: The Pell Institute for the Study of Opportunity in Higher Education.

Fairlie, R. W., & Lofstrom, M. (2013). *Immigration and entrepreneurship*. IZA Discussion Papers, No. 7669. Institute for the Study of Labor (IZA), Bonn, Germany. Retrieved from http://hdl.handle.net/10419/90116

Fishman, R., Ekowo, M., & Ezeugo, E. (2017). *Varying degrees: New America's annual survey on higher education*. Washington, DC: New America. Retrieved from https://www.newamerica.org/in-depth/varying-degrees/

Goldrick-Rab, S., & Kendall, N. (2014). *Redefining college affordability: Securing America's future with a free two year college option*. Retrieved from https://www.luminafoundation.org/files/resources/redefining-college-affordability.pdf

Kim, E., & Díaz, J. (2013). *Immigrant students and higher education: ASHE higher education report 38: 6*. Hoboken, NJ: John Wiley & Sons.

Komives, S. R., & Woodard, D. B., Jr. (2003). *Student services: A handbook for the profession*. San Francisco, CA: John Wiley & Sons.

Kreighbaum, A. (2018). *Trump takes another swipe at community colleges*. Retrieved from https://www.insidehighered.com/news/2018/03/23/president-trump-holds-forth-community-colleges-campus-politics

Lichtman, M. (2010). *Qualitative research in education: A user's guide* (2nd ed.). Thousand Oaks, CA: Sage Publications, Inc.

Ma, J., Pender, M., & Welch, M. (2016). *Education pays 2016: The benefits of higher education for individuals and society*. College Board. Retrieved from https://files.eric.ed.gov/fulltext/ED572548.pdf

McDonough, P. M. (1997). *Choosing colleges: How social class and schools structure opportunity*. Albany, NY: SUNY Press.

McDonough, P. M., & Calderone, S. (2006). The meaning of money: Perceptual differences between college counselors and low-income families about college costs and financial aid. *American Behavioral Scientist*, 49(12), 1703–1718. doi:10.1177/0002764206289140

McDonough, P. M., Lising, A., Walpole, A. M., & Perez, L. X. (1998). College rankings: Democratized college knowledge for whom? *Research in Higher Education*, 39(5), 513–537. doi:10.1023/A:1018797521946

Merriam, S. B., & Tisdell, E. J. (2016). *Qualitative research: A guide to design and implementation*. San Francisco, CA: John Wiley & Sons.

National Science Board. (2018). *Science and engineering indicators 2018*. NSB-2018-1. Alexandria, VA: National Science Foundation.

Nichols, A. H. (2015). *The Pell partnership: Ensuring a shared responsibility for low-income student success*. Washington, D.C: The Education Trust.

Perez, P. A., & McDonough, P. M. (2008). Understanding Latina and Latino college choice: A social capital and chain migration analysis. *Journal of Hispanic Higher Education*, 7(3), 249–265. doi:10.1177/1538192708317620

Perna, L. (2005). The benefits of higher education: Sex, racial/ethnic, and socioeconomic group differences. *The Review of Higher Education, 1*(29), 23–52. doi:10.1353/rhe.2005.0073

Rudgers, L. A., & Peterson, J. A. (2017). *Coming in 2017*. Retrieved from https://www.insidehighered.com/views/2017/01/13/upcoming-trends-2017-colleges-should-prepare-essay

Swartz, D. (1999). *Culture and power: The sociology of Pierre Bourdieu.* The University of Chicago Press.

Teranishi, R. T., Suárez-Orozco, C., & Suárez-Orozco, M. (2011). Immigrants in community colleges. *The Future of Children*, 153–169. doi:10.1353/foc.2011.0009

Yao, C. W., & Vital, L. M. (2016). *Perspectives from U.S. doctoral students on researcher reflexivity and positionality in international contexts.* Paper session presented at the XVIWorld Congress of Comparative Education Societies Conference, Beijing, China.

Crossing the Shapeless River on a Government Craft: How Military-Affiliated Students Navigate Community College Transfer

Saralyn McKinnon-Crowley, Eliza Epstein, Huriya Jabbar, and Lauren Schudde

ABSTRACT
Many community college entrants, attracted by these institutions' variety of academic offerings and low cost, intend to earn a baccalaureate degree but never transfer to a four-year institution. A growing number of researchers seek to understand transfer patterns and behavior, but they often overlook some student groups, including those who receive military benefits. Military-affiliated students may fail to transfer at the same rate as their peers, or their unique supports may help them *navigate* the transfer process more successfully. In this paper, we draw from three years of longitudinal qualitative interviews to investigate the transfer journey of 16 veterans and active duty soldiers in Central Texas, as well as the experiences of nonveteran students who have access to family members' veterans' benefits. We focus on the institutional factors and the individual characteristics that contribute to transfer. Our findings suggest that receiving military benefits increases students' interactions with college staff, limits financial pressures, and encourages students to pursue behaviors that may contribute to a successful transfer process. We conclude with suggestions for practice and future research.

Many community college entrants who intend to earn a baccalaureate degree never transfer to a four-year institution (Jenkins & Fink, 2016). A growing number of researchers seek to understand transfer patterns and behavior (e.g., Backes & Velez, 2014; Crisp & Nuñez, 2014; Cuseo, 1998; Shaw & London, 2001; Wassmer, Moore, & Shulock, 2004), but their research overlooks some student groups, including those who receive military benefits. Military-affiliated students enroll at community colleges in large numbers because of the variety in academic programs and low cost at these broad-access institutions (Rumann, Rivera, & Hernandez, 2011). Despite the strong presence of students receiving military benefits on community college campuses, little is known about how military-affiliated students *navigate* the transfer process. Military-affiliated students may fail to transfer at the same rate as their peers, or they may receive unique supports, due to their military status, that help them navigate the transfer process more successfully.

Many individuals who join the United States military do so because of the educational funding that their military service can provide (Barr, 2016). Military service may offer an avenue to educational attainment and social mobility by providing government funding for educational experiences to eligible veterans and their dependents (Cate, 2014). Veterans benefits include educational funding received through the Post-9/11 GI Bill – discussed below – or obtained through another source, such as vocational rehabilitation, which can be used to receive higher education at a free or deeply discounted rate (McBain, Young, Cook, & Snead, 2012). These benefits also provide funding for housing, living expenses, and books (Rumann et al., 2011). They represent a massive financial investment by the government and a significant educational opportunity for veterans, active duty soldiers, and benefit-eligible family members. Students who used military benefits to fund their education had better college outcomes than students who did not use military benefits (Cate, Lyon, Schmeling, & Bogue, 2017).

A significant number of veteran students enroll in community colleges. For example, one study found that 34.2% of veteran students were enrolled at public two-year institutions (Cate et al., 2017). Veteran students often choose community colleges for their first foray into higher education, due to the open-access educational model of community colleges (Romano & Eddy, 2017). Every community college in the United States enrolls active-duty military students, veteran students, or their dependents (Williams-Klotz & Gansemer-Topf, 2018). On the whole, transfer rates among students who start their higher education at community colleges are quite low, amounting to 10% nationwide (Jenkins, 2018). Students receiving military benefits have access to special support structures that may ease their transfer process, but there is a lack of research examining how students use these resources to navigate transfer.

The purpose of this study is to explore factors which contribute to the successful transfer of military-affiliated students and to identify how those who receive veterans benefits[1] use available resources to navigate the transfer process. Specifically, we ask: (1) How do students who receive veterans benefits use their military experiences and provided resources to navigate the transfer process? (2) What factors contribute to the transfer success of military-affiliated students? To frame our work, we use Scott-Clayton's (2011) research regarding the lack of structure at community colleges and the concept of transfer capital, drawn from Laanan, Starobin, and Eggleston (2010), and Moser (2013).

This study relies on three years of interviews with transfer-intending community college students in Central Texas drawn from a larger, ongoing project. We use the term *military-affiliated* to refer to all students receiving veterans benefits, regardless of their own military status, and *veteran students* to refer to those who have served in the armed forces. By the third round of interviews, nine out of 16 students (56% of the entire military sample) had successfully transferred to a four-year institution. Compared with the 11% of community college students in Texas who had transferred to a four-year institution within six years of entry into higher education (Jenkins, 2018), military-affiliated students appear to have transferred at a higher rate.

The paper proceeds as follows. First, we review the literature concerning veteran and military-affiliated students, including the history and contemporary state of military benefits in the United States. We then describe our methods, including information on the sample and approach. Third, we present our findings regarding how students in the sample navigate and experience transfer. Lastly, we conclude with a discussion of implications for research and practice.

Literature review

In this section, we focus on the GI Bill and the Post-9/11 GI Bill. We then discuss research about veteran students in higher education and the institutional supports that can contribute to their success. This literature provides insight into the experiences of veterans or active duty military in higher education and describes the existing institutional structures to which all students receiving military benefits have access.

Establishment and development of military benefits in the United States: The GI bill

The U.S. government has provided economic benefits to veterans of military service, beginning with those who served in the Revolutionary War and became disabled as a result of their service (Vacchi & Berger, 2014). Subsequently, the Congressional Morrill Land-Grant Act of 1862, known for its impact on the eponymous land-grant colleges, also contained provisions specific to military service. Colleges funded through the Morrill Act were required to offer military training as part of their curricula (Abrams, 1989). Congress passed the Servicemen's Readjustment Act of 1944, more popularly known as the GI Bill – short for *Government Issue* – to stave off a potential post-war economic depression in the United States (Olson, 1973). The GI Bill provided a number of benefits to the 16 million veterans who were returning from military service (Fuller, 2014; Olson, 1973; Vacchi & Berger, 2014). The educational benefits included four years of funding for veterans to receive higher education or vocational training and offered scaled housing stipends based on the veteran's family size (Olson, 1973). By 1954, more than two million veterans – 37% of those eligible – had used their GI benefits to access higher education, far exceeding the government's estimates for enrollment (Olson, 1973). The GI Bill is widely considered to be crucial to the expansion and democratization of American higher education (Fuller, 2014; Olson, 1973).

Post-9/11 GI bill and Forever GI bill

The 1984 Montgomery GI Bill gave veterans approximately $36,000 to fund their college education program. It did not, however, provide sufficient funding to fully finance a veteran's education (Morrill, 2017; Vacchi & Berger, 2014). The Post-9/11 GI Bill attempted to remedy this inadequacy. The Post-9/11 GI Bill provided total coverage of college costs at public institutions for veterans, as well as funding for housing, books, and other fees (Morrill, 2017). Up to 36 months of funding was available, and this could be used for up to 15 years after the date of discharge (Morrill, 2017). Vacchi and Berger (2014) termed this bill "the most generous financial educational benefit package for veterans in our nation's history after adjustments for inflation" (p. 104). The government has invested more than $30 billion into veterans benefits through this bill (Cate, 2014). The Harry W. Colmery Veterans Education Assistance Act of 2017, known as the "Forever GI Bill," went into effect in August 2018. This bill will eliminate the 15-year benefit limit required by the Post-9/11 GI Bill but also decrease the housing benefit for new participants (U.S. Department of Veterans Affairs, n.d.).

Yellow ribbon program

As mentioned above, the Post-9/11 GI Bill provides funding to students attending public institutions of higher education. The Yellow Ribbon program – an opt-in collaboration between the VA and some private institutions – provides funds for veterans who attend private schools (Bagby, Barnard-Brak, Thompson, & Sulak, 2015). The school contributes directly to the cost of the veteran's education (McBain et al., 2012), and the VA matches the school's contribution (Rumann et al., 2011).

Veteran students' transitions to higher education

In the following section, we describe the current state of literature concerning student veterans, their characteristics, and their experiences navigating higher education. Student veterans make the dramatic transition from the military, a highly structured organization (Bagby et al., 2015; Stone, 2017), to the "organized anarchy" of higher education (Vacchi & Berger, 2014, p. 123). Student veterans enrolling in community college encounter an environment that is often decentralized and unstructured (Scott-Clayton, 2011). In addition, students are navigating identity changes. Studies have shown that military students reformulate their identities when entering community college, leaving behind identities associated with their active-duty status and gaining new *student* self-identities (DiRamio, Ackerman, & Mitchell, 2008; Jones, 2017; Rumann & Hamrick, 2010; Wheeler, 2012). Veterans previously deployed outside of the United States also have to readjust to home life while transitioning to higher education (Bagby et al., 2015). Military students may also experience greater mental health difficulties than the overall student population because they may be diagnosed with post-traumatic stress disorder or another illness (Elliott, Gonzalez, & Larsen, 2011; Fortney et al., 2016).

The transition to higher education is complicated by veteran students' status as adult learners, which can be both a boon and a hindrance as they move through this new stage in their lives. According to Cate (2014), 56.3% of all veterans were in their 20s when they began using their veterans benefits for higher education and 12.4% were over 30 years old. As adult learners, veteran students are independent and self-motivated (Persky & Oliver, 2010). They commonly have additional out-of-school responsibilities (Cook & Kim, 2009). More than 60% of student veterans are married or have dependents (Vacchi & Berger, 2014). These challenges do not make veterans' transition into higher education any easier.

Veteran students are, however, strongly committed to higher education (Rumann & Hamrick, 2010). Veterans "view postsecondary education as a necessary step to improving their lives as civilians after military service" (Cook & Kim, 2009, p. 21). Many joined the military because of the education funding that their military service can provide (Barr, 2016), taking advantage of an incentive for enlistment present since the original GI Bill (Angrist, 1993). Many veteran students engage in some form of higher education while enlisted in the military, either by earning credits through their military service (Brown & Gross, 2011) or by enrolling in online or in-person higher education (Williams-Klotz & Gansemer-Topf, 2018). Research suggests that because veterans are used to committing to and carrying out a mission, they often treat degree attainment as a task to be performed with comparable seriousness (Cook & Kim, 2009; De LaGarza, Manuel, Wood, & Harris, 2016; Stone, 2017), decrying the lack of gravitas they see in their younger or less mature classmates (Hammond, 2016).

Institutional supports for veterans

The literature indicates that military students would prefer a simplified, one-stop-shop for all matters dealing with their military status concerning finances, advising, and support services (Brown & Gross, 2011; Persky & Oliver, 2010; Whikehart, 2010; Williams-Klotz & Gansemer-Topf, 2017). Working with the VA to receive benefits in a timely manner can cause military-affiliated students serious difficulties (DiRamio et al., 2008); staff who understand the complexities of the VA, and that federal agencies deadlines and disbursements do not always correspond to the higher education calendar, provide a valuable service to students (Vacchi, 2012). For example, one institution timed military students' tuition bills to correspond to the VA calendar rather than to the traditional institutional calendar so that students were not responsible for paying bills before the VA would do so (Brown & Gross, 2011). Interactions with campus staff, including academic advisors, who are knowledgeable about available payment options may also help this population.

Advising

Degree advising may also present a problem for these students because receipt of funds is contingent upon their following a specific degree plan and being enrolled in courses that adhere to their degree requirements. At the community college level, active-duty or veteran military students are more likely to meet with an advisor than are other students (Center for Community College Student Engagement, 2018). Without this advising knowledge, students may inadvertently enroll in classes that they would have to pay for out-of-pocket, which could affect their receipt of other benefits. Support services, even those as simple as providing a campus lounge for military students or hosting family-friendly mixers for veteran students, have also been found to contribute to student well-being and to increase their campus engagement (Vacchi & Berger, 2014; Williams-Klotz & Gansemer-Topf, 2017).

Student mentors or sponsors who are also military affiliated can provide military-affiliated students with a sense of connection and support. Trained faculty and staff who possess accurate and up-to-date information about veteran students, their benefits, and the requirements of the population would provide a valuable alternative to a one-stop-shop on campuses (Elliott et al., 2011; Kim & Cole, 2013; Persky & Oliver, 2010; Rumann et al., 2011; Wheeler, 2012).

Campus climate concerns

Institutions also shape veteran students' experiences through campus climate. Military students often have difficulty connecting to nonveteran peers in higher education, choosing instead to seek out other students who can relate to their experiences in the military (Kim & Cole, 2013; Rumann et al., 2011; Stone, 2017; Vacchi, Hammond, & Diamond, 2017). Some students choose to hide their military affiliation to avoid being singled out for their service (Hammond, 2016; Rumann et al., 2011; Vacchi, 2012), and to escape inappropriate questions they might receive from others, such as asking if the veterans have ever killed a person (Rumann & Hamrick, 2010).

Veterans may experience a more welcoming campus climate when interacting with their peers, particularly if those peers are also veterans. For some students, sponsorship or mentoring relationships with other veterans are helpful college transition tools (Stone, 2017; Williams-Klotz & Gansemer-Topf, 2017). However, Vacchi and Berger (2014) cautioned that peer mentorships might be less effective for veteran students, who are socialized from their military service to avoid being a "weak link on a team" (p. 132). In cases like this, veteran students may not engage in the mentoring relationships because they fear burdening others.

In the classroom, some veteran students may perceive hostility when faculty share their views on the military or related governmental actions – particularly if faculty and students' opinions differ – or call on military students to offer a representative military opinion (DiRamio et al., 2008). In general, the veteran population has been shown to appreciate tacit recognition for military service, such as institutional messages of support for the military on Memorial Day or Veterans Day, rather than receiving specific attention and awards for their own service (DiRamio et al., 2008).

In summary, research has examined the experiences of veteran students on campus, including some research that explores institutional supports that are helpful to this population. However, little research examines veteran students' experiences with navigating the *transfer* process, from a community college to a four-year university. This transition presents new challenges in terms of selecting transferrable courses, navigating complex inter-institutional agreements, and making decisions about how to apply benefits.

Conceptual framework

We draw on Scott-Clayton's (2011) description of community colleges as a 'shapeless river,' Scott-Clayton argues that community colleges are extremely difficult for students to navigate because of their complexity. There are many opportunities for students to make mistakes due to misinformation or missing information. The current community college structure, in which students are free to make significant academic decisions without consulting an academic advisor, can lead to "mistakes, delay, and dissatisfaction" (Scott-Clayton, 2011, p. 11), namely errors in course choice, waiting to make decisions about academic pathways, and unhappiness with outcomes. The institutional structure is most disadvantageous for low-income students – who are more likely to attend community colleges than their high-income counterparts – because these students may lack the social capital, or "transfer student capital" (Laanan et al., 2010, p. 180), to access the institutional knowledge that would help them be successful.

Transfer student capital includes the institutional and individual characteristics that can drive successful transfer from community college to four-year institution (Laanan et al., 2010). Drawing on Laanan et al.'s (2010) concepts, Moser (2013) developed a six-pronged model of transfer student capital that included academic counseling experiences, learning and study skills developed at the community college, informal contact with community college faculty, formal contact with community college faculty, financial knowledge at the community college, and motivation/self-efficacy. Transfer student capital deepens our understanding of the transfer process by identifying student-level characteristics that can lead to transfer success.

As a potential solution to navigational difficulties at community colleges, Scott-Clayton's (2011) "structure hypothesis" advocated for structural changes to minimize the options offered to students when they make academic decisions (p. 1). Regarding staff, Scott-Clayton suggested using more "intensive" or "high-touch" advising procedures (p. 16), increasing the number of times the institution contacts students, and using technology to simplify the bureaucratic procedures for students. On the structural level, she recommended limiting curricular choices available to students – her work helped to inform the guided pathways model (Bailey, Jaggars, & Jenkins, 2015) – and reorganizing organizational procedures to make information easier to find for students. Leveraging a more intrusive and structured advising model, comparable to that used by private, two-year colleges, could provide fewer opportunities for student error. We use these concepts to frame our analysis of the experiences of the military-affiliated students in our study.

Methods

In this qualitative case study (Yin, 2003), we analyzed interviews with military-affiliated transfer-intending community college students in Texas and examined the resources available to these students at the community college campuses. This paper draws from an ongoing longitudinal study of transfer-intending community college students in Central Texas, of which three years of data collection have been completed; these three years of data are included in this paper.

Participants

Students attended one of three community colleges in Central Texas – two individual colleges within a citywide college system and one urban college in a different city. Working with the institutions and staff, we recruited students by sending messages through e-mail listservs, posting on the institutions' social media websites, attending transfer events, and participating in on-campus tabling events. We targeted recruitment at students whose identities are historically underrepresented in higher education, such as first-generation college students, students of color, and students living near the poverty line. In total, we interviewed in person more than 100 students who intended to transfer to a four-year institution. Subsequently, we followed up with all the students twice over the next two years to see how their transfer plans progressed.

This study focuses on the 16 veteran or military-affiliated students we identified within the larger study. Our sample includes students who intended to transfer to a four-year institution within a year of their initial participation in the study in fall 2015. Out of the 16 military students in our sample, only four (25%) were second- or third-generation college students, and 12 of out 16 (75%) were people of color, which parallels the demographics of many community college students (Ma & Baum, 2016). Five students in our study had not served in the armed forces but funded their higher education through receipt of their parents' Post-9/11 GI Bill benefits.

Data collection

Using semi-structured interview protocols (Patton, 1990), our team sought to interview students three times, that is, once during each year of data collection. We were able to interview nine students three times, two students two times, and five students one time. Based on availability, the research team conducted an in-person or phone interview with the students in the second and third year of data collection. We asked students about their experiences at the community college, their timeline and steps toward transfer, and the barriers and supports they experienced along the way. Each audio-recorded interview lasted approximately 45 minutes. They were subsequently transcribed. Table 1 contains information about the students included in this sample.

Data analysis

To analyze our data, we first coded all transcripts with Dedoose, using a hybrid coding method in which we created codes from both the data and existing theory (Miles, Huberman, & Saldaña, 2014). We used Dedoose's training center to establish interrater reliability. Next, we wrote memos, tracing each student's pathway toward transfer. We conceptualize these memos as condensed analyses,

Table 1. Participants.

Gender (M/F)	Race and Ethnicity	Birth Year	First-Generation College Student	Years Served in Military	Dependents	Years Followed up	Transferred by Year 3
M	White	1992	Y	4	0	3	Y
M	White	1986	N	4	2	1	Unknown
F	Did not report	1994	N	N/A	0	1	Unknown
F	Asian	1985	Y	8	2	1	Y
F	White; Latina	1991	Y	4	0	1	Unknown
F	African American	1986	N	13	1	3	N
F	Asian, Latina	1994	Y	6	0	3	Y
M	White; Latino	1982	Y	10	0	3	Y
F	White; Latina	1997	Y	N/A	0	3	N
F	White	1995	Y	N/A	0	1	N
M	African American	1996	Y	2	1	3	Y
M	White; Latino	1985	Y	12	0	2	Unknown
F	Native American; Latina	1995	Y	N/A	0	3	Y
F	White; Latina	1986	Y	8	2	2	Y
M	White	1986	Y	8	3	3	Y
F	Native American; Latina	1994	N	N/A	0	3	Y

Note: Students without years served (N/A) were using their parents' benefits.

written after a member of the research team had reviewed all interview and survey materials available for each student and coded that student's interview transcripts. For the nine students who had been interviewed in the third year of data collection, the memo contained a section relating to their military experiences. For the others, we reviewed their prior transcripts to seek out data related to their military experiences. From the memos, we created a document that captured students' reasons for joining the military, their military experiences (if applicable), their interactions with the institutions, and how they used their benefits.[2] To analyze students' experiences, we reviewed the memos written about each student, reviewed memos regarding military experiences written in Dedoose during coding, and discussed each student with other members of the research team. We also created a typography for the military-affiliated students, based on their rationale for joining the military, and triangulated those findings by discussing them with other members of the research team. We further triangulated the data by discussing each student's situation with other members of the research team. We created a document to elaborate our findings.

Limitations

This sample was drawn from a larger study of community college students in Central Texas. As such, the sample of 16 military affiliates is not representative of all military students at these institutions. In addition, because the initial focus of our study was not on military-affiliated students, the interview protocol did not explicitly include detailed questions about veterans' military experiences, and the amount of data acquired from the students varied. Nine out of the 16 students spoke with us during each year of the study, but for five students only one year's worth of data was available.

Findings

In this section, we discuss the ways in which students – both veteran and nonveteran – used their military benefits when navigating the transfer process. To answer our research questions – how do students who receive veterans benefits use their military experiences and resources to navigate the transfer process, and what factors contribute to the transfer success of military-affiliated students – we identified three areas in which military-affiliated students had additional help in this process, which we term *guardrails, financial independence*, and *identity characteristics*. We discuss each of these in more detail below. For this group of students, their interactions with the institution structured their transfer experience and made it easier for them to navigate that process.

Guardrails

We define *guardrails* as institutional supports that contribute to a successful transfer process. For instance, to receive funding from the military, military-affiliated students must pick a particular degree plan and can take only courses that are required for their majors. If military-affiliated students take courses that are not required by particular degree plans and drop below the enrollment status required by their funding, they must pay back the money the government has disbursed to them and to their institution. Course choice, therefore, is a high-stakes endeavor for this population. One mistake could result in the removal of financial support, including housing allowances and tuition, for an entire semester. Both veteran and military-affiliated students must adhere to these requirements. One White, male student studying STEM – who was very knowledgeable about transfer – had transferred to a four-year institution. He described course selection in the following manner:

> For me, [my degree plan] mattered just because it's one of the VA requirements – that you have a degree plan and that you're following it... It's just one of the things that the VA has, just to make sure that you're spending the GI bill wisely, not just taking random classes just to get a living stipend or something like that.

Taking care to select courses wisely was, for this student, an arduous but necessary process. However, other students took a different approach to course selection that was motivated by vocational decisions.

Instead of using the strict requirements of veterans benefits to determine their course selection, some students waited to use their veterans benefits until they were certain that courses would apply to their career goals. One Black female student, who had not yet transferred and was taking a break from school until she determined her career path, described how she wanted to take courses that were not part of the Texas Core curriculum or her major requirements but faced constraints. She said,

> Sometimes I want to pick [a course] for fun, but I can't really do that. I won't wanna waste my money ... like, I'm dying to take another art class, but ... it'd have to come out of pocket.

This was the case because of the requirements of the vocational rehab program. The student carefully saved her vocational rehabilitation benefits so that she could use them toward a degree that would match her future career. However, she was limited in her course selection because of these military benefits.

To ensure that each course fulfills a degree requirement, military-affiliated students need to remain in frequent contact with the VA advisor at their institution, if their institution has a staff member in that role, and with their academic advisor. They often need to contact staff members frequently and listen to the staff members' advice because a substantial amount of money is at stake. Most students in our sample spoke about the high quality of advising they received from the veterans' office on their campus. One Native American and Latina student who received her father's military benefits contrasted her experience with veterans'-specific advising with her previous experience:

> I have to go to the veterans' affairs office, so it's a little bit easier, as opposed to when I was going to my advisor the first semester, where I had to go to just the general counselors and advisors and advisors. It's not as long of a wait now. It's going well, my advisor, it seems like she's wanting to work in my best interest, and that she's polite, and she'll break it down into a word or a phrase that I can understand.

As the student's statement indicated, our participants appreciated the designated pool of support staff that afforded them shorter waiting times; in some cases, advisors initiated contact with the veterans and military-affiliated students rather than the other way around. While there were two students who specifically mentioned challenges with the advising they received – in one case lack of information and in another misinformation – most students appreciated the support of their team of staff assigned to advise them. One Mexican-American military-affiliated student receiving benefits from her father's time in the service said that her father, a graduate of the four-year institution she attended, was her main source of information. Unlike others, who spoke highly of the veteran office advisors, she expressed the belief that these advisors were not well-informed about transfer-specific issues: "I'm not allowed to go anywhere else. I could only stay with the veterans, but if I could ... I mean, [I'd see] anybody who knows more about transfers than them, because they don't know at all." In this case, the convenience of having the advisors nearby was complicated by the fact that this particular advisor was not highly literate about the transfer process. This represents another possible inefficiency for veteran and military-affiliated students at community colleges who are seeking transfer.

Broadly, however, because students had so much structure in their course selection process and advising (Scott-Clayton, 2011), they were forced to adhere closely to a schedule that could ultimately help them to transfer or complete their degree efficiently. These requirements also drove students to obtain academic counseling. The guardrails provided by the military benefits thus contributed to and fostered the formation of transfer student capital (Laanan et al., 2010; Moser, 2013).

Financial independence

Military-affiliated students have *financial independence* because their education is financed by the government. The flip side of the stringent course-selection requirements is that military-affiliated students have money to pay for school, and in many cases, they receive housing benefits as well. Compared with other community college students, who work while enrolled in school at higher rates than their four-year counterparts (Ma & Baum, 2016), military-affiliated students effectively trade their past labor (or, in the case of the parent benefit students, their parents' labor) for financial freedom while enrolled in higher education. Theoretically, they do not have to work, outside of attending to their student responsibilities, to live. This freedom is not, however, without costs. Aside from the requirements of the educational guardrails discussed above, some military-affiliated students in our study expressed a sense of responsibility about the funding they received for education. One student said, "I know it's not exactly my money," but she said she still wanted to spend it carefully.

Most students considered the VA benefits to be money they had earned, comparable to their salary or a fringe benefit, not a government handout. For example, the male veteran student studying STEM said,

> I just wanted to use the GI Bill because it is such a great benefit. I did my years, so I earned it. I felt like it would be foolish not to go back to school. I have free education.

One Latina student studying a helping profession who transferred to a four-year private institution that belonged to the Yellow Ribbon Program had mixed feelings about attending that sort of institution:

> I don't want to go to a private school. I know my school's paid for; I still don't want to spend that money. You know, it's stupid to me. I don't want to spend that money on a private school.

This student perceived attending college at a private school as an extravagance because she could get a similar education at a lower cost to the government. She was shocked by the costs she personally incurred upon transferring, particularly as she had to foot the $800 bill for her own books and ran into difficulties with paying tuition. She noted:

> Then I turned everything in, and then of course I had to go get it approved, because the military has a cap on how much you can spend on education. Well, the school costs $14,000 ... well, it cost $13,000 when I started, but it costs $14,000 now, and it costs a semester, so it was kind of expensive ... That was the hardest process, is making sure that they would approve the program, the military.

Even though she viewed the military benefits as her earned benefits, she was aware of the actual financial cost of her education and was overwhelmed by the amount of money the government had spent on her education. She wanted to be a good steward of public funds. Another student's VA advisor had discouraged her from choosing a private school because of the added costs.

Three students in our study were using vocational rehab benefits, which have more restrictions than other types of military benefits. Students take a personality test to find a major they will excel at that will also accommodate their disability. They write a plan with a counselor and must adhere to the plan as they pursue their degree or credential. Although these benefits have fewer time and money constraints, students must attend a public institution (Office of Public and Intergovernmental Affairs, n.d.).

Students were strategic about how to spend their benefits. As the Post-9/11 GI Bill provides only 36 months' worth of higher education funding at most, students used their benefits carefully, even when they experienced financial hardship. Some students wanted to pursue post-baccalaureate education and strategized about how to stretch out the 36 months for as long as possible to defray the costs of a master's degree. In some cases, that meant opting out of using benefits at a community college. Community colleges are usually cheaper than four-year institutions; this meant that the VA would pay for the more expensive educational experiences. The male student studying STEM explained how he planned to parse out his benefits:

> You get 36 months of school. So however you break that up, you know, like a semester is four months, there's four months down. You take summer, two and a half months or whatever, that subtracts that off. And that's why the first, I think, maybe first two semesters and I think the summer at [community college], I didn't use the GI bill, because tuition at [community college] is a lot cheaper, one-fifth what it is at [the four-year university]. So, I figured, if there was a chance I would run out of GI Bill at [the four-year university], I'd rather not use it at [community college]. So, I did that in order to make sure I would have enough GI Bill to carry me through [to my master's degree].

This student's comments reflect a sentiment shared by others who were thoughtful about how long they intended to study and about what benefits they should access and when. As mentioned earlier, the vocational rehab benefits are more restrictive and cannot be used for a master's degree. One student stated that he would use his GI Bill to get an MA in business after using his rehab benefits during his community college and undergraduate education. Optimal use of VA benefits – maximizing the amount the government would pay for school while minimizing the students' own out-of-pocket costs – required students to possess a precise understanding of VA benefits and engage in long-term, strategic cost-benefit analyses.

Identity characteristics

We define *identity characteristics* as the traits students possess that can ease or hinder their transfer process. The students in our sample who were veterans largely did not express having had difficulty with the transfer process; some of them attributed this lack of obstacles to their military status. When explaining her behavior while interacting with faculty and staff at the community college, the Black female student veteran student quoted above who had not yet transferred said: "The military would give me directions. I had specific, straight to the point. If I have a problem, let me do my thing. If I have a problem I will raise my hand. I have no problem doing that." Her training had provided her with skills that enabled her to advocate for herself and solve her own problems. This and similar participant statements echoed the literature about the bureaucratic know-how students must have to receive veterans benefits (DiRamio et al., 2008; Rumann & Hamrick, 2010; Rumann et al., 2011; Stone, 2017; Wheeler, 2012; Williams-Klotz & Gansemer-Topf, 2017). These students also had facility with transferring between two-year and four-year schools. A White and Latino veteran who has since transferred to a four-year, in-state public institution reported no issues at all with the application and transfer process. He told us that the process "felt normal." He called the VA office at his destination institution only once during the "easy" transfer and application process and said that the process "wasn't complicated. It's not like I'm applying to an Ivy League, you know." One student veteran said he knew he had to monitor how credits transferred between his transfer destination and his home school but felt ill-equipped to do this successfully.

In contrast, one American Indian student who had not served, who was using her parents' benefits, did run up against bureaucratic hurdles. After she transferred to a four-year university, there was a mix-up with her VA benefits and she received notice that she owed tuition for the semester. As a result, she had to complete her VA paperwork twice, and the university prevented her from registering for classes until she finished the paperwork. The student described this process as "super frustrating" and "annoying." A Latina student using her parents' benefits expected difficulty interacting with faculty and staff at her intended four-year destination and told us her opinion of faculty and staff: "they don't wanna be helpful but they are. They don't have a right to say no because it's their job." This student relied on her father to ask appropriate questions about veteran benefits and said that on campus visits "he'll ask those questions that I won't even know [to ask]." Although it is impossible to disentangle student identities and military training as facilitators of college transfer, we observed that for the students in our sample who had served, navigation of higher education logistics was fairly seamless.

Discussion

The military-affiliated students in our study provide a test case for Scott-Clayton's (2011) "structure hypothesis" – when students have more structure in their course-selection process, the "shapeless river" begins to take on a more coherent form (p. 1). This configuration, with more prescribed course choices and additional mandated check-ins with advising staff, keeps students moving efficiently towards their educational goals. The students in our sample were functionally required to interact with many staff members in order to receive their college funding, and that interaction may have facilitated their acquisition of transfer capital (Laanan et al., 2010). In addition, because they had to enroll exclusively in courses that met specific degree requirements, the students did not experience the boundless choices and lack of structure that Scott-Clayton described.

In these ways, the benefits provided to military-affiliated students helped them overcome other conditions, such as first-generation status, that might affect their ability to transfer and increased their transfer capital through increased contact with academic advisors and information about their education financing (Moser, 2013). Veteran students were also motivated to complete their schooling and were confident in their own abilities to navigate the higher education bureaucracy (Moser, 2013). The high level of transfer rates in this subsample, comprised of military students with additional structural supports, is consistent with Scott-Clayton's (2011) structure hypothesis. Of course, the military-affiliated students' college experiences were not entirely free of difficulties or hurdles. The highly structured college experience had some drawbacks. It did not encourage course experimentation or an exploratory college experience because it was so narrowly focused on degree attainment.

Implications for practice and future research

The high rate of transfer success for the military-affiliated students in our sample indicates that community colleges may be able to help other transfer-intending students by providing a similarly high level of structure for that population (Scott-Clayton, 2011). Our findings suggest that military students' mandatory interactions with community college staff members, use and commitment to a degree plan, course selection dictated by the demands of the degree plan, and required interactions of military-affiliated students with staff could contribute to their transfer success. Requiring other community colleges students to participate in similar kinds of structured engagement with the institution could lead to more positive transfer outcomes for non-military-affiliated students. Perhaps these interactions could be mandated in order for students to continue at the institution or to receive financial aid, building in this structure for advising could help community college students to make informed decisions, in conversations with staff members, about their academic choices at the institution. Making sure these decisions are informed ones could then improve their chances for successful transfer.

Military-affiliated students are frequently required to interact with community college staff because the financial stakes for failing to do so are so high. Other students may benefit from similar practices, though implementing them would require substantial financial investment by the community college. High-touch advising practices, such as required meetings with staff and mandatory consulting with academic advisors each semester, might improve transfer or degree attainment. Encouraging students to commit to a degree plan or follow a transfer guide each semester and promoting regular interactions with their advisors to ensure that their courses are applicable to that degree plan may also contribute to transfer success. This commitment, which aligns with recommendations of the guided pathways model, might ensure that students take fewer courses that are not relevant to their transfer plans (Bailey et al., 2015). Check-ins with advisors and clear degree plans could serve as guardrails against course choices that are not optimal for transfer goals, as they appear to do for veteran students. While this could require additional per-student financial expenditures at the community college level, adding structures that encourage student engagement with staff could improve students' transfer outcomes. However, for community colleges to effectively serve as places of exploration (Rose, 2012), addressing financial constraints by providing additional financial assistance, including housing stipends and benefits, may be necessary (Broton & Goldrick-Rab, 2016).

A substantial body of work on veteran students exists, but more quantitative and qualitative research is needed on military-affiliated nonveteran students and on veteran students who intend to transfer from a community college to a four-year institution. Further research at the national level on veteran students' paths through higher education could fill in further details about these students' trajectories. Research about workforce outcomes for military-affiliated students who begin at community colleges would enrich our understanding of this population.

This qualitative study explored the transfer process for military-affiliated students in Central Texas. We found that the stringent requirements of using veterans benefits may have helped these students in the transfer process. The students had the advantage of what we term guardrails, structures that create frequent interactions with community college staff and financial flexibility afforded by government stipends for living and tuition. It is also possible that veterans, specifically, benefit from their prior experiences and identity characteristics, which make it easier for them to navigate the transfer process. Our work bolsters support for the guided pathways model (Bailey et al., 2015), as students appeared to benefit from the additional structures offered to military affiliates. We recommend that, to improve transfer rates for the student population as a whole, community colleges consider implementing programs and institutional structures similar to those offered for military-affiliated students for all transfer-intending students.

Acknowledgments

We would like to acknowledge Andrea Chevalier, Wesley Edwards, Marisol Garza, Catherine Hartman, Joanna Sánchez, and Elif Yucel for their research assistance. Data collection and analysis were supported by the Greater Texas Foundation through their Faculty Fellows program and a grant for the project "Tell me what I need to do": How Texas Community College Students Experience and Interpret State Transfer Policies

Funding

This work was supported by the The Greater Texas Foundation.

Notes

1. The term "veterans benefits" applies to students who are using those benefits, regardless of whether they served in the armed forces.
2. One student in the study had already transferred when the team conducted her initial interview and was therefore ineligible for participation in years two and three of the study; a memo had not been completed for her, so we relied solely on her interview and survey for the first year of the study.

ORCID

Saralyn McKinnon-Crowley http://orcid.org/0000-0002-5553-1744

References

Abrams, R. M. (1989). The U.S. military and higher education: A brief history. *The ANNALS of the American Academy of Political and Social Science, 502*(1), 15–28. doi:10.1177/0002716289502001002

Angrist, J. D. (1993). The effect of veterans benefits on education and earnings. *Industrial and Labor Relations Review, 46*(4), 637–652. doi:10.1177/001979399304600404

Backes, B., & Velez, E. D. (2014). *Who transfers and where do they go? Community college students in Florida.* Retrieved from http://capseecenter.org/labor-market-returns-michigan/

Bagby, J. H., Barnard-Brak, L., Thompson, L. W., & Sulak, T. N. (2015). Is anyone listening? An ecological systems perspective on veterans transitioning from the military to academia. *Military Behavioral Health, 3*(4), 219–229. doi:10.1080/21635781.2015.1057306

Bailey, T., Jaggars, S. S., & Davis, J. (2015). *Redesigning America's community colleges: A clearer path to student success.* Cambridge, MA: Harvard University.

Barr, A. (2016). Enlist or enroll: Credit constraints, college aid, and the military enlistment margin. *Economics of Education Review, 51,* 61–78. doi:10.1016/j.econedurev.2015.06.003

Broton, K., & Goldrick-Rab, S. (2016). The dark side of college (un) affordability: Food and housing insecurity in higher education. *Change: the Magazine of Higher Learning, 48*(1), 16–25. doi:10.1080/00091383.2016.1121081

Brown, P. A., & Gross, C. (2011). Serving those who have served—Managing veteran and military student best practices. *Journal of Continuing Higher Education, 59*(1), 45–49. doi:10.1080/07377363.2011.544982

Cate, C. A. (2014). *Million records project: A review of veteran achievement in higher education.* Washington, DC: Student Veterans of America.

Cate, C. A., Lyon, J. S., Schmeling, J., & Bogue, B. Y. (2017). *National veteran education success tracker: A report on the academic success of student veterans using the Post-9/11 GI Bill.* Student Veterans of America: Washington, D.C.

Center for Community College Student Engagement. (2018, April). Not all advising services are created equally. *Re-Engaging Data, 2,* 1. Retrieved from www.ccsse.org/center/resources/docs/publications/Re-Engaging_Data_April_2018.pdf

Cook, B. J., & Kim, Y. (2009). *From soldier to student: Easing the transition of service members on campus.* Washington, DC: American Council on Education. Retrieved from http://www.acenet.edu/news-room/Pages/From-Soldier-to-Student.aspx

Crisp, G., & Nuñez, A.-M. (2014). Understanding the racial transfer gap: Modeling underrepresented minority and nonminority students' pathways from two-to four-year institutions. *Review of Higher Education, 37*(3), 291–320. doi:10.1353/rhe.2014.0017

Cuseo, J. B. (1998). *The transfer transition: A summary of key issues, target areas and tactics for reform.* Retrieved from http://eric.ed.gov/?id=ED425771

De LaGarza, T. R., Manuel, M. A., Wood, J. L., & Harris, F. I. (2016). Military and veteran student achievement in postsecondary education: A structural equation model using the Community College Survey of Men (CCSM). *Community College Enterprise, 22*(1), 43–54. Retrieved from: http://works.bepress.com/jluke_wood/93/

DiRamio, D., Ackerman, R., & Mitchell, R. L. (2008). From combat to campus: Voices of student-veterans. *NASPA Journal, 45*(1), 73–102. doi:10.2202/0027-6014.1908

Elliott, M., Gonzalez, C., & Larsen, B. (2011). U.S. military veterans transition to college: Combat, PTSD, and alienation on campus. *Journal of Student Affairs Research and Practice, 48*(3), 279–296. doi:10.2202/1949-6605.6293

Fortney, J. C., Curran, G. M., Hunt, J. B., Cheney, A. M., Lu, L., Valenstein, M., & Eisenberg, D. (2016). Prevalence of probable mental disorders and help-seeking behaviors among veteran and non-veteran community college students. *General Hospital Psychiatry, 38,* 99–104. doi:10.1016/j.genhosppsych.2015.09.007

Fuller, M. B. (2014). A history of financial aid to students. *Journal of Student Financial Aid, 44*(1), 42–68. Retrieved from: https://publications.nasfaa.org/cgi/viewcontent.cgi?article=1078&context=jsfa

Hammond, S. P. (2016). Complex perceptions of identity: The experiences of student combat veterans in community college. *Community College Journal of Research and Practice, 40*(2), 146–159. doi:10.1080/10668926.2015.1017891

Jenkins, D. (2018, July). *From articulation agreements to regional talent pathways partnerships.* Presentation at the San Antonio/Austin Regional Summer Transfer Pathway Forum, San Marcos, TX.

Jenkins, D., & Fink, J. (2016). *Tracking transfer: New measures of institutional and state effectiveness in helping community college students attain bachelor's degrees.* New York, NY: Community College Research Center, Aspen Institute, and the National Student Clearinghouse Research Center.

Jones, K. C. (2017). Understanding transition experiences of combat veterans attending community college. *Community College Journal of Research and Practice, 41*(2), 107–123. doi:10.1080/10668926.2016.1163298

Kim, Y. M., & Cole, J. S. (2013). *Student veterans/service members' engagement in college and university life and education.* Washington, DC: American Council on Education. Retrieved from http://www.acenet.edu/news-room/Pages/Student-Veterans-Service-Members-Engagement.aspx

Laanan, F. S., Starobin, S. S., & Eggleston, L. E. (2010). Adjustment of community college students at a four-year university: Role and relevance of transfer student capital for student retention. *Journal of College Student Retention, 12*(2), 175–209. doi:10.2190/CS.12.2.d

Ma, J., & Baum, S. (2016). *Trends in community college: Enrollment, prices, student debt, and completion*. New York, NY: The College Board. Retrieved from https://trends.collegeboard.org/sites/default/files/trends-in-community-colleges-research-brief.pdf

McBain, L., Young, M. K., Cook, B. J., & Snead, K. M. (2012). *From soldier to student II: Assessing campus programs for veterans and service members*. Washington, DC: American Council on Education. Retrieved from http://www.acenet.edu/news-room/Pages/From-Soldier-to-Student-II.aspx

Miles, M. B., Huberman, A. M., & Saldaña, J. (2014). *Qualitative data analysis: A methods sourcebook* (3rd ed. ed.). Thousand Oaks, CA: SAGE.

Morrill, S. M. (2017). *From benefits to service: Post-9/11 student veterans' educational outcomes at a Texas community college* (Unpublished doctoral dissertation). The University of Texas at Austin, Austin, TX. Retrieved from https://repositories.lib.utexas.edu/bitstream/handle/2152/47301/MORRILL-DISSERTATION-2017.pdf

Moser, K. M. (2013). Exploring the impact of transfer capital on community college transfer students. *Journal of the First-Year Experience & Students in Transition, 25*(2), 53–75. Retrieved from: https://eric.ed.gov/?id=EJ1031678

Office of Public and Intergovernmental Affairs. (n.d.). *Chapter 3 vocational rehabilitation and employment (VR&E)*. Retrieved from https://www.va.gov/opa/publications/benefits_book/benefits_chap03.asp

Olson, K. W. (1973). The GI Bill and higher education: Success and surprise. *American Quarterly, 25*(5), 596–610. doi:10.2307/2711698

Patton, M. Q. (1990). *Qualitative evaluation and research methods*. Newbury Park, CA: SAGE.

Persky, K. R., & Oliver, D. E. (2010). Veterans coming home to the community college: Linking research to practice. *Community College Journal of Research and Practice, 35*(1–2), 111–120. doi:10.1080/10668926.2011.525184

Romano, R. M., & Eddy, P. L. (2017). Community colleges and social mobility. *Change: the Magazine of Higher Learning, 49*(6), 55–62. doi:10.1080/00091383.2017.1399041

Rose, M. A. (2012). *Back to school: Why everyone deserves a second chance at education*. New York, NY: The New Press.

Rumann, C. B., & Hamrick, F. A. (2010). Student veterans in transition: Re-enrolling after war zone deployments. *Journal of Higher Education, 81*(4), 431–458. doi:10.1353/jhe.0.0103

Rumann, C. B., Rivera, M., & Hernandez, I. (2011). Student veterans and community colleges. *New Directions for Community Colleges*, (155), 51–58. doi:10.1002/cc.457

Scott-Clayton, J. (2011). *The shapeless river: Does a lack of structure inhibit students' progress at community college?* (Working Paper No. 25). New York, NY: Community College Research Center.

Shaw, K. M., & London, H. B. (2001). Culture and ideology in keeping transfer commitment: Three community colleges. *Review of Higher Education, 25*(1), 91–114. doi:10.1353/rhe.2001.0015

Stone, S. M. (2017). Internal voices, external constraints: Exploring the impact of military service on student development. *Journal of College Student Development, 58*(3), 365–384. doi:10.1353/csd.2017.0028

U.S. Department of Veterans Affairs. (n.d.). *Forever GI Bill - Harry W. Colmery Veterans Educational Assistance Act*. Retrieved from https://www.benefits.va.gov/GIBILL/FGIBSummaries.asp

Vacchi, D. T. (2012). Considering student veterans on the twenty-first-century college campus. *About Campus, 17*(2), 15–21. doi:10.1002/Abc.21075

Vacchi, D. T., & Berger, J. B. (2014). Student veterans in higher education. In M. B. Paulsen (Ed.), *Higher education: Handbook of theory and research* (Vol. 29, pp. 93–151). Dordrecht, The Netherlands: Springer Science+Business Media.

Vacchi, D. T., Hammond, S., & Diamond, A. (2017). Conceptual models of student veteran college experiences. *New Directions for Institutional Research, 2016*(171), 23–41. doi:10.1002/ir.20192

Wassmer, R., Moore, C., & Shulock, N. (2004). Effect of racial/ethnic composition on transfer rates in community colleges: Implications for policy and practice. *Research in Higher Education, 45*(6), 651–672. doi:10.1023/B:RIHE.0000040267.68949.d1

Wheeler, H. A. (2012). Veterans' transitions to community college: A case study. *Community College Journal of Research and Practice, 36*(10), 775–792. doi:10.1080/10668926.2012.679457

Whikehart, J. (2010). Mission graduation: A student military and veteran organization. *Community College Journal of Research and Practice, 34*(11), 920–922. doi:10.1080/10668926.2010.509261

Williams-Klotz, D. N., & Gansemer-Topf, A. M. (2017). Identifying the camouflage: Uncovering and supporting the transition experiences of military and veteran students. *Journal of the First-Year Experience & Students in Transition, 29*(1), 83–98. Retrieved from: https://eric.ed.gov/?id=EJ1139413

Williams-Klotz, D. N., & Gansemer-Topf, A. M. (2018). Examining factors related to academic success of military-connected students at community colleges. *Community College Journal of Research and Practice, 42*(6), 422–438. doi:10.1080/10668926.2017.1339647

Yin, R. K. (2003). *Case study research: Design and methods*. Thousand Oaks, CA: Sage.

Historically Black Community Colleges: A Descriptive Profile and Call for Context-Based Future Research

Kayla C. Elliott, Jarrett B. Warshaw, and Crystal A. deGregory

ABSTRACT
Much of the research and discussion of Historically Black Colleges and Universities (HBCUs) focuses on four-year institutions, impeding the significance of their two-year counterparts. Using extant literature and data from the National Center for Education Statistics' *Integrated Postsecondary Education Data System* (IPEDS), this paper elucidates Historically Black Community Colleges (HBCCs). By providing nuanced perspectives on this group of community colleges, we situate these institutions in their unique context. The paper provides a historical background of HBCCs, a review of relevant literature, and a descriptive profile of HBCCs' organizational characteristics. Finally, we discuss topical and theoretical recommendations for future research. This paper is a call for further research situated in the distinctive context of HBCCs, and carries both scholarly and practical significance for HBCCs, as well as other HBCUs, Minority Serving Institutions (MSIs), and community colleges.

Introduction

All too often, discussion of Historically Black Colleges and Universities (HBCUs) focuses on four-year institutions and precludes consideration of their two-year counterparts. The purpose of this scholarly paper is to describe and highlight Historically Black Community Colleges (HBCCs), a seldom-discussed and -studied category of institutions. This paper leverages research and available data in order to situate these institutions in their unique context. This work provides nuanced perspectives on the context and complexity of this group of community colleges, and carries both scholarly and practical significance. In centering HBCCs, scholars may launch novel lines of inquiry, which can benefit not only HBCCs, but other HBCUs, Minority Serving Institutions (MSIs), and community colleges. Studies of HBCCs can also help other higher education leaders and policymakers learn about different and possibly innovative approaches to serving students of color at community colleges, in particular Black American community college students. Researchers and policymakers could potentially group HBCCs together and categorize them as a sector without knowing how much diversity and variation exists amongst these institutions. Thus, this paper is a call for further research situated in the distinctive context of HBCCs.

The paper begins with a history of HBCCs and continues with a review of relevant literature. As there are relatively few *empirical* studies on HBCCs, it is important to provide a profile of the institutions. We expound upon the current state of HBCCs with discussion of organizational characteristics, including time-invariant characteristics and descriptive statistics for selected time-variant characteristics. Finally, we provide topical and theoretical recommendations for future research based on the extant literature and HBCC characteristics.

History of HBCCs

The history of HBCCs, like all HBCUs, began against the backdrop of Black sufferings and strivings in the American experience (Lovett, 2011). It is a remarkable story of educational persistence in the face of insurmountable odds including not only slavery but the unfreedoms resulting from white supremacy and its manacles of *de facto* and *de jure* racism. Access to literacy for those enslaved which had been, at best, a subject of much-debate during the enlightenment of the colonial period, had become an imagined and real threat to slavery by the antebellum period (Anderson, 1988). These realities, coupled with the challenges that all educational institutions face, make the founding of the earliest HBCUs even more noteworthy.

The nation's three oldest surviving HBCUs, Cheyney University, Lincoln University of Pennsylvania, and Wilberforce University, were all founded well-before the Civil War. However, the first-known institution dedicated to the higher education of Blacks in the United States, Avery College, was established even before them (Lovett, 2011). Avery College was founded in Pittsburgh, Pennsylvania in 1849 as the Allegheny Institute and Mission Church. The college was renamed in honor of its founder Charles Avery, an immigrant shopkeeper-turned-cotton merchant. Avery's benevolence was not unlike that of scores of white northern philanthropy to Black schools who followed (Avery College Historical Marker, 2011).

In facilitating their eventual freedom as well as unparalleled cultural and social progress, no single event in the nation's history more affected the fate and futures of Blacks in the United States than the Civil War (Lovett, 2011). The same is true of Black educational institutions. Even so, it was religious motivation for support of Black education that was most apparent in the years immediately following the war. Northern Whites and their benevolent or religious institutions including the Congregationalist's American Missionary Association (AMA), Baptist's American Baptist Home Mission Societies (as well as the Congregational, Presbyterian and Methodist's Freedmen's Aid Society teamed up with other agencies like the Freedman's Bureau to found many of the freedmen's schools that would eventually grow into black colleges (Fairclough, 2007; Sterling, 1984). Early on, they sought to imbue the then-emergent culture of Black schools and Black students with their missionary ethos. Their efforts led the historiography to ignore the role of Black self-reliance and self-determination in Black educational pursuits (Anderson, 1988; deGregory, 2011).

Equally, if not more important, was the federal government's adoption of a *laissez-faire* stance on race and education nationally, each state was permitted to set their own racial agenda. This position allowed southern legislatures to enact laws enforcing *de jure* segregation (Minor, 2008). Still, it was the *Plessy v. Ferguson* ruling of 1896 which legally enshrined the social, economic, political, and cultural code of separate but equal. In doing so, *Plessy* provided a damning legal means for Jim Crow, and in consequence, supported the further marginalization of Black people and the educational institutions which served them (Brown, 1999).

Table 1 shows that by the year of the Plessy ruling, Avery College had long been closed. In the more than century since then, more black colleges have likewise closed (Lovett, 2011). Within less than the last 15 years alone, four historically black colleges – Morristown College, Mary Holmes College, Lewis College of Business, and St. Paul's College – have closed. Founded as a high school for girls in 1892, Mary Holmes College, a two-year private college in Jacksonville, Mississippi filed for bankruptcy before closing in 2004. Today, several others, including Knoxville, Barber-Scotia, and Morris Brown colleges, having lost their accreditation, remain open in name only (Schexnider, 2017; Suggs, 2019).

Similarly, 19 HBCCs continued their mission of educating African Americans by the year of the *Plessy* ruling. These early HBCCs were private and religiously-affiliated, with the African Methodist Episcopal Church as the most common HBCC partner. Other founding affiliates unsurprisingly included the American Baptist Home Mission Societies (ABHMS), AMA, and Home Missionary Society as well as the Baptist church, the Church of God in Christ, the Christian Methodist Episcopal Church, and the Freewill Baptist Missionary Society.

Table 1. Closed Historically Black Community Colleges.

School	City	State	Founded	Closed	Type	Religious Affiliation
Avery College	Pittsburgh	Pennsylvania	1849	1873	Private	African Methodist Episcopal Church
Southern Christian Institute	Jackson	Mississippi	1872	1932	Private	Disciples of Christ
Storer College	Harpers Ferry	West Virginia	1865	1955	Private	Freewill Baptist Missionary Society
Carver Junior College	Cocoa	Florida	1960	1963	Public	None
Collier-Blocker Junior College	Palatka	Florida	1960	1964	Public	None
Booker T. Washington Junior College	Pensacola	Florida	1949	1965	Public	None
Roosevelt Junior College	West Palm Beach	Florida	1958	1965	Public	None
Volusia County Junior College	Daytona Beach	Florida	1958	1965	Public	None
Gibbs Junior College	St. Petersburg	Florida	1957	1966	Public	None
Hampton Junior College	Ocala	Florida	1958	1966	Public	None
Rosenwald Junior College	Panama City	Florida	1958	1966	Public	None
Suwannee River Junior College	Madison	Florida	1959	1966	Public	None
Johnson Junior College	Leesburg	Florida	1960	1966	Public	None
Lincoln Junior College	Fort Pierce	Florida	1960	1966	Public	None
Jackson Junior College	Marianna	Florida	1961	1966	Public	None
Kittrell College	Kittrell	North Carolina	1886	1975	Private	African Methodist Episcopal Church
Friendship College	Rock Hill	South Carolina	1891	1981	Private	Baptist
Natchez College	Natchez	Mississippi	1885	1993	Private	Baptist
Morristown College	Morristown	Tennessee	1881	1994	Private	Methodist Episcopal
Mary Holmes College	West Point	Mississippi	1892	2005	Private	Presbyterian
Lewis College of Business	Detroit	Michigan	1928	2013	Private	None
Conroe Normal and Industrial College	Conroe	Texas	1903	?	Private	Baptist

Sources: Barr (1996). Black Texans: A History of African Americans in Texas, 1528–1995. Norman, Okla: University of Oklahoma Press. Smith (2003). Black Firsts, Second Edition, 191–196; Smith (1994). The magnificent twelve: Florida's Black junior colleges. Winter Park, Fla. (P.O. Box 2249, Winter Park 32790): FOUR-G Publishers, 1994. Herd-Clark, D. J. (2012). Appendix: Profiles of closed HBCUs. In V. R. Newkirk (Ed.), New Life for Historically Black Colleges and Universities: A 21st century perspective. (239–244). Jefferson, NC: McFarland.

Though there have been 25 private HBCCs, many closed due to financial issues. A few were able to merge with nearby four-year HBCUs. The only public HBCCs or HBCUs to be closed were the 12 Black junior colleges in Florida. Eleven of the 12 were founded after the passage of *Brown v. Board* in full defiance of the case's call for integration. All 12 were abruptly closed and merged with local white junior colleges between 1964 and 1966.

Before we discuss the contemporary characteristics and contexts of HBCCs, we address the research literature, albeit scant, on institutions in this sector. In the next section, we review research on student experiences and outcomes at HBCCs, institutional differentiation and missions, and the professional work and academic careers in these settings.

Literature review

This paper seeks to demonstrate how HBCCs have been studied in their unique context, but to our knowledge, the research literature on HBCCs is extremely limited. To locate HBCCs in the literature, we conducted boolean searches for research that addressed Historically Black junior colleges, community colleges, or two-year colleges. There are relatively few *empirical* studies on these institutions and as situated in their unique contexts. Given the dearth of research, we also sought works such as book chapters, scholarly essays, news articles, and policy reports. Much of the extant literature that directly mentions HBCCs is to note their existence in higher education, or their exclusion from the study because they are outliers substantively different from others and thus liable to skew research findings and results (Allen, 2016; Benítez & DeAro, 2004; Davis & Markham, 1991; Shorette & Arroyo, 2015).

In some studies, such as Abelman, (2013), researchers included HBCCs in larger datasets without noting their distinction from four-year institutions. In other research, authors erased HBCCs by creating a false dichotomy between HBCUs and community colleges (Dervarics, 1997), or failing to distinguish between HBCCs and other community colleges (Abraham, Slate, Saxon, & Barnes, 2014). The false dichotomy created between HBCUs and Hispanic Serving Institutions erases only one institution, St. Philip's College (TX), which holds both designations (Glover, Simpson, & Waller, 2009). The research which specifically centers HBCCs falls primarily into four areas: student attainment (Bailey et al., 2004; Bailey, Calcagno, Jenkins, Kienzl, & Leinbach, 2005; Bailey, Calcagno, Jenkins, Leinbach, & Kienzl, 2006; Benítez & DeAro, 2004; DePass & Chubin, 2015); student experience (Meléndez, Falcón, & Bivens, 2003; Ruffins, 2008); organizational considerations such as mission statements and institutional advancement (Abelman & Dalessandro, 2009; Carter, 2018; Harris, 2012); and faculty development (Chubin & DePass, 2015; Opp & Gosetti, 2002).

Student experiences

Several researchers and analysts have focused on the student experience at HBCCs and on selected student populations with particular needs and challenges. Ruffins (2008) addressed services and structured programs offered to students with learning disabilities. Ruffins found few mentions of HBCUs in publications created by independent associations. Ruffins also found few mentions of HBCUs in two guidebooks widely used by guidance counselors, namely the Petersons Colleges for Students with Learning Disabilities or ADD, and The K&W Guide to Colleges for Students with Learning Disabilities or Attention Deficit/Hyperactivity Disorder. Bishop State Community College in Alabama was the only HBCC listed as providing services for students with learning disabilities.

In contrast to Ruffins's (2008) conclusions on limited HBCC resources for students with special needs, Meléndez et al. (2003) found special-needs programs for student welfare recipients with low reading or math skills at 78.4% of "Black-servicing" two-year colleges, consisting of HBCCs and other community colleges serving 25% or more Black students. Other special needs programs by Black-servicing two-year colleges with welfare-to-work initiatives included those for students with poor work history (52.2%), no high school diploma or GED (62.7%), young children (45.1%), and substance abuse problems (26.7%). Meléndez et al. focused on HBCC participation in Temporary Assistance to Needy Families (TANF) and the colleges' offerings to TANF recipients. In all, 6% of students at community colleges are also TANF recipients. At 4.4%, student participation in TANF at HBCCs and other Black-serving two-year institutions is lower than the average. Additionally, 95% of Black-serving two-year institutions offered nondegree programs to welfare-to-work recipients, while 79% offered degree programs. Both are higher than the community college average of 83% and 71%, respectively. The authors noted that: "Even with many institutional impediments to creating career advancement opportunities, many colleges allow students to transfer part of the credits taken in nondegree programs to degree programs" (Meléndez et al., 2003, p. 213). While helpful, these studies do not expound on institutional barriers or levers in order to influence internal procedures and public policy.

Student outcomes

Meanwhile, student-related outcomes at HBCCs have captured some scholarly and analytical attention over the years. Bailey and colleagues have particularly focused on student attainment at HBCCs, analyzing both institutional graduation rates and individual student outcomes (Bailey et al., 2004, 2005, 2006). In 2004 and 2005, they found no significant difference between the performance of HBCCs and the performance of other institutions. However, in a later study the researchers created a unique dependent variable by combining the institutional graduation rate and the rate of students who transferred to other institutions. Using this as the determinant of success, HBCCs performed approximately 13% higher than all other institutions (Bailey et al., 2006). This is aligned to a study focused on student attainment at multiple HBCCs in Alabama (Chubin & DePass, 2015). Leticia McCain, dean of instructional services at Bishop State Community College in Mobile, Alabama, noted that HBCCs "do a very good job of transferring students to four-year colleges or universities," (DePass & Chubin, 2015, p. 21). The qualitative study offered insight into 15 students' academic progress, persistence, and integration, revealing the effectiveness of interventions such as the field trips, tutoring, and research opportunities. The same study found trends in student experience as well, revealing the importance of mentoring from faculty, as well as the importance of forming friendships which helped students collaborate and study together.

Faculty development

The last theme of research on HBCCs focuses on faculty development. In the study of Alabama HBCCs, McCain found that the student support program created faculty development at all of the participating institutions (DePass & Chubin, 2015). The participating students reported faculty contact and availability as a key aspect of their connection to their HBCC. Specifically, the students believed they would not have persisted through their HBCC without a faculty member as a mentor and guide (Chubin & DePass, 2015).

While faculty development arose in the findings of McCain's study, Opp and Gosetti (2002) aimed to study the progress of HBCC faculty, specifically women of color faculty. Using trend analyses, the authors found that full-time Asian American female faculty had limited growth across institutions, and small declines at HBCCs. Additionally, HBCCs were significant positive predictors of a change in the proportional representation of women faculty of color.

Organizational considerations and outcomes

The literature on HBCC organizational contexts is currently limited to research on HBCC mission and vision statements. Abelman and Dalessandro (2009) studied HBCUs to ascertain which had vision statements. Most of the institutions with vision statements – both HBCUs (91%) and nonHBCUs (75%) – were four-year institutions. Where the majority of nonHBCU community colleges (66.3%) had a vision statement, only 15.4% of HBCCs had one. In a study of HBCU mission statements, Harris (2012) sought to determine if HBCUs explicitly and intentionally "foster communal education environments" (p. 333). To ascertain the presence of this communal pedagogy or "village pedagogy," Harris (2012) studied HBCU mission statements for the presence of: village pedagogy terms, references to diversity, a reference to Blackness or African heritage, and a reference to Blackness or African heritage that was not a historical statement (p.335). He found that only three of the 13 HBCCs referred to their African American heritage, and only one Denmark Technical College, mentioned its Black American heritage outside of a historical context. Additionally, seven HBCCs' mission statements refer to diversity and, ultimately, seven had terminology associated with village pedagogy.

In a recent dissertation on institutional advancement at HBCCs, Carter (2018) noted the importance of the internal and external communities' beliefs in the HBCC mission statement and vision. Carter (2018) gathered the perspectives of four institutional advancement professionals at three different HBCCs: Trenholm State Community College (AL), Coahoma Community College (MS), and St. Philip's College (TX). The study revealed common themes across institutions such as the importance of the president as a strategic leader, the role of alumni and friends, and specific fundraising challenges. However, there were distinct difference in the organization and operation of each HBCC and its institutional advancement office, resulting in different fundraising strategies as well. It follows that with different strategies, the HBCCs in the study also had differing definitions of success.

Finally, a one-off study addressed the broader economic impacts of HBCCs (Humphreys & Korb, 2006). This research examined the overall economic activity associated with 101 HBCUs, including estimates for wages and salaries, other institutional spending, undergraduate student spending, and graduate and professional students spending. In all, the 101 HBCUs in the study spent a combined $6.6 billion in their respective communities and the total economic impact for 2001 was $10.2 billion. Narrowing in on two-year institutions, public HBCCs generated 9,353 jobs, and private HBCCs specifically created 522 jobs (Humphreys & Korb, 2006).

Summary of the literature review

This review of the literature enhances the understanding of the context and complexity of HBCCs. The review provides insight into important issues impacting the success of the students, faculty, and organizational context of HBCCs. However, to our knowledge, there has been little study of HBCCs' administration, governance, and policy contexts. Though the institutions have historically extended educational opportunity like the four-year and predominantly white counterparts, we found limited research on how HBCCs support social mobility. These ongoing knowledge gaps provide scholarly opportunities for researchers and analysts, who can generate evidence-based recommendations to practitioners and policymakers. Elucidating HBCCs can better integrate the institutions into existing research and advocacy platforms, and to study them may also lead to practical implications, such as building capacity and fostering collaboration with other HBCUs, MSIs, and community colleges. In a later section, we suggest several potential directions to inform research on HBCCs. The next section discusses the distinctive organizational characteristics of HBCCs

A descriptive profile of organizational characteristics of HBCCs

Data and variables for descriptive profile

To offer a descriptive profile of organizational characteristics of HBCCs, we collected and analyzed data from the Penn Center for Minority-Serving Institutions, the American Association of Community Colleges (AACC), and the National Center for Education Statistics' *Integrated Postsecondary Education Data System* (IPEDS). The Penn Center focuses on elevating the visibility of MSIs nationally and, among other initiatives, advancing scholarship on them (Penn Center for Minority-Serving Institutions Penn Center for Minority-Serving Institutions, 2018a). It provides a current directory of all four-year and two-year MSIs, and also lists MSIs by specific categories including HBCUs, Hispanic-Serving Institutions, and Asian American and Native American Pacific Islander-Serving Institutions (Penn Center for MSI, 2018b). AACC offers through its website general information about the total number of its institutional members and the scope and scale of students served (American Association of Community Colleges [AACC], 2018). The AACC website helps to contextualize the relative size of the HBCC sector.

IPEDS comprises publically available qualitative and numeric information that postsecondary institutions report on their organizational characteristics (National Center for Education Statistics [NCES], 2018). As IPEDS captures institutional data over time, it supports longitudinal, time-dynamic perspectives of change and adaptation among campuses. We downloaded from IPEDS separate data files for the institutional characteristics, student enrollment, and financial subcomponents of the IPEDS survey for 1995 and 2015. These time-points were selected as 2015 featured the most recent, complete data, and by extending back in time to 1995, we were able to indicate how selected variables changed for HBCCs over two decades.

Specifically, we pulled IPEDS data for selected time-invariant and time-variant characteristics. The time-invariant variables were founding year, public or private status, Carnegie classification, geographical location/region, and urbanicity. Time-variant characteristics were number of degree/certificate-seeking students, race/ethnicity of students, number of Pell Grant recipients, federal, state, and local appropriations, tuition and fee revenue, and number of associate and certificate degrees awarded. Financial data from 1995 was adjusted for inflation using the Consumer Price Index and reported in 2015 constant dollars. Analogous to many community colleges, HBCCs serve a wide range of students who may not necessarily be degree/certificate-seeking or full- or part-time. A key consideration, then, for researchers, analysts, and policymakers entails how to scale-adjust various organizational characteristics of HBCCs relative to size and scale. Though perhaps an imperfect proxy for full-time equivalent student, and while available data in IPEDS is limited, we focused on the grand total of full- and part-time degree/certificate-seeking undergraduate students enrolled in credit in the fall semester as a way to measure organizational capacity. We thus constructed ratios of, for instance, the amount of federal appropriations per full- and part-time degree/certificate seeking student (e.g., FTE student).

The descriptive profile, presented below, offers a snapshot of organizational characteristics of HBCCs at two points in time. As noted, it includes information on both time-invariant and time-variant characteristics to inform a dynamic understanding of distinctive aspects of HBCCs and how those aspects have changed over time. We highlight the wide variety and diversity of HBCCs by calculating and reporting percentages and statistical means, standard deviations, minimums, and maximums on variables of interest. These data do not tell us why or how HBCCs are the way they are or the specific challenges and prospects ahead for them. From our interpretation of them, however, they suggest that research and policy attention may benefit from considering the *variation and distinctive, time-dynamic qualities* that may differentiate HBCCs from others and also from each other.

Overview of the HBCC sector

The Penn Center's directory of MSIs indicates 12 HBCCs (Penn Center for MSIs, 2018b). These 12 institutions are listed in Table 2. In relation to all MSIs featured in the Penn Center directory, our calculations show that HBCCs constitute about 12% of all HBCUs (n=98) and about 4% of all two-year minority-serving institutions (n=357). AACC (2018) reported that it has approximately 1,200 institutions members, and thus, in this national-level context, the 12 HBCCs constitute fewer than 1% of America's community colleges. To highlight for researchers and analysts some of the commonalities and differences among these 12 institutions, we discuss next the selected time-invariant characteristics that remain relatively stable over the years. Then we address time-variant features that indicate an array of changes across two decades from 1995 to 2015.

Time-invariant characteristics

Table 3 presents selected time-invariant characteristics of the 12 HBCCs. Each institution was founded prior to 1964, which, in addition to their student demographics and institutional missions, qualified them to receive the federal designation as HBCUs (Gasman, 2008). Ten of the 12 were established in the first-half of the 20th century, with most of these formed at least 30 years after the passage of the second Morrill Land Grant Act in 1890, and two – 17% – began in the 1800s. In their source of

Table 2. Current Historically Black Community Colleges.

Institution	State	Founded	Control
Bishop State Community College	AL	1927	Public
Coahoma Community College	MS	1924	Public
Denmark Technical College	SC	1948	Public
Gadsden State Community College	AL	1925	Public
H. Councill Trenholm State Community College	AL	1961	Public
Hinds Community College at Utica	MS	1903	Public
J.F. Drake State Community and Technical College	AL	1961	Public
Lawson State Community College-Birmingham Campus	AL	1949	Public
Shelton State Community College	AL	1952	Public
Shorter College	AR	1886	Private
Southern University at Shreveport	LA	1967	Public
St Philip's College	TX	1898	Public

Note: Institutions identified from data from the Penn Center for Minority-Serving Institutions.

Table 3. Selected descriptive statistics for time-invariant variables.

Variables	Number of Institutions	Percent of Institutions
Founded before 1900	2	17%
Founded after 1900	10	83%
Public	11	92%
Private	1	8%
Associate's Colleges: High Transfer-Mixed Traditional/Nontraditional	1	8%
Associate's Colleges: Mixed Transfer/Career & Technical-High Traditional	3	25%
Associate's Colleges: Mixed Transfer/Career & Technical-Mixed Traditional/Nontraditional	1	8%
Associate's Colleges: High Career & Technical-High Traditional	1	8%
Associate's Colleges: High Career & Technical-Mixed Traditional/Nontraditional	4	33%
Associate's Colleges: High Career & Technical-High Nontraditional	2	17%
New England (CT, ME, MA, NH, RI, VT)	0	0%
Mid-Atlantic (DE, DC, MD, NJ, NY, PA)	0	0%
Great Lakes/Plains (IL, IN, MI, OH, WI, IA, KS, MN, MO, NE, ND, SD)	0	0%
Southeast/Southwest (AL, AR, FL, GA, KY, LA, MS, NC, SC, TN, VA, WV, AZ, NM, OK, TX)	12	100%
Rocky Mountains/Far West (CO, ID, MT, UT, WY, AK, CA, HI, NV, OR, WA)	0	0%
Urbanicity – Small City	3	25%
Urbanicity – Midsize City	5	42%
Urbanicty – Large City	1	8%
Urbanicity – Rural (Fringe)	3	25%

Note: This table presents descriptive statistics for 12 Historically Black Community Colleges. Carnegie Classification was based on the 2015 basic groupings. Urbanicity was based on data reported in IPEDS in 2015.

institutional control, 11 are public, and one, Shorter College in Arkansas, is private, non-profit and is also religiously affiliated with the African Methodist Episcopal Church. The HBCCs are spread across the range of Carnegie categories for Associate's Colleges. Perhaps owing to their origins in extending educational opportunity for technical training and career preparation, five of the 12 (about 41%) are grouped in High Career & Technical classifications. Meanwhile, the other seven indicate variation in the extent to which their students transfer and are traditional or adult learners.

In the context of strong sociopolitical and economic barriers to postsecondary education for Black communities in the South, all HBCCs are located in the Southeast and Southwest. Half are in Alabama, a state typically associated with strong resistance to complying with the Civil Rights Act of 1964 that replaced separate-but-equal education with a legal mandate for racial integration throughout all levels of schooling (Cohen & Kisker, 2010). Though not depicted in the table, two of the public HBCCs, Southern University at Shreveport (LA) and St. Philip's College (TX), are in states with performance-based funding models for two-year institutions. They face funding environments where criteria for performance are not always sensitive to their unique missions, histories, or student populations, and tend to perpetuate contexts of resource constraints and underfunding (Jones et al., 2017; Li, Gándara, & Assalone, 2018). Nine HBCCs are situated in urban environments, with almost half (about 42%) in mid-sized cities, and three are in rural-fringe settings. The geographical locations of HBCCs suggest a concentration of institutions in more populous areas and access-points for students in their states and postsecondary systems.

Time-variant characteristics of HBCCs

To inform an understanding of organizational changes over time among HBCCs, Table 4 shows descriptive statistics for selected time-variant characteristics in 1995 and 2015. A note of caution, though, is warranted. Hinds Community College at Utica constitutes one campus within a multi-campus system, and its data in IPEDS is aggregated and reported through the main campus (for a related methodological discussion, see Jaquette & Parra, 2014). As such, the numeric information for Hinds Community College at Utica would skew the averages, standard deviations, and minimums and maximums for the group of HBCCs as a whole. Due to limitations in available

Table 4. Selected descriptive statistics for time-variant characteristics.

	1995				2015			
	Mean	SD	Min	Max	Mean	SD	Min	Max
Number of Degree/Certificate-seeking Students	2,339	2,210	261	5,658	2,779	2,267	236	8,111
Black or African American Students	61.81%	31.55%	17.85%	97.22%	63.42%	30.43%	11.42%	98.31%
Hispanic/Latino Students	4.46%	13.47%	0.00%	45.04%	6.33%	17.47%	0.21%	58.94%
American Indian or Alaska Native Students	0.18%	0.24%	0.00%	0.64%	0.43%	0.46%	0%	1.34%
Asian, Native Hawaiian, or Pacific Islander Students	0.50%	0.62%	0.00%	2.04%	0.91%	0.90%	0%	2.98%
White Students	28.83%	27.75%	0.38%	76.76%	25.69%	22.63%	1.27%	69.78%
Female Students	58.16%	8.98%	45.29%	71.97%	59%	5%	49.14%	66.58%
Number of Undergraduate Pell Grant Recipients	1,264	846	293	2,718	1,574	889	211	2,659
Federal appropriations, contracts, & grants per degree/certificate-seeking student (2015 dollars)	$3,904.97	$2,046.15	$1,627.89	$4,668.57	$2,245.16	$1,217.58	$495.69	$3,660.19
State appropriations, contracts, & grants per degree/certificate-seeking student (2015 dollars)	$6,111.22	$4,236.93	$929.47	$11,128.85	$4,410.84	$2,198.53	$0.00	$7,607.19
Local appropriations & grants per degree/certificate-seeking student (2015 dollars)	$389.83	$573.96	$0.00	$1,537.34	$1,968.88	$1,684.73	$0.00	$6,603.60
Tuition and fee revenue per degree/certificate-seeking student (2015 dollars)	$2,084.67	$649.34	$1,311.50	$2,862.08	$1,968.88	$1,684.73	$1,304.85	$6,603.60
Number of Associate/Certificate Degrees Awarded	330.82	245.33	32	792	577.64	513.90	29	1,809

Note: Descriptive statistics calculated for 11 HBCCs using IPEDS data reported in 1995 and 2015. Number of degree/certificate-seeking students was based on total full- and part-time undergraduate enrollment in the fall semester. The percentages for race/ethnicity and gender were derived by dividing the number of undergraduate degree/certificate-seeking students in each category by the total number of undergraduate degree/certificate-seeking students. IPEDS grouped Asian students together with Native Hawaiian and Pacific Islander students until the 2009 survey, and while breakouts by each group was available in 2015 it was not in 1995. Financial data were adjusted for inflation and reported in 2015 constant dollars using the December-to-December Consumer Price Index. In 1995, institutions reported in IPEDS the dollars expended on Pell grant awards; to calculate the approximate number of undergraduate federal Pell grant recipients, an institution's expenditures was divided by the average Pell grant award for recipients that year in the U.S. ($1,502) (U.S. Department of Education, 1995).

longitudinal datasets, we omitted the institution from our calculations and acknowledge that further research and policy attention to Hinds Community College at Utica is warranted.

The average number of degree/certificate-seeking undergraduate students increased by about 19% from 2,339 in 1995 to 2,779 in 2015, suggesting enrollment growth among HBCCs. Even so, the size of these institutions still varied considerably (ranging from 236 to 8,111 degree/certificate-seeking students in 2015). During that time period, the average HBCC increased its overall racial diversity across ethnic groups with the exception of white students. The percentage of Black degree/certificate-seeking students increased slightly from about 62% in 1995 to 63% in 2015. St. Philip's College (TX) enrolled the fewest Black students and instead, reflecting broader demographics of its state and region, had a disproportion number of Hispanic/Latino students. Throughout the HBCC sector as a whole, there were notable gains in the average enrollment among HBCCs for Hispanic/Latino students from about 4.5% in 1995 to 6% in 2015, American Indian or Alaskan Native students from .18% to .43%, and Asian, Native Hawaiian, or Pacific Islander students from .50% to .90%. Enrollment trends reported here could reflect broader patterns in postsecondary education in the United States (U.S.), in which participation rates among minorities have increased over time but not in the historically stratified, selective private and public flagship four-year institutions (Warshaw & Hearn, In press). Despite longstanding resource inequities for HBCUs, HBCCs are, on average, expanding educational opportunity for underrepresented minorities in general and Black students in particular.

Compositionally, the average percentage of female degree/certificate-seeking students grew slightly, by about 1%, from 58.16% in 1995 to 59% in 2015. The data suggest increasing socioeconomic diversity at the average HBCC as measured through the total number of undergraduates receiving federal Pell grant awards (any dollar amount). For example, the federal Pell grant program entails the largest need-based financial aid initiative in the U.S., and nearly three-quarters of dependent Pell recipients are from families whose income is near or below the U.S. poverty line (U.S. Department of Education, 2016). The federal poverty threshold for a household of four was $24,250 in 2015 (U.S. Department of Health & Human Services, 2015). For the remaining share of Pell recipients, they were from families earning less than the national median household income of $56,516 (in 2015) (U.S. Census Bureau, 2016). At HBCCs, the average number of Pell recipients increased by about 25% from 1,264 in 1995 to 1,574 in 2015. While there continues to be some variation among the institutions, ranging from 211 to 2,659 Pell recipients in 2015, HBCCs have on the whole expanded access to racially diverse students from backgrounds of strong socioeconomic disadvantage.

Turning attention to financial and resource considerations, there are several striking trends in the data. HBCCs, analogous to four-year HBCUs, are eligible to receive federal funding through Title III of the Higher Education Act (and subsequent reauthorizations), and even private, non-profit HBCUs may receive specialized forms of state support. The average amount of federal appropriations, contracts, and grants per degree/certificate-seeking student decreased from $3,904.97 in 1995 (in 2015 constant dollars) to $2,245.16 in 2015, indicating a 43% drop. Indeed, the average amount of state appropriations, contracts, and grants per degree/certificate-seeking student decreased as well from $6,111.22 (in 2015 constant dollars) in 1995 to $4,410.84 in 2015, a 28% drop. Even when we analyzed state funding trends for 10 public HBCCs, omitting Shorter College as the private, non-profit institution, the retrenchment in these resources indicated a 27% decrease. Such funding dynamics could be due to fluctuations and shifts in the economy (e.g., the worldwide market crash of 2008 and ensuing economic malaise). Even if federal and state governments could in any given fiscal year increase their funding of HBCUs, those potential increases, data here suggest, may not keep pace with inflation or the increases in enrollment (and thus size and capacity) at these institutions.

Perhaps in keeping to their historic missions of access, diversity, and equity, the average HBCC has drawn less revenue over time from tuition and fees. For instance, tuition and fee revenue per degree/certificate-seeking student fell from $2,084.67 in 1995 (in 2015 constant dollars) to $1,968.88 in 2015, yielding a 6% decline. Within a context of resource constraints, HBCCs have become increasingly reliant on local appropriations and grants through governing municipalities and, for the public HBCCs, the ability to levy, analogous to public schools in the K-12 arena, taxes for revenues.

The average amount of local appropriations and grants per degree/certificate-seeking student increased from $389.83 in 1995 (in 2015 constant dollars) to $1,968.88 in 2015, a striking 405% increase. What is more, the average number of degrees and certificates awarded, a measure of productivity, also increased by a margin of about 75% from 330.82 in 1995 to 792 in 2015.

A holistic, time-dynamic view of these data suggest that the average HBCC has shown resilience and broader patterns of growth despite operating from a position of sociopolitical and financial disadvantage. As the data further suggest, HBCCs are a diverse group of institutions that differ some in size, enrollment composition, socioeconomicdiversity, resource providers and revenues, and extent to which they serve degree/certificate-seeking students and award these credentials. Thus, research and policy attention in this arena may require nuance suitable to the range and complexity of organizational characteristics of HBCCs.

Recommendations for future research

At best, our review of the literature and organizational characteristics reveal the basic history and context of HBCCs. These unique institutions are ripe for future research on students, faculty, organizational considerations, and public policy. Here, we suggest several possible directions to inform work on this topic.

With such limited research literature on HBCCs, there is not only a breadth of potential topics, but also *potential theoretical frameworks to apply to studies of these institutions*. Theoretical considerations may be drawn from student development theory, organizational theory, leadership theory, critical theory, and public policy. Student development theories on student transition would be particularly relevant to HBCCs as two-year institutions which prepare students for transfer to careers and to four-year institutions. Organizational theories would provide insight into the administration and governance of HBCCs, an untapped topic. As institutions built for the education of Black Americans, critical perspectives would center students' intersectionality and the institution's mission and climate. Research on public policy issues relevant to HBCCs would reveal whether these uniquely positioned institutions are uniquely impacted by federal and state laws and policies.

Researchers who study HBCUs, or community colleges more generally, may consider *replicating studies for HBCCs*. For example, researchers might consider replicating or drawing from studies on students' racial identity development at four year HBCUs. Cokley (1999, 2001, 2002) has provided robust quantitative analyses on HBCU students' Black identity development. Adapting this to the HBCC context would account for the growing increase in Latino students at HBCCs. Allen (2016) studied the experiences of Latino students at four-year HBCUs and provides recommendations for future study.

In addition to Latino students, the literature review revealed *a number of HBCC student populations that have not been studied*. Expanding Ruffins (2008) work on HBCC services for students with learning disabilities, researchers may consider examining how students with learning disabilities navigate HBCC student services, HBCC students who enroll in developmental education courses, and how faculty and staff are prepared to work with remedial students or students with special needs. While Meléndez et al. (2003) focused on TANF recipients' enrollment in nondegree programs and degree programs, no study currently addresses how other populations of students do the same. Higher education scholars have focused on the college choice and college experience of other high-needs populations such as foster care alumni, homeless students, formerly incarcerated students, nontraditional students, and veterans. Certainly research on these populations at HBCCs would provide important insight for student success.

The literature review also exposed *opportunities to research student success and attainment within distinctive HBCC settings*. McCain insisted that HBCCs excel at helping students transfer to four-year colleges and universities, and there is room for additional research on the topic (DePass & Chubin, 2015). There has been much research on the transfer of STEM students to four-year HBCUs (Jackson, 2013), but none conducted specifically on the transition from two-year HBCUs. In addition to transition, more research can be conducted on student retention and graduation. Scholars can provide more nuanced, and perhaps more accurate, research by using data and methods more suitable to HBCCs and their students.

For example, Bailey et al. (2006) defined student success for two-year colleges by combining the institutional graduation rate and the rate of students who transferred to other students. Using this as the determinant of success, HBCCs outperformed all other institutions. Scholars have already done this for their four-year counterparts (Espinosa, Turk, & Taylor, 2017). Federal data show a graduation rate for four-year HBCUs of 34.1%. Using data from the National Student Clearinghouse and considering mixed enrollment students who move between attending college both full time and part time, Espinosa et al. (2017) determined a 43% total completion rate, and the completion rate for full-time students was nearly 62%. As scholars pursue new modes of analysis for HBCCs, there is an opportunity to contextualize them by using alternative metrics, data sources, and methods that better suit the institutions and the students they serve.

Through the literature review, we discovered a theme *highlighting HBCCs' unique institutional contexts to inform understandings of professional work and careers in the academy*. Opp and Gosetti (2002) pointed out that studies which do not consider institutional race, size, urbanicity, and locale an obscure the strong positive influence of HBCCs on the progress of women faculty of color. Their supposition that organizational climate and faculty climate are part of this positive relationship is ideal for empirical study. Organizational context was a key finding in Carter's (2018) multi-case study. The HBCCs included in the study had strong institutional cultures of giving, but saw a need for improving the relationships with their institutional boards. Thus, examining HBCCs within their unique institutional context reveals strengths, weaknesses, opportunities and challenges. For example, Meléndez et al. (2003) discussed how institutional barriers impede welfare-to-work students' career opportunities. Future study which examines these organizational obstacles can help to influence internal procedures and public policy. Accordingly, HBCCs' organizational contexts are not limited to internal institutional contexts. Future research must also consider the institutions' positioning in the state and local communities. Earlier, we suggested further research and policy attention to Hinds Community College at Utica as the institution's data was reported as part of a larger district of community colleges. St. Philip's College (TX) is also part of the greater Alamo Colleges District, which consists of five colleges in the San Antonio area.

Moreover, researchers could aim *to include rather than omit HBCCs from their quantitative analyses*. With the growing number of Latino students nationally, but particularly in community colleges, HBCC researchers and practitioners alike should seek to better understand the positioning of St. Philip's College (TX) as the only institution to simultaneously hold the designation of HBCU/HBCC and Hispanic-Serving Institution (HSI). This particular line of study has implications for both two-year HBCCs and four-year HBCUs. Like St. Philip's College (TX), other institutions in Texas are seeing increases in Latino student enrollment (Allen, 2016). Finally, when conducting research on HBCUs, HSIs, and community colleges, researchers must be careful to call out and distinguish HBCCs from their peer institutions because of their distinctive characteristics, histories, and missions. By eliminating the false dichotomies, and centering HBCCs, scholars open up new, untapped lines of inquiry.

The descriptive profile we have provided offers guidance for newer lines of research on resources, revenues, and various aspects of student enrollment. Future research could address changes in HBCC size and composition related to this growth, such as the increase in the average number of HBCC Pell students, socioeconomic stratification, and racial diversity. Scholars may also address the extent to which HBCCs serve degree/certificate-seeking students and award these credentials. As mentioned, HBCCs enroll a number of students who may not be degree/certificate-seeking. Future research may address how to scale-adjust various organizational characteristics of HBCCs relative to size and scale. Finally, researchers may explore the impact and influence of resource providers and revenues on HBCCs' operations and services.

Conclusion

Research on HBCCs can inform responsive policy action at the governmental and institutional level. Policymakers may consider how to differentiate approaches and strategies relative to the diversity of HBCCs. Policymakers may consider the role of HBCCs in reaching the state's workforce and education goals alongside public HBCCs' increasing dependence on local appropriations and taxes. Such consideration may yield efforts to enhance HBCCs institutional capacity to generate revenues through public-private partnerships and grants. Policy attention can be directed to particularly unique situations such as Hinds Community College at Utica existence within a broader community college system, and St. Philip's College's designation as both an HBCU and an HSI. Practitioners at these institutions, including both HBCC administrators and faculty, should also consider these nuances and how to tailor their work to the local campus context.

Like their four-year counterparts, HBCCs have long-been conduits of social mobility, particularly for Black Americans. HBCCs provide educational opportunity within a higher education landscape of growing disparity and stratification between elite and less prestigious institutions, and among students based on race, socioeconomic status and other identities and experiences. Context-based research on HBCCs will inform policy and practice at the institutional level. However, there is much for policymakers and leaders of HBCUs, HSIs, and community colleges to learn from HBCCs, such as different or innovative practices or operational and financial initiatives that serve their student populations well.

References

Abelman, R. (2013). On the horns of a dilemma: The institutional vision of church-affiliated HBCUs. *Religion & Education*, 40(2), 125–154. doi:10.1080/15507394.2013.786622

Abelman, R., & Dalessandro, A. (2009). The institutional vision of historically Black colleges and universities. *Journal of Black Studies*, 40(2), 105–134. doi:10.1177/0021934707307828

Abraham, R. A., Slate, J. R., Saxon, D. P., & Barnes, W. (2014). Math readiness of Texas community college developmental education students: A multiyear statewide analysis. *Community College Enterprise*, 20(2), 25–44.

Allen, T. O. (2016). In)validation in the minority: The experiences of Latino students enrolled in an HBCU. *Journal of Higher Education*, 87(4), 661–687. doi:10.1353/jhe.2016.0021

American Association of Community Colleges. (2018). *Membership*. Retrieved from https://www.aacc.nche.edu/about-us/membership/

Anderson, J. (1988). *The education of Blacks in the south, 1860-1935*. Chapel Hill: UNC Press.

Avery College Historical Marker. (2011)Retrieved from http://explorepahistory.com/hmarker.php?markerId=1-A-37E

Bailey, T., Alfonso, M., Calcagno, J. C., Jenkins, D., Kienzl, G., & Leinbach, T. (2004). *Improving student attainment in community colleges: Institutional characteristics and policies*. Community College Research Center, Teachers College, Columbia University. Retrieved from https://ccrc.tc.columbia.edu/publications/improving-student-attainment.html

Bailey, T., Calcagno, J. C., Jenkins, D., Kienzl, G., & Leinbach, T. (2005). *The effects of institutional factors on the success of community college students*. Community College Research Center, Teachers College, Columbia University. Retrieved from https://eric.ed.gov/?id=ED484345

Bailey, T., Calcagno, J. C., Jenkins, D., Leinbach, T., & Kienzl, G. (2006). Is student-right-to-know all you should know? An analysis of community college graduation rates. *Research in Higher Education*, 47(5), 491–519. doi:10.1007/s11162-005-9005-0

Barr, A. (1996). *Black Texans: A history of African Americans in Texas, 1528-1995*. Norman, Okla: University of Oklahoma Press.

Benítez, M., & DeAro, J. (2004). Realizing student success at Hispanic-serving institutions. *New Directions for Community Colleges*, 2004(127), 35–48. doi:10.1002/cc.162

Brown, M. C., II. (1999). *The quest to define collegiate desegregation: Black colleges, title VI compliance, and post-Adams litigation*. Westport, CT: Bergin & Garvey. Retrieved from http://web.a.ebscohost.com.ezproxy.fau.edu/ehost/detail/detail?sid=78152ed2-b644-4648-a2f9013bb7f2d993%40sessionmgr4008&vid=0&hid=4206&bdata%3d%3d#AN=63673&db=nlebk

Carter, L. (2018). Institutional advancement at Historically Black Community Colleges: A multi-case study. (Theses and Dissertations). Retrieved from https://rdw.rowan.edu/etd/2537

Cohen, A. M., & Kisker, C. (2010). *The shaping of American higher education: Emergence and growth of the contemporary system* (2nd ed.). San Francisco, CA: Jossey-Bass.

Cokley, K. (1999). Reconceptualizing the impact of college racial composition on African American students' racial identity. *Journal of College Student Development*, 40, 235–246.

Cokley, K. O. (2001). Gender differences among African American students in the impact of racial identity on academic psychosocial development. *Journal of College Student Development*, 42(5), 480. Retrieved from http://ezproxy.fau.edu/login?url=http://search.proquest.com/docview/195181617?accountid=10902

Cokley, K. O. (2002). Testing Cross's revised racial identity model: An examination of the relationship between racial identity and internalized racialism. *Journal of Counseling Psychology*, 49, 476–483. doi:10.1037/0022-0167.49.4.476

Davis, J. J., & Markham, P. L. (1991). Student attitudes toward foreign study at historically and predominantly Black institutions. *Foreign Language Annals; New York, 24*(3), 227–237. doi:10.1111/j.1944-9720.1991.tb00467.x

deGregory, C. (2011). Raising a nonviolent army: Four Nashville black colleges and the century-long struggle for civil rights, 1830s-1930s. (Vanderbilt University Electronic Theses and Dissertations). Retrieved from https://etd.library.vanderbilt.edu/available/etd-03272011-230413/unrestricted/RaisingANonviolentArmyFINAL.pdf

DePass, A. L., & Chubin, D. E. (Eds.). (2015). *Understanding interventions that broaden participation in science careers: Growing the community* (Vol. 6). Baltimore, MD: Understanding-Interventions.org.

Dervarics, C. (1997). Robbing Peter to pay Paul. *Black Issues in Higher Education, 14*(16), 26.

Espinosa, L. L., Turk, J. M., & Taylor, M. (2017). *Pulling back the curtain: Enrollment and outcomes at minority-serving institutions.* Washington, DC: American Council on Education. Retrieved from http://www.acenet.edu/news-room/Documents/Pulling-Back-the-Curtain-Enrollment-and-Outcomes-at-MSIs.pdf

Fairclough, A. (2007). *A class of their own: Black teachers in the segregated south.* Cambridge, MA: Harvard University Press.

Gasman, M. (2008). Minority-serving institutions: A historical backdrop. In M. Gasman, B. Baez, & C. S. V. Turner (Eds.), *Understanding minority-serving institutions* (pp. 18–27). Albany: State University of New York Press.

Glover, L. C., Simpson, L. A., & Waller, L. R. (2009). Disparities in tuition: A study of tuitions assessed by Hispanic Serving community colleges versus non-Hispanic Serving community colleges in Texas. *Academic Leadership (15337812), 7*(4), 6.

Harris, O. D., III. (2012). From margin to center: Participating in village pedagogy at historically Black colleges and universities. *The Urban Review, 44*(3), 332–357. doi:10.1007/s11256-012-0199-0

Herd-Clark, D. J. (2012). Appendix: Profiles of closed HBCUs. In V. R. Newkirk (Ed.), *New life for historically black colleges and universities: A 21st century perspective* (pp. 239–244). Jefferson, NC: McFarland.

Humphreys, J., & Korb, R. (2006). *Economic impact of the nation's Historically Black Colleges and Universities.* Washington, DC: National Center for Education Statistics. Retrieved from https://nces.ed.gov/pubs2007/2007178.pdf

Jackson, D. L. (2013). A balancing act: Impacting and initiating the success of African American female community college transfer students in STEM into the HBCU environment. *The Journal of Negro Education, 82*(3), 255–271.

Jaquette, O., & Parra, E. E. (2014). Using IPEDS for panel analyses: Core concepts, data challenges, and empirical applications. In J. Smart (Ed.), *Higher education: Handbook of theory and research* (Vol. 29, pp. 467–533). Dordrecht, Netherlands: Springer.

Jones, T., Jones, S., Owens, L., Assalone, A. E., Elliott, K. C., & Gándara, A. (2017). *Outcomes based funding and race in higher education: Can equity be bought?* New York, NY: Palgrave Macmillan.

Li, A. Y., Gándara, D., & Assalone, A. (2018). Equity or disparity: Do performance funding policies disadvantage 2-year minority-serving institutions? *Community College Review, 46*(3), 288–315. doi:10.1177/0091552118778776

Lovett, B. L. (2011). *America's historically Black colleges and universities: A narrative history, from the nineteenth century into the twenty-first century.* Macon, GA: Mercer University Press.

Meléndez, E., Falcón, L., & Bivens, J. (2003). Community college participation in welfare programs: Do state policies matter? *Community College Journal of Research and Practice, 27*(3), 203–223. doi:10.1080/713838121

Minor, J. T. (2008). Segregation residual in higher education: A tale of two states. *American Educational Research Journal, 45*(4), 861–885. Retrieved from http://www.jstor.org/stable/27667156

National Center for Education Statistics. (2018). *Integrated postsecondary education data system.* Retrieved from https://nces.ed.gov/ipeds/.

Opp, R. D., & Gosetti, P. P. (2002). Women full-time faculty of color in 2-year colleges: A trend and predictive analysis. *Community College Journal of Research and Practice, 26*(7–8), 609–627. doi:10.1080/10668920290102743

Penn Center for Minority-Serving Institutions. (2018a). *Mission and purpose.* Retrieved from https://cmsi.gse.upenn.edu/content/mission-purpose.

Penn Center for Minority-Serving Institutions. (2018b). *MSI directory.* Retrieved from https://cmsi.gse.upenn.edu/content/msi-directory.

Ruffins, P. (2008). Creating an atmosphere of acceptance. *Diverse: Issues in Higher Education, 25*(9), 14–16.

Schexnider, A. J. (2017, December 20). *Governance and the future of Black colleges.* Inside Higher Ed. Retrieved from https://www.insidehighered.com/views/2017/12/20/struggling-hbcus-must-consider-new-options-survival-opinion

Shorette, C. R., & Arroyo, A. T. (2015). A closer examination of white student enrollment at HBCUs. *New Directions for Higher Education, 2015*(170), 49. doi:10.1002/he.20131

Smith, J. C. (2003). *Black firsts: 4,000 ground-breaking and pioneering historical events* (2nd ed.). Canton, MI: Invisible Ink Press.

Smith, W. L. (1994). *The magnificent twelve: Florida's Black junior colleges.* Winter Park, FL: FOUR-G Publishers.

Sterling, D. (1984). *We are your sisters: Black women in the nineteenth century.* New York, NY: W. W. Norton & Company.

Suggs, E. (2019, January 14). *17 HBCUs that didn't make it.* The Atlanta Journal-Constitution. Retrieved from https://www.ajc.com/news/local/hbcus-that-didn-make/BnmRJgnxwnBV8yXqqtsWcP/

U.S. Census Bureau. (2016). *Income and poverty in the United States: 2015.* Retrieved from https://www.census.gov/library/publications/2016/demo/p60-256.html

U.S. Department of Education. (1995). *1994–1995 Federal Pell grant program end of year report.* Retrieved from https://www2.ed.gov/finaid/prof/resources/data/pell-data.html

U.S. Department of Education. (2016). *2015–2016 Federal Pell grant program end of year report*. Retrieved from https://www2.ed.gov/finaid/prof/resources/data/pell-data.html

U.S. Department of Health & Human Services. (2015). *2015 poverty guidelines*. Retrieved from https://aspe.hhs.gov/2015-poverty-guidelines

Warshaw, J. B., & Hearn, J. C. (In press). Federal spending on higher education: A system of opportunity and stratification. In G. R. Serna & J. M. Cohen (Eds.), *Administration, finance, and budgeting in higher education and student affairs: Theory, research, and practice* (pp. 1–33). Springfield, IL: Charles C. Thomas Publisher.

Two-Year Institution and Community College Web Accessibility: Updating the Literature after the 2018 Section 508 Amendment

Z. W. Taylor and Ibrahim Bicak

ABSTRACT
On January 18th, 2018, the Americans with Disabilities Act (ADA) required all federal aid-receiving institutions of higher education (Title IV) to publish web accessible websites for people with disabilities. To be compliant with federal law, Title IV institutions must now adhere to Web Content Accessibility Guidelines (WCAG) 2.0 standards at the Level-A and Level-AA threshold. This study examined the web accessibility of a random sample of 325 two-year Title IV institutions in the United States and found all institutions had at least one Level-A error on their homepage, potentially violating new ADA guidelines. This study also found private, for-profit institutions published the least web accessible websites, while public institutions published the most web accessible websites. Implications for future research and practice are addressed.

Introduction

According to the most recent per the Integrated Postsecondary Education Data System (IPEDS), students with their disabilities documented by their institution comprised less than 3% of the overall student population at 79% of all institutions of higher education in the United States in fall 2016. In all, roughly 215,000 students with disabilities studied at two-year institutions in the United States in fall 2016, comprising less than 4% of nearly 6.5 million community college students in the United States (National Center for Education Statistics, 2018). As students with disabilities are often marginalized and under-supported during their transition from high school to postsecondary education (Brinckerhoff, 1996; Eckes & Ochoa, 2005; Garrison-Wade & Lehmann, 2009; Janiga & Costenbader, 2002; White et al., 2017), a large, longitudinal body of research has demonstrated that students with disabilities do not access higher education – at two- and four-year institutions – at the same level as their peers (Evans, Broido, Brown, & Wilke, 2017; Getzel, 2008; Getzel & Thoma, 2008; Hong, 2015; Madaus, Grigal, & Hughes, 2014).

For as influential and powerful as Internet technologies have become for informing student choice (Burdett, 2013; Daun-Barnett & Das, 2013; Dettling, Goodman, & Smith, 2018), researchers have criticized institutions of higher education for not producing web accessible materials for students with disabilities (Erickson et al., 2013; Hackett & Parmanto, 2005; Harper & DeWaters, 2008; Thompson, Burgstahler, & Comden, 2003; Thompson, Burgstahler, & Moore, 2010). This lack of web accessibility has contributed to students with disabilities being excluded from postsecondary education in the U.S. (Bradbard, Peters, & Caneva, 2010), including from community colleges (Erickson, Trerise, VanLooy, Lee, & Bruyère, 2009; Flowers, Bray, & Algozzine, 2011; Wisdom et al., 2006).

Subsequently, hundreds of people with disabilities have brought lawsuits against institutions of higher education (Carlson, 2018). These lawsuits have alleged that institutions of higher education have violated Section 508 of the Rehabilitation Act of 1973, which mandated that electronic and information technology used by the federal government, including federally-funded institutions of higher education, be accessible to all people with disabilities (LaGrow, 2017). In response, beginning on January 18, 2018, U.S. Government updated Section 508 requirements. These Section 508 requirements now hold all federally-supported U.S. institutions of higher education (Title IV institutions) to Level-A and Level-AA compliance according to Web Content Accessibility Guidelines (WCAG) 2.0 standards (United States Access Board, 2018).

Section 508 of the Americans with Disabilities Act adopted the WCAG as the official standard of web accessibility, setting accessibility conformance at three levels. Level-A is the minimum level of conformance and satisfies all Level-A success criteria defined by WCAG, such as ensuring all audio content is captioned for those hard of hearing (W3C, 2018b). Level-AA is the standard level of conformance and the threshold Title IV institutional websites must meet to be deemed web accessible and in compliance with ADA (United States Access Board, 2018). Level-AA success criteria encompasses all Level-A criteria, plus an additional level of conformance, such as color contrast minimums and using unique headings and labels to allow students to differentiate between webpages (W3C, 2018b). Finally, Level-AAA is the optimal level of conformance, including all Level-A and Level-AA success criteria (W3C, 2018b). Title IV institutions do not need to meet Level-AAA conformance, as "It is not recommended that Level AAA conformance be required as a general policy for entire sites because it is not possible to satisfy all Level AAA Success Criteria for some content" (W3C, 2018c, para. 11).

Ultimately, WCAG 2.0 requires websites to be perceivable, operable, understandable, and robust for people with disabilities, as these four categories encompass diverse elements of a webpage, such as audio, video, images, text, hyperlinks, buttons, toolbars, and menus (W3C, 2018b). As a result, an institution's website can be considered ADA and WCAG 2.0 compliant if a wide variety of assistive technologies are able to read the data in the website's markup language – typically HTML or hypertext markup language – and render the content intelligible to a person with a disability (W3C, 2018b). For instance, a person who is blind may require an assistive technology which can vocalize text and visual elements of a website, while a deaf person may require an assistive technology which can caption audial elements of a website.

Extant research has examined web accessibility at four-year (Bradbard et al., 2010; Hackett & Parmanto, 2005; Harper & DeWaters, 2008; Kelly, 2002) and two-year institutions (Erickson et al., 2009; Flowers et al., 2011; Wisdom et al., 2006). These studies have found that postsecondary websites are rarely compliant with WCAG standards. The most recent studies of two-year institutional web accessibility are the works of Flowers et al. (2011) and Erickson et al. (2013). Flowers et al. (2011) found only 58 of 253 (23%) community college home pages were accessible to people with disabilities, while Erickson et al. (2013) found less than 1% of webpages from 30 community college websites met Section 508 guidelines. Since the January 18, 2018 deadline, no research has updated previous work to learn if postsecondary websites – specifically, two-year institutional websites – comply with new Section 508 guidelines and the most recent WCAG 2.0 standards (W3C, 2018b). In addition, it is important to update previous studies related to web accessibility, as assistive technologies and web accessibility can frequently change and become more advanced (Kurt, 2018). Therefore, this study seeks to update and expand upon previous work by answering two critical research questions pertinent to community college students with disabilities:

(1) After the January 18, 2018 deadline, are two-year, Title IV-receiving institutional websites compliant with new Section 508 guidelines and WCAG 2.0 standards?
(2) If not, which WCAG 2.0 standards are most abundant?

Answering these questions will not only inform the scholarly community but also inform institutions as to whether their websites are compliant with federal law and accessible for a marginalized population in higher education, namely community college students with disabilities.

Literature review

Since the proliferation of the Internet, educational researchers have examined the web accessibility of postsecondary websites. Kelly's (2002) study of the web accessibility of United Kingdom (U.K.) university websites ($n = 162$) found only four U.K. universities were Level-AA compliant per WCAG 1.0 standards. Using the web-based Bobby™ accessibility tool, Kelly (2002) also asserted the primary source of web accessibility errors were made when images were missing alt element attributes, or text that specifies what should be rendered on a screen when the element cannot be rendered (i.e., screen reader technology reading text to a person who is blind). Similarly, in a longitudinal study from 1997 until 2002, Hackett and Parmanto (2005) evaluated archived institutional higher education webpages and found that as Internet technology advanced, institutional websites became increasingly inaccessible for people with disabilities.

Thompson et al. (2003) provided an early audit of four-year U.S. institutional websites when they applied WCAG 1.0 standards to 102 public research university websites using a five-point accessibility scale employed by two human evaluators. In total, their work evaluated 1,103 different webpages on 102 different websites and found one evaluator to determine that 182 webpages were entirely web accessible, while another evaluator found 42 webpages to be entirely web accessible using the same scale. Thompson et al. (2003) asserted that human evaluators may differ in their perceptions of web accessibility, yet human judgement should be used in tandem with web accessibility software to provide a more accurate assessment of web accessibility.

Shortly after Thompson et al.'s (2003) foundational work, Wisdom et al. (2006) examined web accessibility knowledge of staff members at Oregon community colleges. Wisdom et al. (2006) found information technology (IT) professionals and disability/student services staff members were the most knowledgeable about disability laws including web accessibility guidelines, yet IT professionals and disability staff members rarely collaborated to ensure web accessibility. This finding led Wisdom et al. (2006) to encourage communication between IT and disability/student services departments to collaboratively publish web accessible websites. Closely related to web accessibility, other studies have examined web accessibility policies at land-grant universities (Bradbard et al., 2010) and community colleges (Erickson et al., 2009). Both studies found many institutions either did not have web accessibility policies, or these policies were weak or poorly distributed among practitioners working at the institution (Bradbard et al., 2010; Erickson et al., 2009).

Once WCAG 2.0 standards were updated and published in 2008, Harper and DeWaters (2008) found that one of 12 four-year U.S. institutions met Level-AAA standards, while four of the 12 institutions did not comply with Level-A, Level-AA, or Level-AAA standards. At the community college level, Erickson et al. (2009) found that although 90% of a sample of nearly 700 community colleges reported offering online courses, catalogs, and class schedules, only 50% of respondents reported their institution having written requirements for web accessibility. Examining institutional websites, Flowers et al. (2011) asserted that only 23% of a sample of 253 community college homepages were web accessible to people with disabilities. Using a different sample, Erickson et al. (2013) later found less than 1% of webpages from 30 community colleges met Section 508 guidelines.

Beyond community colleges, Thompson et al. (2010) performed a longitudinal, five-year study of 127 four-year U.S. institutions and asserted advances in web technology made it difficult for institutions to reach or maintain WCAG 2.0 compliance. The authors found a decline in keyboard accessibility across the sample, likely owed to technology advances, yet web accessibility training did help improve the web accessibility of institutional websites. However, near the end of their study, Thompson et al. (2010) reasoned that there was no significant difference in the web accessibility between institutions that had received training and those that had not.

Outside of the United States, related studies have found Turkish university websites (Kurt, 2017) and Israeli university websites (Nir & Rimmerman, 2018) to be not accessible for people with disabilities to varying degrees. In a cross-continent comparison, Lorca, De Andrés, and Martínez (2018) recently articulated the relationship between efforts to improve web content and efforts to improve web accessibility. Therein, the researchers learned Anglo-Saxon institutions paid more attention to web accessibility while improving and adding web content, while Germanic institutions published higher quality web content. Meanwhile, Latin American institutions published both higher quality web content, while maintaining high levels of web accessibility (Lorca et al., 2018).

Ultimately, given the mutability of Internet technologies and web accessibility (Kurt, 2018; Thompson et al., 2010), this study updated and expanded upon extant research to learn whether prospective community college students with disabilities still face technology hurdles on their path to a postsecondary education in the form of inaccessible institutional websites.

Methods

The following sections will detail how the research team identified the population and sample, gathered data, analyzed data, and delimited the study so that the study could be completed in a timely, efficient manner.

Population and sample

To address this study's primary research questions of whether two-year institution websites are web accessible, we gathered institutional-level data from the Integrated Postsecondary Education Data System (IPEDS). The research team identified a sampling frame of all public and private nonprofit and for-profit two-year higher education institutions in the U.S. receiving Title IV funding. As the new Section 508 update requires all Title IV institutions to publish web accessible websites, the research team identified only Title IV two-year institutions in the U.S. In all, the research team narrowed the scope of the population to 2,088 two-year institutions receiving Title IV funds during the 2016–2017 academic year according to IPEDS.

After the research team established this population, we randomly selected a sample size of 325 institutions by using the random number generation function in Microsoft Excel. A sample size of 325 reflects a 95% confidence level to prove strong enough for quantitative analysis in subsequent studies or meta-analysis of this study. Furthermore, Flowers et al. (2011) examined a sample of 253 community college homepages. The research team wanted to expand and update this work, thus requiring a larger sample size. An overview of the sample in this study can be found in Table 1 below.

Data collection and analysis

To collect website accessibility data, the research team gathered institutional hyperlinks or URLs to each institution's homepage. Once the research team located these URLs, the team employed Tenon™ accessibility software, a robust freeware program capable of running 99 total tests of web accessibility at the Level-A, Level-AA, and Level-AAA standards (Tenon LLC, 2018). However, any Level-AAA errors discovered in this study were removed from the analysis, as Title IV institutions are not required to meet Level-AAA conformance. In addition, Tenon™ allows practitioners to download a .csv report detailing which accessibility errors are most prevalent and the HTML location at which to remedy to error. Recent comparisons of web accessibility software have found Tenon™ to be a reliable, accurate, and efficient web accessibility tool (Ismail, Kuppusamy, & Nengroo, 2017; Timbi-Sisalima, Amor, Otón, Hilera, & Aguado-Delgado, 2018); thus, the research team employed Tenon™.

Table 1. Sectors of institutions (n = 325).

Sector	Number of institutions (% of sample)
Public	185 (57%)
Private	140 (43%)
For-profit	116 (36%)
Non-profit	24 (7%)

Once the research team gathered web accessibility data, the team merged institutional IPEDS variables with Tenon's™ error reports to analyze the data by institution type and error type. This merge allowed the research team to understand what the most frequent error types were, and which institutions were responsible for the least web accessible and most web accessible websites. As a result, Tables 2 and 3 in the findings section of this study clearly explain the overall sample mean, median, high, low, and standard deviation of errors, as well as descriptive statistics of errors by institution type. In addition, the research team analyzed the merged dataset and created Table 3 to clearly display the most frequent error types across all four strands of WCAG 2.0 web accessibility: perceivable, operable, understandable, and robust web elements (W3C, 2018b).

Delimitations

The research team delimited this study in three ways: by sample size, web accessibility evaluation tool, and webpage.

First, the research team delimited this study to 325 two-year, Title IV-receiving U.S. institutions of higher education in order to complete the study and report its findings in a timely, efficient manner, given the mutability of Internet and web accessibility technologies. The research team acknowledges the web accessibility work performed by other researchers choosing to focus on different institution types,

Table 2. Descriptive statistics of web accessibility errors (n = 22,523*) of homepages/landing pages for two-year institutions of higher education (n = 325), by institution type.

Institution type	Web accessibility errors
All institutions (*n* = 325)	
Mean	69**
Median	41
High	1065
Low	1
Standard deviation	112
Public (*n* = 185)	
Mean	59
Median	36
High	430
Low	1
Standard deviation	68
Private, For-profit (*n* = 116)	
Mean	87**
Median	44
High	1065
Low	2
Standard deviation	166
Private, Non-profit (*n* = 24)	
Mean	60
Median	52
High	145
Low	2
Standard deviation	44

* This study found 70 Level AAA, 1.4.8 errors; however, these errors were removed from our analysis, as ADA guidelines only require Level-A and Level-AA web accessibility compliance.
**In the private, for-profit sample, there were three outliers (1000 or more errors). After removing these outliers from the analysis, private, for-profit mean was lowered to 62 errors per page and overall mean was lowered to 60 errors per page.

Table 3. Descriptive statistics of web accessibility errors (n = 22,523*) of homepages/landing pages for two-year institutions of higher education (n = 325), by error type.

Errors, by type, all institutions	# of errors
Perceivable	
Level-A, 1.1.1, Non-text content	2289
Level-A, 1.3.1, Information and relationships	4187
Level-A, 1.3.2, Meaningful sequence	142
Level-AA, 1.4.5, Images of text	2
Operable	
Level-A, 2.1.1, Keyboard	3668
Level-A, 2.3.1, Three flashes or below threshold	4
Level-A, 2.4.1, Bypass blocks	418
Level-A, 2.4.2, Page titled	7
Level-A, 2.4.3, Focus order	321
Level-A, 2.4.4, Link purpose (in context)	6443
Level-AA, 2.4.6, Headings and labels	425
Understandable	
Level-A, 3.1.1, Language of page	59
Robust	
Level-A, 4.1.1, Parsing	1936
Level-A, 4.1.2, Name, role, value	2622

*This study found 70 Level AAA, 1.4.8 errors; however, these errors were removed from our analysis, as ADA guidelines only require Level-A and Level-AA web accessibility compliance.

such as land-grant universities (Bradbard et al., 2010), Turkish universities (Kurt, 2017), and regional U.S. institutions (Thompson et al., 2010). However, since the work of Flowers et al. (2011) and Erickson et al. (2013), no research has examined the web accessibility of two-year U.S. institutions. In addition, this study's sample of 325 institutions is the largest study of two-year institutional websites to date, rendering this study an important and updated contribution to the literature.

Second, the research team delimited this study by using Tenon™ instead of using multiple web accessibility technologies or a combination of software and human input (Thompson et al., 2003). The decision to use Tenon™ was informed by extant research demonstrating Tenon's™ quality (Ismail et al., 2017; Timbi-Sisalima et al., 2018), and practitioner-focused research asserting that Tenon's™ technology is user-friendly for two-year institutional professionals who are unfamiliar with web design, coding, or web accessibility (Taylor, 2018).

Finally, similar to other studies, this study only examines the homepage or landing page of each institution in the sample, following the logic that if a student with a disability cannot navigate past the homepage, they may be unlikely to navigate through the rest of the website. This study focused on homepages, as many other studies have done the same and made important contributions to the research community (Flowers et al., 2011; Hackett & Parmanto, 2005; Harper & DeWaters, 2008; Kelly, 2002; Kurt, 2017).

Acknowledging these delimitations, future research should continue to examine the web accessibility of all types of educational institutions, including those in the K-12 pipeline. In addition, future studies could use different web accessibility technologies or a combination of software and human input akin to Thompson et al.'s (2003) work. Finally, beyond homepages, future research could address multi-level websites and multiple webpages to learn how web accessibility may improve or worsen as a student navigates deeper into a website. These suggestions for future research could inform practitioners working with students with disabilities to provide a more accessible website for prospective and current educational stakeholders, including students, faculty, staff, and their support networks.

Findings

Table 2 indicates that across 325 institutions, a total of 22,523 Level-A and Level AA errors were detected on institutional homepages. Across all institutions, the average homepage included 69 errors, while one institution published a homepage with only one Level-A error. In addition, public institutions (*n* = 185) published the most web accessible websites, with a mean of 59 errors per homepage. Private, for-profit institutions (*n* = 116) published the least web accessible websites, with a mean of 60 errors per landing page. Outliers in the study, three private, for-profit institutions published homepages with over 1,000 Level-A and Level-AA errors. As mentioned in the note below Table 2, after removing these errors, the overall sample mean was lowered to 60 errors per page, and the private, for-profit mean was lowered to 62 errors per page. Inversely, the most web accessible homepage in this study's sample was Southern Union State Community College (public), publishing a homepage with one Level-A error.

Table 3 indicates the most frequent errors were Level-A, including 3,668 keyboard-related errors, echoing previous research that found keyboard-related errors were often due to advances in technology that were not reflected on institutional websites (Thompson et al., 2010). According to WCAG 2.0 guidelines, Level-A 2.1.1 keyboard standards require, "All functionality of the content is operable through a keyboard interface without requiring specific timings for individual keystrokes, except where the underlying function requires input that depends on the path of the user's movement and not just the endpoints" (W3C, 2018a, para. 26). For example, in HTML, a programmer can add an attribute called an event handler to a HTML element, such as a hyperlink, image, button, or menu. However, in some types of Level-A 2.1.1 errors, an element may be missing an attribute – such as an event handler – causing a keyboard-focused assistive technology to parse over the element, thus failing to read it. This finding indicates students with disabilities who use assistive technologies relying on keyboard navigation may face an unfair disadvantage when attempting to access information on two-year institutional websites.

Findings in Table 3 also suggest Level-A 2.4.4 errors related to the purpose of links embedded on webpages are abundant on two-year institutional websites. In total, this study found 6,443 of these types of errors. Errors related to the purpose of links often mean that alt element text or another form of metadata is missing from a webpage element, rendering that element difficult or impossible to understand depending on the type of assistive technology the person is using. For instance, one institution added alt element text to every hyperlink on their website, but these hyperlinks were simply titled "link." In all, there were five Level-A 2.4.4 errors on this particular institution's homepage because all of their hyperlinks contained generic alt element text that did not adequately describe the hyperlink and concisely inform the Internet user about where the hyperlink will take them. This lack of metadata renders it impossible for an assistive technology to discern where a hyperlink may lead. Subsequently, an Internet user may be searching for admissions criteria but may be compelled to click on every hyperlink on this institution's homepage because none of the hyperlinks were accurately or adequately described.

Similarly, Level-A 1.1.1 errors (2,289 in total) and 1.3.1 errors (4,187 in total) are related to the description and detail of non-text content and other webpage elements. Here, many of these errors may be owed to an image not containing text to describe it or a fillable form that is not described. For instance, one institution's embedded search tool was missing metadata to describe its function. For a user to input information, such as "apply for financial aid" and for the internal search engine to find the financial aid webpage included on that institution's website. Typically, in HTML, an embedded search tool can be considered a form element, or, an HTML element that can be filled with information by the Internet user. As a Level-A 1.1.1 error, this form element (the search tool) was missing an HTML label, alerting the Internet user as to what types of information could be entered in the field (the blank space) of the form element (the search tool). Here, an Internet user may be unable to find the content they need and want to perform a search on the institutional website, but the assistive technology would be unable to tell the Internet user what type of information could be entered in the search tool. These errors may render websites inaccessible, as students who are blind or have low vision may need text to be read to them in order to understand an image or form element on the screen.

Similarly, to inadequate and uninformative text included in hyperlink metadata, many Level-A 1.1.1 errors in this study pertained to images with no metadata or uninformative metadata. For example, one institution embedded 11 different images on their homepage, with each image having its own file name. In

HTML, an image's file name is part of the language, as HTML code will include the digital location of the file being used on the website. For this particular institution, all 11 images had different file names but the same alt text. Here, an Internet user with a vision impairment could hover their mouse all 11 images on the homepage and be unable to discern what each image was and where its hyperlink – if applicable – directed them. Alternatively, an Internet user with a hearing impairment and unfamiliar with postsecondary education may be unfamiliar about an image's contents. In this instance, the assistive technology would display the same caption – the same alt text – over 11 all images – potentially confusing the student as to what was included in each image. Here, students who are deaf or hard of hearing may need images and video to include text descriptions in order to better understand the multimedia content on the webpage, and these text descriptions should be unique, accurate, and understandable.

Finally, this study finds the robustness of two-year institutional websites to be problematic, as this study found 1,936 Level-A 4.1.1 and 2,622 Level-A 4.1.2 robust errors. For example, one institution's homepage included 162 Level-A 4.1.1 errors pertinent to parsing, or the way assistive technologies can read HTML and convey it to users. The main problem with this homepage was that each HTML element contained the same "id" attribute, or, a unique value of an HTML element. Within HTML documents, each HTML element should have a unique "id" attribute in order for a wide range of assistive technologies to parse the elements and distinguish each element from one another. However, nearly every HTML element on this particular institution's homepage had the same "id" attribute, rendering it difficult for multiple assistive technologies to parse the HTML and discern different elements. Level-A 4.1.1 errors fall under the category of WCAG robust standards (W3C, 2018b), ensuring that webpages can be accessed by a wide range of diversity assistive technologies, given that students possess a wide range of diverse disabilities. This study suggests many two-year websites are simply not robust enough to be accessed by a wide range of assistive technologies, as robust errors comprised over 4,000 total errors in this study.

Discussion and implications

After analyzing 325 two-year institution websites, data in this study suggest that no one website was entirely Level-A and Level-AA compliant. As a result, not a single two-year institution website entirely satisfied the new Section 508 guidelines. Building upon the previous work of Flowers et al. (2011) and Erickson et al. (2013), a number of themes emerge pertinent to web accessibility, advances in technology, and students with disabilities' equal access to higher education.

First, this study found keyboard-related errors were problematic, echoing prior research (Thompson et al., 2010). Subsequently, students with disabilities who rely on assistive technologies including keyboard usage may be unfairly disadvantaged when accessing postsecondary websites. Expanding on prior research, this study found robustness to be a critical area of emphasis from which community college websites could improve, as over 4,000 Level-A and Level-AA errors fell underneath the robust WCAG 2.0 standard. Given the variability of error amount from website to website, our data suggest students with disabilities may experience varying levels of web accessibility when navigating community college websites. For example, 30 institutions in this study had 10 or fewer errors on their homepage. In these instances, students with disabilities accessing these websites may not struggle to access these institutions' content. Inversely, 55 institutions in this study had 100 or more error on their homepage. Ultimately, this study suggests aspiring community college students with disabilities may experience vastly different experiences when navigating institutional websites depending on the student's disability, their assistive technology, and which institutions they are exploring.

In addition – although this study does not examine institutional websites over time – this study's data suggests web accessibility continues to be an elusive goal. For two decades or longer, extant research has asserted postsecondary websites are often not accessible to people with disabilities (Flowers et al., 2011; Hackett & Parmanto, 2005; Harper & DeWaters, 2008; Kelly, 2002; Kurt, 2017). This study continues this narrative. However, one common hurdle facing all institutions of higher education is the nature of an ever-changing technology landscape, especially Internet technologies.

Twenty years ago, uploading a 10-minute video to the Internet could take hours. Now, it takes minutes, if not seconds. For institutions of higher education to be truly web accessible for all people, institutions must find ways to keep up with technology (Kurt, 2017; Thompson et al., 2010). If not, a student with a disability may be able to access an institution of higher education, but without technology and accessibility maintenance, the same student may find themselves struggling to access digital content only one or two years into their postsecondary career. Here, the topic of web accessibility should enter discussions of student persistence and retention, as assistive technologies may play a much larger role in students with disabilities' persistence and retention.

Finally, understanding that institutions of higher education are frequently targets of lawsuits and others forms of litigation for failing to comply with ADA laws (Carlson, 2018), all members of institutions should explore web accessibility. As technology has allowed for voluminous amounts of data to be uploaded onto a website in short time, both faculty and staff members should be aware of how this ease of technology must be counterbalanced by an eye toward web accessibility. Akin to the foundational work of Erickson et al. (2009) and Thompson et al. (2010), institutions should alert their employees and greater campus community to the issue of web accessibility and their campus web accessibility policies. Subsequently, institutions should work to distribute the responsibility of web accessibility across multiple units to better serve students with disabilities (Wisdom et al., 2006). If this responsibility cannot be shared, web accessibility will likely continue to be problematic for both institutions and students alike, perpetuating the underrepresentation of students with disabilities at community colleges (National Center for Education Statistics, 2018).

Ultimately, this study, along with decades of extant research, demonstrates that publishing web accessible websites is difficult for community colleges (Erickson et al., 2013; Flowers et al., 2011) and other types of institutions (Bradbard et al., 2010; Hackett & Parmanto, 2005; Harper & DeWaters, 2008; Kelly, 2002; Kurt, 2017; Lorca et al., 2018; Nir & Rimmerman, 2018; Thompson et al., 2003; Wisdom et al., 2006). However, if researchers and practitioners can prioritize web accessibility – even though technology will continue to evolve – perhaps students with disabilities will access higher education to a greater degree, rendering the U.S. higher education landscape a more tech-savvy and inclusive one.

ORCID

Z. W. Taylor http://orcid.org/0000-0002-6085-2729

References

Bradbard, D. A., Peters, C., & Caneva, Y. (2010). Web accessibility policies at land-grant universities. *The Internet and Higher Education*, 13(4), 258–266. doi:10.1016/j.iheduc.2010.05.007

Brinckerhoff, L. C. (1996). Making the transition to higher education: Opportunities for student empowerment. *Journal of Learning Disabilities*, 29(2), 118–136. doi:10.1177/002221949602900202

Burdett, K. R. (2013). *How students choose a college: Understanding the role of internet based resources in the college choice process* (Doctoral dissertation). Lincoln, NE: University of Nebraska at Lincoln. Available from ProQuest database. (UMI No. 3590306)

Carlson, L. L. (2018). *Higher ed accessibility lawsuits, complaints, and settlements*. Retrieved from http://www.d.umn. edu/~lcarlson/atteam/lawsuits.html

Daun-Barnett, N., & Das, D. (2013). Unlocking the potential of the Internet to improve college choice: A comparative case study of college-access Web tools. *Journal of Marketing for Higher Education*, 23(1), 113–134. doi:10.1080/08841241.2013.805708

Dettling, L. J., Goodman, S., & Smith, J. (2018). Every little bit counts: The impact of high- speed internet on the transition to college. *The Review of Economics and Statistics*, 100(2), 260–273. doi:10.1162/REST_a_00712

Eckes, S. E., & Ochoa, T. A. (2005). Students with disabilities: Transitioning from high school to higher education. *American Secondary Education*, 33(3), 6–20. Retrieved from http://www.jstor.org/stable/41064551

Erickson, W., Trerise, S., Lee, C., VanLooy, S., Knowlton, S., & Bruyère, S. (2013). The accessibility and usability of college websites: Is your website presenting barriers to potential students? *Community College Journal of Research and Practice*, 37(11), 864–876. doi:10.1080/10668926.2010.484772

Erickson, W., Trerise, S., VanLooy, S., Lee, C., & Bruyère, S. (2009). Web accessibility policies and practices at American community colleges. *Community College Journal of Research and Practice, 33*(5), 403–414. doi:10.1080/10668920802505561

Evans, N. J., Broido, E. M., Brown, K. R., & Wilke, A. K. (2017). *Disability in higher education: A social justice approach.* San Francisco, CA: Jossey-Bass.

Flowers, C., Bray, M., & Algozzine, R. F. (2011). Content accessibility of community college websites. *Community College Journal of Research and Practice, 25*(7), 475–485. doi:10.1080/10668920152407874

Garrison-Wade, D. F., & Lehmann, J. P. (2009). A conceptual framework for understanding students' with disabilities transition to community college. *Community College Journal of Research and Practice, 33*(5), 415–443. doi:10.1080/10668920802640079

Getzel, E. E. (2008). Addressing the persistence and retention of students with disabilities in higher education: Incorporating key strategies and supports on campus. *Exceptionality: A Special Education Journal, 16*(4), 207–219. doi:10.1080/09362830802412216

Getzel, E. E., & Thoma, C. A. (2008). Experiences of college students with disabilities and the importance of self-determination in higher education settings. *Career Development and Transition for Exceptional Individuals, 31*(2), 77–84. doi:10.1177/0885728808317658

Hackett, S., & Parmanto, B. (2005). A longitudinal evaluation of accessibility: Higher education web sites. *Internet Research, 15*(3), 281–294. doi:10.1108/10662240510602690

Harper, K. A., & DeWaters, J. (2008). A quest for website accessibility in higher education institutions. *The Internet and Higher Education, 11*(3–4), 160–164. doi:10.1016/j.iheduc.2008.06.007

Hong, B. S. S. (2015). Qualitative analysis of the barriers college students with disabilities experience in higher education. *Journal of College Student Development, 56*(3), 209–226. doi:10.1353/csd.2015.0032

Ismail, A., Kuppusamy, K. S., & Nengroo, A. S. (2017). Multi-tool accessibility assessment of government department websites: A case-study with JKGAD. *Disability and Rehabilitation: Assistive Technology,* 1–10. doi:10.1080/17483107.2017.1344883

Janiga, S. J., & Costenbader, V. (2002). The transition from high school to postsecondary education for students with learning disabilities: A survey of college service coordinators. *Journal of Learning Disabilities, 35*(5), 463–470. doi:10.1177/00222194020350050601

Kelly, B. (2002). Web watch: An accessibility analysis of UK university entry points. *Ariadne, 33*. Retrieved from http://www.ariadne.ac.uk/issue33/web-watch

Kurt, S. (2017). Accessibility of Turkish university web sites. *Universal Access in the Information Society, 16*(2), 505–515. doi:10.1007/s10209-016-0468-x

Kurt, S. (2018). Moving toward a universally accessible web: Web accessibility and education. *Assistive Technology,* 1–10. doi:10.1080/10400435.2017.1414086

LaGrow, M. (2017). The Section 508 refresh and what it means for higher education. *Educause Review.* Retrieved from https://er.educause.edu/articles/2017/12/the-section-508-refresh-and-what-it-means-for-higher-education

Lorca, P., De Andrés, J., & Martínez, A. B. (2018). The relationship between web content and web accessibility at universities. *Social Science Computer Review, 36*(3), 311–330. doi:10.1177/0894439317710435

Madaus, J. W., Grigal, M., & Hughes, C. (2014). Promoting access to postsecondary education for low-income students with disabilities. *Career Development and Transition for Exceptional Individuals, 37*(1), 50–59. doi:10.1177/2165143414525037

National Center for Education Statistics. (2018). *Use the data: Population of students with disabilities in United States institutions of higher education.* Retrieved from https://nces.ed.gov/ipeds/use-the-data

Nir, H. L., & Rimmerman, A. (2018). Evaluation of web content accessibility in an Israeli institution of higher education. *Universal Access in the Information Society,* 1–11. doi:10.1007/s10209-018-0615-7

Taylor, Z. W. (2018). Web accessibility: Not just for tech experts anymore. *Disability Compliance for Higher Education, 23*(9), 5. doi:10.1002/dhe.30416

Tenon LLC. (2018). *Tenon: Services.* Retrieved from https://tenon.io/services.php#testing

Thompson, T., Burgstahler, S., & Comden, D. (2003). Research on web accessibility in higher education. *Information Technology and Disabilities Journal, 9,* 2. Retrieved from http://itd.athenpro.org/volume9/number2/thompson.html

Thompson, T., Burgstahler, S., & Moore, E. J. (2010). Web accessibility: A longitudinal study of college and university home pages in the northwestern United States. *Disability and Rehabilitation: Assistive Technology, 5*(2), 108–114. doi:10.3109/17483100903387424

Timbi-Sisalima, C., Amor, C. I. M., Otón, S., Hilera, J. R., & Aguado-Delgado, J. (2018). Comparative analysis of online web accessibility evaluation tools. *Information Systems Development: Complexity in Information Systems Development.* Retrieved from http://aisel.aisnet.org/isd2014/proceedings2016/CreativitySupport/3

United States Access Board. (2018). *Text of the standards and guidelines.* Retrieved from https://www.access-board.gov/guidelines-and-standards/communications-and-it/about-the-ict-refresh/final-rule/text-of-the-standards-and-guidelines

W3C. (2018a). *Guideline 2.1: Keyboard accessible.* Retrieved from https://www.w3.org/WAI/WCAG21/quickref/?versions=2.0#keyboard-accessible

W3C. (2018b). *Web content accessibility guidelines (WCAG) overview.* Retrieved from https://www.w3.org/WAI/standards-guidelines/wcag/

W3C. (2018c). *Web content accessibility guidelines: Understanding conformance requirements.* Retrieved from https://www.w3.org/TR/UNDERSTANDING-WCAG20/conformance.html

White, S. W., Elias, R., Capriola-Hall, N. N., Smith, I. C., Conner, C. M., Asselin, S. B., … Mazefsky, C. A. (2017). Development of a college transition and support program for students with autism spectrum disorder. *Journal of Autism and Developmental Disorders, 47*(10), 3072–3078. doi:10.1007/s10803-017-3236-8

Wisdom, J. R., White, N. A., Goldsmith, K. A., Bielavitz, S., Davis, C. E., & Drum, C. (2006). An assessment of web accessibility knowledge and needs at Oregon community colleges. *Community College Review, 33*(3–4), 19–37. doi:10.1177/009155210603300302

A Document Analysis of Student Conduct in Florida's Community Colleges

Allyson Miller and Cristobal Salinas Jr.

ABSTRACT
Student disciplinary systems have been operating in higher education for decades and their role in furthering an institution's educational mission continues to raise. Almost all institutions have a Code of Conduct section in their handbook which describes all rules and regulations students must comply with in addition to federal, state, and local laws. The student conduct process varies as each university or college has their own unique set of standards and methods for adjudicating misbehaviors. Through a document analysis, we examined the history of student conduct and analyzed the mission of student conduct offices at community colleges in the state of Florida.

A document analysis of student conduct in Florida's Community Colleges

The definition and meaning of student conduct varies by institution and, thus, leaves ambiguity in higher education. Since the collapse of *in loco parentis*[1] in the 1960s, colleges and universities have received limited guidance from the government on the handlings of student disciplinary issues (Chun & Evans, 2016). While student misbehavior is displayed in several forms including academic dishonesty, violation of housing policies, alcohol and drug use, and sexual misconduct, this document analysis serves to provide an overview of the mission and purpose of student conduct offices in community colleges[2] in the state of Florida. Currently, there are over 100 community colleges across the United States that are under investigation by the Department of Education's Office of Civil Rights ("Pending Cases Currently", 2018). The allegation for each institution varies but the common theme of why these institutions are under investigation is due to student conduct matters. Student conduct plays a large role on any college campus as it can have an impact on graduation rates and retention rates which are evaluated by the state, the federal government, and prospective students. It is also important to note that the literature surrounding mission statements for student conduct policy and departments, both at the two-year and four-year institutions level is limited. More research is needed to examine whether a clear mission statement and student conduct policy helps to improve campus culture and reduce lawsuits and allegations of mishandling.

Students or organizations who have alleged to have violated a university policy will be referred to an administrator to determine responsibility of their actions and impose appropriate sanctions if necessary (Smith, 1994). Although some institutions use student judicial affairs or community standards, we will refer to this area of higher education as student conduct. Policies are created and established based on the needs of the individual institution, state and federal laws, and previous situations that have threatened the safety of the students (Smith, 1994). Some examples include the use of alcohol, the ban on candles in the residence halls as it poses a fire hazard, and hazing policies as they are often unclear (Salinas & Boettcher, 2018). Higher education institutions will often seek advice from others in student conduct offices to update their handbooks in hopes of preventing any unexpected circumstances (Lancaster & Waryold, 2008).

Since the 1600s, it has been the responsibility of the higher education institution to ensure the safety and monitor the behavior of the members of a college or university community (Chun & Evans, 2016). However, the expectation of the college or university to do more than provide a *safe space* for adults to learn has expanded due to a rise in mental health, social media, and student activism. The purpose of this document analysis was to examine the history of student conduct and to analysis the mission statements of student conduct offices at community colleges in the state of Florida. Through this document analysis, we hope to create an exchange of ideas and start the conversation of the value student conduct offices might bring to educational settings and its importance of student learning directed by misbehavior.

Student conduct defined

Although the act of disciplining students has been around for centuries, colleges and universities have not agreed on a formal definition and term for this practice (Lancaster & Waryold, 2008). Each higher education institution has their own definition and methodology based on the values and mission in which the college or university was founded upon. Yet, there are some higher education institutions that have not institutionalized a code of conduct. The process of adjudicating conduct cases are often reflected in higher education institutions' code of conduct which should be made public to students, faculty, and staff members. In addition to the outlined student conduct process, the code of conduct consists of all policies and violations in which students have consented to abide by including housing guidelines, classroom and community etiquette, state and federal laws, and off-campus behavior.

Moreover, there are two common outcomes to any student conduct case in which an alleged individual is found responsible for a violation(s): punitive sanctions and educational sanctions (Martin-Anderson, 2009). Punitive or sometimes called administrative sanctions include written warnings, disciplinary probation, suspension, and expulsion. Disciplinary probation and suspension can range in length of time and include other restrictions such as studying abroad, living on campus, and/or the ability to hold a leadership position within a student organization. Educational sanctions can range in format from research papers, meetings with campus partners, restitution, apology letters, alcohol or drug courses, community service, and other creative ideas in which the hearing officer feels is appropriate (Martin-Anderson, 2009). Most college administrators agree that the disciplinary process, including sanctions, should be educational in nature and help the student(s) learn from their past behavior (Kompalla & McCarthy, 2001).

A common misconception by students and faculty members is the idea that the code of conduct of higher education institutions is similar, if not entirely, the same as a court of law. Despite the fact that courts have ruled students must have due process, right to appeal and other constitutional rights, Bostic and Gonzalez (1999) pointed out the failure of courts to "communicate a consistent, clear approach to guide higher education administrators" (p. 166). This obscurity allows institutions to create their own technique for handling student disciplinary issues including the manner in which evidence is weighed (Taylor, Thrasher, & Wilfong, 2012). Some institutions will base their conduct decisions on preponderance of the evidence, meaning more likely than not, while others will use clear and convincing as the standard of proof (Loschiavo & Waller, n.d.). Additionally, each college and university has their own boundaries regarding student organizations and academic integrity cases.

Further, numerous code of conduct mission statements analyzed for this paper includes the development of students, encouragement of displaying citizenship and self-discipline, and ensuring the safety of the community members. However, when examining the code of conduct mission statements for Florida's community colleges, we noted some differences between each institution. For example, Seminole State College (2018) Office of Student Conduct defined their process to be an "educational opportunity that foster individual growth, ethical development, and personal accountability while promoting the core values of the college: integrity, respect, excellence, academic freedom and learning" (para. 2). Moreover, Broward College's (2018) Student Code of Conduct states, "Upon admission to Broward College, students and student organizations agree to act responsibility in all areas of personal and social conduct and to take full responsibility for their individual and collective action" (p.67).

History of student conduct

The evolution of student conduct in higher education can be aligned with the transformation and development of colleges and universities (Smith, 1994). During the Colonial Era (1636–1789), young men attended universities to study clergy beginning at age 12 or 13 years-old. The President and faculty members of higher education institutions were responsible for instilling morals and ethics, and handled all student discipline. Colleges and universities in the United States followed the pathway established by British Common Law and adopted *in loco parentis*, meaning in place of parent. For students who misbehaved during the Colonial Era, punishment could range from fines, loss of privileges, extra assignments, flogging, and expulsion (Smith, 1994). Harvard University considered flogging to be inhumane and was replaced with "boxing" where a student would kneel before a faculty member and receive slaps on the side of the head (Smith, 1994, p.78). These actions reflected on punishments people would receive during this time for violating any laws.

By the end of the 1700s and beginning of the 1800s, student discipline was at its deadliest (Smith, 1994). Students were rebelling against the sanctions and began to fight for their constitutional rights. Buildings were burned, professors were killed, and student protest was a weekly occurrence (Smith, 1994). Thomas Jefferson wanted to combat the violence in higher education by treating students with respect and as adults by having a student court (Smith, 1994). However, this led to numerous legal problems and outbursts from students, turning the 1830s into one of the worst student violence scenes in American higher education.

With the passing of the Morrill Land Grant Act in 1862, higher education began to see a shift in student population to meet the needs of the working class by opening public junior colleges and technical schools (Lancaster & Waryold, 2008). With a higher enrollment rate and the development of student organizations and student athletes, faculty members had a difficult time balancing student relationships with their disciplinary roles. In the nineteenth century, the first "disciplinary specialist" was employed (Chun & Evans, 2016, p. 34). Counseling was added to the options of punishment for misbehaved students and the President along with faculty members transitioned into a hands-off approach to student conduct (Smith, 1994). In 1883, Amherst College created the first student government which allowed students to act as judicial bodies, but the president was able to veto any decision made (Smith, 1994). Several colleges and universities mirrored the "Amherst system" and hired college deans to assist with the disciplinary responsibilities (Smith, 1994, p. 81).

The 1900s served as a pivotal moment in the history of student conduct. In the beginning of the century, each college or university conducted student disciplinary meetings as they saw fit. The lack of uniformity across higher education raised concerns among students. In reaction to the protests, institutions began to create committees or councils with bipartisan representation, allowing students to be seen as "whole" (Smith, 1994, p. 84). By the 1940s, the American Council of Education emphasized that higher education should focus on "the development of the student as a person rather than upon his intellectual training alone" (Smith, 1994, p.82). Student activism on college campuses brought about some of the biggest changes to student conduct. The *Dixon v. Alabama* (1960) case marked the beginning of the end for *in loco parentis*. The courts ruled public higher education institutions were required to give students due process. In addition, the majority of age was lowered from 21 to 18. Since then, several students have brought their conduct case to a courtroom and many have won.

Above all, on June 23, 1972, Title IX of the Education Amendment of 1972 was enacted into law. This law prohibits any school – elementary to university level – who is receiving federal funds to discriminate against an individual based on sex. Originally, the law was passed to afford equal rights for women in athletic programs (Helper, 1999). However, the shift of focus to sexual misconduct came from *Davis v. Monroe County Board of Education* (1999). The Supreme Court ruled educational institutions can be held liable in private suits for student-to-student sexual harassment if the behavior is "so severe, pervasive, and objectively offensive that it can be said to deprive the victims of access to the educational opportunities or benefits provided by the school" (Lieberwitz et al., 2016, p. 75).

Today, students continue to contest for their civil liberties on college campuses, while the line between student conduct and the judicial system grow thin. Pierce College, a community college in California, is under fire for allegedly violating student's First Amendment rights (Svrluga, 2017). Kevin Shaw, a student, was passing out copies of the US Constitution when an administrator told him he would need to move to the designated free speech area and obtain a permit if he wished to continue. Shaw hired an attorney from the Foundation for Individual Rights in Education (FIRE) and filed a lawsuit against the college, citing the free speech zone is unconstitutional (Svrluga, 2017). Virginia, Missouri, Arizona, Kentucky, Colorado, Utah, North Carolina, and Tennessee have explored the possibility of banning free speech zones on public college campuses. For example, a recent proposed bill (SB 4) in the state of Florida hopes to ban free speech zones on college campuses. The Florida Excellence in Higher Education Act of 2018 would prohibit the use of free speech zones and would allow students to actively protest anywhere on campus as long as it does not disrupt the process of learning (Blake, 2018). The bill came about from hundreds of students calling upon their state politicians.

In 2017, hundreds of students at The Evergreen State College in Washington State protested the removal of campus leaders for racism and gender discrimination (Pemberton, 2017). As student activism boosts, the spotlight on student conduct intensifies. Almost all institutions have a conduct process and minor violations tend to be informal and focus on education, while more serious actions take on a formal process to protect the rights of students involved. Title IX creates hefty pressure on the field of student conduct as the rise in lawsuits and investigations into alleged violations remains a concern for higher education administrators. As the shift in viewpoint advances toward students as private consumers, the identity crisis of student conduct cultivates (McKay, 1968).

Methods

We used document analysis to identify and examine the mission statements and purpose of student conduct policies and office in community colleges in the state of Florida. According to Bowen (2009), a document analysis is a procedure in which both paper and electronic documents are analyzed. A document may contain words and varies in format from websites, agendas, and journals (Bowen, 2009). In this work, we assessed the mission statements of student conduct policies and offices to evaluate the similarities and differences amongst Florida's community colleges.

Document analysis is best suited for qualitative research to "elicit meaning, gain understanding, and develop empirical knowledge" (Corbin & Strauss, 2008, p. 377). The utilization of this method to understand and compare the mission statements and purpose of student conduct offices in community colleges across the state of Florida was advantageous. The ambiguity in this area of higher education is seen through the contrasting mission statements of the individual community colleges; thus, leaving an opportunity for further research and deeper questioning.

The data collection process for document analysis was conducted in three steps: (1) research all 28 community colleges in Florida; (2) explore the institution's website for student conduct office; (3) scan the college's code of conduct to identify their mission statement; and (4) compare and contrast mission statements among the community colleges.

Results: Student conduct offices & mission statements

Through this document analysis, we found that only four community colleges in the state of Florida have a specialized office for handling student and organizational misconduct: Daytona State College, Pensacola State College, Seminole State College, and Tallahassee Community College. However, 20 community colleges have mission statements specifically relating to their Code of Conduct and student conduct process.[3] Most of the mission statements discuss the process to be educational and developmental in nature, while promoting civility among community members. Integrity, responsibility, and citizenship are common values seen throughout the community colleges examined. Yet, there are eight community colleges with no clear mission statement regarding the student conduct process, leaving ambiguity to the campus community.[4]

One major difference among all of the community colleges studied is the individual serving as the hearing officer for conduct matters. From this study, we discovered several institutions utilize the Dean of Students or Director of Student Services to adjudicate conduct cases with the President serving as the appellate officer. St. Petersburg College and Eastern Florida State College, model colonial times by having a provost or a member of academic affairs adjudicate conduct matters. Only two colleges, Daytona State College and Pensacola State College, have Directors whose job is to oversee the student conduct process. In contrast to community colleges, most four-year universities in Florida have a student conduct office with multiple full-time staff members including a Director, Associate Director, and Assistant Director to aid in adjudication of conduct cases. It is rare for a four-year university to have the President hear and rule on appeals; this is typically the job of the Dean of Students or Vice President for Student Affairs.

Although individual hearing officers are popular among the community colleges, there are five community colleges (Chipola College, Gulf Coast State College, Santa Fe College, St. Johns River State College, and State College of Florida) that utilize a student conduct committee, board, or student court to assist in the adjudication of conduct. Chipola College, Gulf Coast State College, and St. Johns River State College have adopted a committee model; whereas, State College of Florida operates with a student court. Based on the information within the student code of conduct or student handbook provided by each community college, a committee consists of faculty, administration personnel, and students who have been appointed and approved by the President of the college. Santa Fe College is the only community college to have a student conduct board in their practice. This board is made up of three members selected by the vice president for student affairs. Specific qualifications were not listed within Santa Fe's Student handbook. According to each community colleges website, their appeals are often heard by the vice president of student affairs. The lack of consistency in mission statements, offices, and hearing officers demonstrates the autonomy of student conduct in higher education.

Implications for practice and future research

Community colleges should work to create an office for student conduct and communicate a definitive mission statement to the campus community. To combat stereotypical notions associated with this area, institutions should have a strong presence in the community by hosting programs and educational sessions and being accessible to students. Additionally, community colleges should establish a committee consisting of faculty, staff, and students to aid in the creation and annual revision of a mission statement and campus policies. Student discipline has been in higher education for centuries and is only increasing in needs. Procedure, charges, and potential sanctions relating to the student conduct process are exclusive to each institution. Without a clearly defined mission statement and administrator to adjudicate student and organizational misbehavior, community colleges could face lawsuits, loss of funding, and other consequences outlined by the Department of Education.

Students and student organizations misbehavior remain an issue within higher education. As student conduct can impact student success, graduation and retention rates, it is crucial for further research to be conducted with respect to how conduct cases are adjudicated and the role a conduct office plays in a student's college experience. Institutions need to have a clearly defined mission statement and process relating to the student disciplinary system in which they enact to ensure the rights of alleged students are protected and the safety of the community is at the forefront of the framework. By installing a thorough mission statement, colleges and universities can ensure their goals and community standards are mutually understood while promoting a positive campus culture.

The majority of the literature on student conduct focuses on Title IX or sexual misconduct (Hepler, 1997; Lieberwitz et al., 2016). However, it is imperative to further study student conduct in other subcategories to gain knowledge in the function and the value it has in various institutional settings. Research in sanctioning, standard of evidence, substance abuse and methodology would greatly benefit practitioners and other campus stakeholders. Additionally, studies concerning restorative justice programs and student development through the conduct process will aid in the future success of students. Annual or biennial assessment of an institution's student conduct procedure should be conducted to safeguard best practices and equal opportunities for students.

It is important for campus administrators, faculty members, and students to be well educated on campus policies and violations, the conduct process, and the rights afforded to them. Student conduct hearing officers or administrators should be knowledgeable on the potential implications their institution can face including lawsuits and governmental fines. By continuing with research efforts, colleges and universities can have a better understanding of the needs of their students in order to provide support while securing the safety of the community. Throughout this document analysis, we have defined what student conduct is, the history of this phenomenon, and evaluated the mission statements of conduct offices in Florida's community colleges.

Notes

1. *In loco parentis* in Latin means "in place of parent".
2. Community colleges primarily offer two-year degrees, and some offer four-year degrees and these institutions may be referred as state colleges (Floyd & Walker, 2008).
3. Institutions include Broward College, College of Central Florida, Chipola College, Daytona State College, Edison State College, Florida State College at Jacksonville, Florida Keys Community College, Gulf Coast State College, Hillsborough Community College, Indian River State College, Lake-Sumter State College, North Florida Community College, Palm Beach State College, Pensacola State College, Santa Fe College, Seminole State College, South Florida State College, State College of Florida, Tallahassee Community College, and Valencia College.
4. Colleges include Eastern Florida State College (formerly Brevard Community College), Florida Gateway College (formerly Lake City Community College), Miami Dade College, Northwest Florida State College, Pasco-Hernando Community College, Polk State College, St. Johns River State College, and St. Petersburg College.

References

Blake, A. (2018, March). Florida lawmakers ban 'free speech zones' on college campuses. *The Washington Times*. Retrieved from https://www.washingtontimes.com/news/2018/mar/6/florida-lawmakers-ban-free-speech-zones-college-ca/
Bostic, D., & Gonzalez, G. (1999). Practices, opinions, knowledge, and recommendations from judicial officers in public higher education. *NASPA Journal, 36*(3), 166–183. doi:10.2202/0027-6014.1085
Bowen, G. A. (2009). Document analysis as a qualitative research method. *Qualitative Research Journal, 9*(2), 27–40. doi:10.3316/QRJ0902027
Chun, E., & Evans, A. (2016). Rethinking cultural competence in higher education: An ecological framework for student development. *ASHE Higher Education Report, 42*(4), 7–162. doi:10.1002/aehe.20102
Corbin, J., & Strauss, A. (2008). *Basics of qualitative research: Techniques and procedures for developing grounded theory* (3rd ed.). Thousand Oaks, CA: Sage.
Davis, V. Monroe County Board of Education, 526 US 629 (1999)
Dixon, V. Alabama State Board of Education, 186 F. Supp. 945 (M.D. Ala. 1960)
Floyd, D. L., & Walker, K. P. (2008). The community college baccalaureate: Putting the pieces together. *Community College Journal of Research and Practice, 33*(2), 90–124. doi:10.1080/10668920802564667

Hepler, C. I. (1997). A bibliography of title IX of the education amendments of 1972 and its impact on intercollegiate athletics. *SSRN Electronic Journal.* doi:10.2139/ssrn.1116692

Kompalla, S. L., & McCarthy, M. C. (2001). The effect of judicial sanctions on recidivism and retention. *College Student Journal, 35*(2), 223–225.

Lancaster, J. M., & Waryold, D. M. (2008). *Student conduct practice: The complete guide for student affairs professionals.* Sterling, VA: Stylus.

Lieberwitz, R. L., Jaleel, R., Kelleher, T., Scott, J. W., Young, D., Reichman, H., & Runyan, A. S. (2016). The history, uses, and abuses of Title IX. *Academe, 102,* 69.

Loschiavo, C., & Waller, J. (n.d.). The preponderance of evidence standard: Use in higher education campus conduct processes. *Association of Student Conduct Administration,* 1–6. Retrieved from https://www.theasca.org/files/The%20Preponderance%20of%20Evidence%20Standard.pdf

Martin-Anderson, K. A. (2009). Student conduct practice: The complete guide for student affairs professionals. *Journal of College Student Development, 50*(1), 133–135. doi:10.1353/csd.0.0056

McKay, R. B. (1968). The student as private citizen. *Denver Law Journal, 45*(4), 558–570.

Pemberton, L. (2017, March). Students allege racism, protest administrators at The Evergreen State College. *The Olympian,* para. 7.

Pending Cases Currently Under Investigation. (2018, March 30). Retrieved from https://www2.ed.gov/about/offices/list/ocr/docs/investigations/open-investigations/index.html

Salinas, C., & Boettcher, M. L. (2018). *Critical perspectives on hazing in colleges and universities: A guide to disrupting hazing culture.* New York, NY: Routledge.

Seminole State College. (2018). About the office of student conduct. Retrieved from https://www.seminolestate.edu/student-conduct/about

Smith, D. B. (1994). Student discipline in American college & universities a historical overview. *Educational Horizons, 72*(2), 78–85.

Student Code of Conduct. (2018). *Broward college student handbook.* Retrieved from https://reader.mediawiremobile.com/BrowardCollege/issues/203632/viewer?page=1

Svrluga, S. (2017, October). Justice department supports student's claim that his free-speech rights were violated. *The Washington Post.*

Taylor, T., Thrasher, R. R., & Wilfong, M. (2012). A study of current student conduct investigation practices. *Journal of Student Conduct Administration, 4,* 1–34.

Experiential Learning as a Strategy for Student Completion and Course Success in the Community College

Carolyn Walker

ABSTRACT
Community college leaders seeking best practices to improve completion rates and student success have a strategy to consider – experiential learning as part of a course. An accounting business course, at a mid-sized community college in the southeast, recently implemented an experiential learning activity to determine the association with students obtaining a degree and completing a course successfully. A comparison of graduation rates and end-of-course grades, between experiential and non-experiential learning participants, yielded positive benefits for the experiential learning participants.

The completion rates of students at two-year colleges are an important area of focus for community college leaders. Completion, which is defined as obtaining a degree, has declined among community college students. The United States led the world in college degree completion for many years; however, currently ranks 16th in the world in completion rates for 25- to 34-year-olds (American Association of Community Colleges [AACC], 2014, p. 4). Colleges may offer support methods to assist students from entry to completion such as first-year experience programs, orientation, and holistic advising (Center for Community College Student Engagement [CCCSE], 2012). Although these support methods may be in place, the issue of low completion rates remains. This dilemma led the American Association of Community Colleges (AACC) and five other national community college organizations to commit to a 50% increase of student completion by the year 2020 (AACC, 2014).

A strategy that may contribute to increased completion rates is experiential learning opportunities within programs. Experiential learning affords the opportunity to apply concepts learned in a hands-on, real-world environment. This article discusses experiential learning and its positive association with student completion, which is obtaining a degree, and successful course completion. The results from an experiential learning activity involving accounting students serving as tax preparers to the local community further support this strategy.

Experiential learning

Experiential learning combines theory, hands-on application, and reflection, which allow the learner to develop new ideas and thoughts (Peterson, 2017). Experiential learning is not a new method of pedagogy. John Dewey, in 1938, began the movement of experiential learning with a laboratory school. According to Pegg (2017), children were encouraged to learn through experience, clarify the key points, and apply the lessons to obtain practical results. David Kolb (1984) expanded on the works of Dewey and partnered with Roger Fry to develop an *Experiential Learning Cycle*. The cycle has four sequential components which begin with an initial experience and, with reflection, leads to similar or new experiences. The components consist of (a) concrete experience, (b) observation and reflection, (c) forming abstract concepts, and (d) testing new situations (Coffey, n.d.). Astin's (1999) theory of student involvement emphasizes active participation of the student in the learning process and encourages instructors to focus more on the student's time and energy in the learning process. The theory aligns with experiential learning.

Student completion

Community colleges, public and private, enrolled 38% of the nation's undergraduates in the fall of 2015 (Grinder, Kelly-Reid, & Mann, 2017). The benefits and options available at a community college may lead students to enroll; however, the issue of low completion rates exists nationwide (AACC, 2014). According to Cohen, Brawer, and Kisker (2014), recent efforts to increase college completion have prompted new scrutiny and strategies to improve the rate of completion. A recent report from the Center for Community College Student Engagement (CCCSE) revealed several strategies to help increase completion rates, and experiential learning was among the strategies (CCCSE, 2012). Castellano (2015) discussed a Gallup survey which points to experiential learning as a benefit to career success. The survey revealed graduates who participate in experiential learning opportunities, such as internships, extracurricular activities (which are aligned with career goals), and long-term projects will double the odds of being engaged as an employee.

Successful course completion

Achieving The Dream (2017), a product of the Lumina Foundation, began with 27 colleges collaborating to improve student success. Colleges pledged to increase the percentages of students who complete courses with a C or higher, persist from one term to the next, and earn certificates and degrees (McClenney, 2014). National programs, as well as best practices implemented by community colleges such as experiential learning, assist with student course success. Some common advantages of utilizing experiential learning as part of instruction are:

- sharpens student skills at setting strategic plans and goals;
- aids in teaching and learning analytical techniques;
- provides opportunities for students to work with, and through, others in a team;
- provides timely, meaningful, and quick feedback facilitating reinforcement of concepts;
- offers experiences for students with concepts rather than merely reading and talking about concepts;
- encourages active learning and participation; and
- lends excitement to the learning experience (Devasagaya, Johns-Masten, & McCollum, 2012, p. 2).

Further, Hart Research Associates (2013) conducted a study of 318 employers whose organizations have at least 25 employees and reported 25% or more of new hires hold an associate degree from a two-year college or a bachelor's degree from a four-year college. The study revealed employers recognize the importance of preparing students for workplace success and endorse the following educational practices:

- requiring students to conduct research and use evidence-based analysis,
- gaining in-depth knowledge in the major and analytics,
- problem-solving,
- increasing communication skills, and
- applying learning in a real-world setting (Hart Research Associates, 2013, p. 1)

The components of experiential learning – theory, hands-on application, and reflection align with the endorsed educational practices.

An accounting business course

A mid-sized community college in the southeast implemented a required experiential learning activity in an accounting business course to enhance course content. Students partnered with a local United Way organization in support of the Volunteer Income Tax Assistance (VITA) Initiative. The experiential learning activity was conducted during the spring semester of each year, February through April, and required students to serve 10 hours as a tax preparer at a VITA site on the college campus. The activity counted as 30% of the students' final grade.

Methodology

A study was conducted on the accounting experiential learning activity to determine if experiential learning had a positive influence on student completion and course success. The following research questions were considered:

(1) How did completion rates compare between accounting students who participate in experiential learning and those who did not?
(2) How did end-of-course grades compare for the semester of experiential learning between accounting students who participate in experiential learning and those who did not?

The sample population, of this study, consisted of (a) accounting graduates in spring 2015 and 2016 – experiential learning participants, and (b) accounting graduates in spring 2010 and 2011 – non-experiential learning participants. A comparison of graduation rates and end-of-course grade data were measured between the two cohorts for the semesters identified.

Findings

Comparison results revealed a higher completion rate (84%) among experiential learning participants versus non-experiential learning participants (75%). The end-of-course grade comparison revealed a higher course success rate (96%) among experiential learning participants versus a (91%) course success rate among non-experiential learning participants.

Recommendations

The recommendations of this study are (a) provide experiential learning within more business programs as part of a course and (b) the accounting faculty involved in this experiential learning activity could provide an information session to other business faculty on including experiential learning as part of a course. It would be interesting to see the results of other business programs including experiential learning as part of a course such as management or marketing.

Conclusion

This experiential learning activity revealed a positive association between experiential learning, student completion, and course success. Community college leaders seeking best practices to improve completion rates and course success may consider the strategy of experiential learning as part of a course.

ORCID

Carolyn Walker http://orcid.org/0000-0001-7743-8375

References

Achieving The Dream. (2017). *About us*. Retrieved from http://achievingthedream.org/about-us

American Association of Community Colleges. (2014). *Empowering community colleges to build the nation's future: An implementation guide*. Washington, DC: Author.

Astin, A. (1999). Student involvement: A developmental theory for higher education. *Journal of College Student Development, 40*(5), 522.

Castellano, S. (2015, March) Setting up for career success: Mentoring and experiential learning are shown to benefit future workers. *TD Magazine*. Retrieved from http://link.galegroup.com/apps/doc/A413786045/AONE?U=gvltec_main&sid=AONE&xid=05707096.

Center for Community College Student Engagement. (2012). *A matter of degrees: Promising practices for community college student success (A first look)*. Austin: The University of Texas at Austin, Community College Leadership Program.

Coffey, H. (n.d.). Experiential education. Retrieved from http://web.archive.org/web/20180124233130/http://www.learnnc.org/lp/pages/4967.

Cohen, A. M., Brawer, F. B., & Kisker, C. B. (2014). *The American community college* (6th ed.). San Francisco, CA: Jossey-Bass.

Devasagayam, R., Johns-Masten, K., & McCollum, J. (2012). Linking information literacy, experiential learning, and student characteristics: Pedagogical possibilities in business education. *Academy of Educational Leadership Journal, 16*(4), 2. GALE|A322780944.

Grinder, S. A., Kelly-Reid, J. E., & Mann, F. B. (2017). *Enrollment and employees in postsecondary institutions, fall 2015; and financial statistics and academic libraries, fiscal year 2015: First look (Provisional Data) (NCES 2017-024)*. U.S. Department of Education. Washington, DC: National Center for Education Statistics. Retrieved from http://nces.ed.gov/pubsearch

Hart Research Associates. (2013). It takes more than a major: Employer priorities for college learning and student success. *Liberal Education, 99*(2), 1. Retrieved from https://www.aacu.org/publications-research/periodicals/it-takes-more-major-employer-priorities-college-learning-and

Kolb, D. (1984) Experiential learning cycle. Retrieved from https://www.simplypsychology.org/learning-kolb.html.

McClenney, B. N. (2014). Leadership matters: Addressing the student success and completion agenda. *New Directions for Community Colleges, (2014)*(164), 8. doi:10.1002/cc.20076

Pegg, M. (2017). D is for Dewey: His approach to education. Retrieved from http://www.thepositiveencourager.global/john-deweys-approach-to-doing-positive-work/).

Peterson, D. (2017). What is experiential learning? Experiential learning is more than learning by doing. Retrieved from https://www.thoughtco.com/what-is-experiential-learning-31324.

Texas Community Colleges Respond to the Threatened End of DACA: A Document Analysis

Nicholas Tapia-Fuselier and Jemimah L. Young

ABSTRACT
Undocumented students continue to face unique barriers in American higher education. Community colleges are being challenged to enhance the ways in which they serve, support, and advocate for undocumented students in order to become undocu-competent. Through qualitative document analysis, this study evaluated Texas community colleges' institutional responses to the announcement of the end of Deferred Action for Childhood Arrivals (DACA). The findings of this study demonstrate that although there were themes discovered in the institutional responses, there were differences in the superficiality or depth with which they were presented. Further, we propose the Undocu-Competent Institutional Response (UCIR) Framework – a practical framework for administrators to consider utilizing when crafting future undocu-competent institutional responses on major issues impacting undocumented students.

In 2012, President Obama passed Deferred Action for Childhood Arrivals (DACA) – an executive order that permitted undocumented immigrants who arrived in the United States before the age of 16 to stay in the United States to work or attend school without fear of deportation (Krogstad, 2017). Five years later, President Trump ordered DACA to be rescinded in September of 2017 (Shear & Davis, 2017). Although the future of DACA is being debated in the courts (National Immigration Law Center, 2018), Trump's action prompted the American Council on Education (ACE) and the American Association of Community Colleges (AACC) to release public statements condemning the decision (AACC Letter, 2017; ACE, 2017).

The potential end of DACA is not the only issue undocumented students face in higher education. Undocumented students in the United States continue to face unique barriers to success including navigating disparate in-state resident tuition policies (Ali, 2017; Oseguera, Flores, & Burciaga, 2010), facing hostile campus climates (Muñoz & Maldonado, 2012), and dealing with insensitive and uninformed staff and faculty (Contreras, 2009; Nienhusser, Vega, & Carquin, 2016). Considering these barriers, Valenzuela, Perez, Perez, Montiel, and Chaparro (2015) called on community colleges to establish Institutional Undocu-Competence (IUC). IUC, an institutional capacity framework, is the conceptual framework guiding this study. Informed by social justice principles, IUC calls on institutions to engage in action-oriented steps to equitably serve undocumented students in different areas of campus life (Valenzuela et al., 2015). For the purposes of this study, we build on the recommendations related to the area of *visible and open advocacy* (Valenzuela et al., 2015). According to Valenzuela at el. (2015), institutions should advocate for undocumented students in clear and public ways. Moreover, "advocacy… should include recognition of the ways that the legal and policy contexts off campus shape community college students' lives" (Valenzuela et al., 2015, p. 90).

Purpose of the study and methods

After the decision to wind down DACA was announced, many higher education institutions released public responses about the decision. Some of these responses were sent to the campus community. Others were posted in various news outlets. The purpose of this study was to examine how Texas community colleges publicly responded to the Trump administration's decision to rescind DACA by answering the following two research questions:

1) What themes are present in community colleges' institutional responses to the rescinding of DACA? and
2) How do these themes align with IUC?

Texas, only behind California, leads the country with 121,000 DACA recipients (Krogstad, 2017). In 2013, over 70% of undocumented students who qualified for in-state resident tuition in Texas were studying at community colleges (Ura & McCullough, 2015). Of the 10 post-secondary institutions serving the largest numbers of undocumented students, eight were community college districts and campuses (Ura & McCullough, 2015). These eight institutions were chosen as a purposive sample.

We began to gather the public institutional responses of these eight institutions through online searches. If no response was found through our search, we requested it directly through the institutions' public relations officers. Through this process, we obtained the public institutional responses of five institutions; these were utilized as the dataset. We conducted a qualitative document analysis as the method for this study. Document analysis is a "systematic procedure for reviewing or evaluating documents… [including] electronic material" (Bowen, 2009, p. 27). Because public institutional responses were the unit of analysis for this study, this method was deemed appropriate. We organized the data by first identifying sections of the institutional responses most relevant to the research questions; these were identified as meaning units (Graneheim & Lundman, 2004). Then, we thematically analyzed the content of the meaning units and constructed respective categories (Bowen, 2009; Graneheim & Lundman, 2004). Finally, five major themes were identified.

Findings

There were five major themes discovered through our analysis: institutional commitment; community resources; context; emotionality; and public support and advocacy. Critical to each theme is the level of superficiality or depth with which it was present in the institutional response. As we present in our discussion, the combination of the five themes presented deeply in an institutional response best aligns with IUC.

Institutional commitment

First, institutional commitments to mission, values, and history were the most prevalent theme throughout the data. For example, one institution's response included "our commitment to creating and sustaining a safe, respectful, welcoming, and equitable environment for all students and employees has always been and remains unwavering." The ways in which institutional commitments are presented in the statements are superficial and largely speak to nonperformative commitments (Ahmed, 2012). Signaling to institutional commitments in a public statement is deeper if it is explained how these commitments have been operationalized.

Community resources

Second, nearly each statement directed students to available resources on campus or links to resources in the community including on-campus counseling centers, student affairs departments, and websites with DACA updates. Referring students to available campus resources is critical. However, IUC requires that institutions form collaborative partnerships with local, state, or national undocumented immigrant-specific community resources (Valenzuela et al., 2015). A richer statement would include where undocumented students can find support off campus and in their community.

Context

Third, each response addressed the context of the moment: the Trump administration's decision to end DACA. This is essential information sharing, a necessary component to institutional responses. However, only one statement was deeper and acknowledged the historical context, specifically on undocumented students in Texas and in-state resident tuition policies. Setting the historical context displays a sustained awareness of the issues impacting undocumented students locally and nationally.

Emotionality

Fourth, the majority of the institutional responses named the emotionality that existed immediately following the DACA announcement. Statements like, "we understand that this may be an emotional and uncertain time for many of our students" were present. However, one response was deeper and shared in the emotions of the moment: "The… Board of Trustees and Administration are disappointed and saddened by the recent termination of the Deferred Action for Childhood Arrivals (DACA) program." The empathy captured in this statement is a meaningful display of sincere support for undocumented students.

Public support and advocacy

Finally, some responses addressed what their campus is doing to provide support for undocumented students. For example, one response included, "please know that you and your families are safe on our campuses and that we are prepared to help support you during this time of uncertainty regarding our nation's immigration policy." This support is expected. Some statements were deeper and pledged to advocate for legislation that would protect undocumented immigrants from deportation. This level of advocacy best aligns with IUC.

Discussion

As we concretized the themes discovered in our analysis, we found that these themes were not singular concepts. Rather, we found that there were varying levels of superficiality or depth with which each theme was presented. None of the responses evaluated in this study captured all five themes with depth. Therefore, we propose an Undocu-Competent Institutional Response (UCIR) Framework – a practical framework for administrators to consider when crafting institutional responses about issues impacting undocumented students. More specifically, the UCIR Framework can guide the process of developing future public institutional responses in a way that deeply captures the institutional commitments of the college, available community resources, overarching context, complex emotionality, and the promise of public support and advocacy; these types of responses best align with IUC.

Implications

The findings from this study add an additional layer to IUC that includes institutional responses. However, we contend that IUC is far greater than releasing institutional responses to events that impact undocumented students. Rather, institutional responses are a part of visible and open advocacy, and should be in addition to providing adequate training to faculty and staff, developing more opportunities for financial aid, creating space and support for undocumented student groups, and transforming the campus culture to inclusive and equitable (Valenzuela et al., 2015).

Additionally, we are interested in understanding if this framework could be adapted for institutional responses not related to undocumented students. For example, is this framework useful for crafting and assessing responses related to on-campus racial-bias incidents? Further, researchers interested in effective, justice-oriented institutional responses could replicate our study in alternative contexts, including the four-year college or university context.

Conclusion

We recognize that the decision to release institutional responses to major policy decisions is complicated, particularly considering the ways in which these responses are written, reviewed, and approved by governing bodies. However, the current political climate in the United States respective to immigration includes toxic debates around immigration reform (Hulse, 2018), a sustained fight against sanctuary cities and campuses (Chokshi, 2017), and hard line, zero-tolerance immigration policies that have led to family separation (Montanaro, 2018). Therefore, we join the existing calls for community colleges to establish IUC and, in turn, publicly advocate for undocumented students.

ORCID

Jemimah L. Young http://orcid.org/0000-0001-6598-9196

References

AACC Letter. (2017). DACA institutional sign-on letter. Retrieved from https://www.aacc.nche.edu/wp-content/uploads/2017/10/DACA_Institutional_Sign-On_Letter-1.pdf

ACE. (2017). Statement by ACE president Ted Mitchell on the Trump administration's reported decision to end DACA. Retrieved from http://www.acenet.edu/news-room/Pages/Statement-by-ACE-President-Ted-Mitchell-on-the-Trump-Administrations-Reported-Decision-to-End-DACA.aspx

Ahmed, S. (2012). *On being included: Racism and diversity in institutional life*. Durham, NC: Duke University Press. doi:10.1215/9780822395324

Ali, D. (2017). In-state tuition for undocumented students: 2017 state-level analysis. Retrieved from https://www.naspa.org/rpi/posts/in-state-tuition-for-undocumented-students-2017-state-level-analysis

Bowen, G. A. (2009). Document analysis as a qualitative research method. *Qualitative Research Journal, 9*(2), 27–40. doi:10.3316/QRJ0902027

Chokshi, N. (2017, May 7). Texas governor signs a ban on sanctuary cities. *New York Times*. Retrieved from https://www.nytimes.com/2017/05/07/us/texas-governor-signs-ban-sanctuary-cities.html

Contreras, F. (2009). Sin papeles y rompiendo barreras: Latino students and the challenges of persisting in college. *Harvard Educational Review, 79*, 610–631. doi:10.17763/haer.79.4.02671846902gl33w

Graneheim, U. H., & Lundman, B. (2004). Qualitative content analysis in nursing research: Concepts, procedures and measures to achieve trustworthiness. *Nurse Education Today, 24*(2), 105–112. doi:10.1016/j.nedt.2003.10.001

Hulse, C. (2018, February 15). No room for debate: Senate floor fight over immigration is a bust. *New York Times*. Retrieved from https://www.nytimes.com/2018/02/15/us/politics/senate-immigration-debate.html

Krogstad, J. M. (2017). DACA has shielded nearly 790,000 young unauthorized immigrants from deportation. Retrieved from http://www.pewresearch.org/fact-tank/2017/09/01/unauthorized-immigrants-covered-by-daca-face-uncertain-future/

Montanaro, D. (2018). Family separation is Trump's immigration policy. Retrieved from https://www.npr.org/2018/06/20/621489166/family-separation-is-trumps-immigration-policy-here-s-why-he-won-t-own-it

Muñoz, S. M., & Maldonado, M. M. (2012). Counterstories of college persistence by undocumented Mexicana students: Navigating race, class, gender, and legal status. *International Journal of Qualitative Studies in Education, 25*(3), 293–315. doi:10.1353/rhe.2017.0021

National Immigration Law Center. (2018). DACA. Retrieved from https://www.nilc.org/issues/daca/

Nienhusser, H. K., Vega, B. E., & Carquin, M. C. S. (2016). Undocumented students' experiences with microaggressions during their college choice process. *Teachers College Record, 111*(2), 1–33.

Oseguera, L., Flores, S. M., & Burciaga, E. (2010). Documenting implementation realities: Undocumented immigrant students in California and North Carolina. *Journal of College Admission, 206*, 37–43.

Shear, M. D., & Davis, J. H. (2017, September 5). Trump moves to end DACA and calls on congress to act. *New York Times*. Retrieved from https://www.nytimes.com/2017/09/05/us/politics/trump-daca-dreamers-immigration.html

Ura, A., & McCullough, J. (2015, April 16). Where undocumented students pay in-state tuition. *Texas Tribune*. Retrieved from https://www.texastribune.org/2015/04/16/colleges-undocumented-students-with-state-tuition/

Valenzuela, J. I., Perez, W., Perez, I., Montiel, G. I., & Chaparro, G. (2015). Undocumented students at the community college: Creating institutional capacity. *New Directions for Community Colleges, 2015*(172), 87–96. doi:10.1002/cc.2015.2015.issue-172

Reflections on Publishing Graduate Students' Research: Advice and Lessons Learned

Deborah L. Floyd, Cristobal Salinas Jr., Ethan C. Swingle, María-Jose Zeledón-Pérez, Sim Barhoum, and Gianna Ramdin

This book featured chapters about community college research that were written by graduate students and faculty who participated in mentor-mentee relationships throughout the publication process. Chapter 1 described the processes implemented, along with offering practical tips, advice, and recommendations about the publishing process. The other 12 chapters followed featuring research about community colleges and authored by 15 graduate students or recent graduate mentees and 9 faculty scholar mentors. This final chapter aims to summarize authors' lessons learned, including advice and tips, after completion of this mentor-mentee project.

The methods utilized included a survey of authors inviting them to respond to the open-ended questions about advice they would offer a graduate student publishing and lessons learned as a result of this publishing process. Of the 24 authors 13 offered responses to at least one of the four questions.

Advice about Publishing

Authors offered advice to graduate students who wanted to publish, which reaffirmed much of the advice and tips described in Chapter 1. Several authors stressed the importance of following published editorial guidelines, reaching out to editors for assistance, selecting an appropriate journal or publisher, meeting deadlines and expectations in a timely fashion, and soliciting reviewers for feedback before submitting to editors. They also emphasized the importance of finding the right mentor for guidance throughout the process. Authors advised to not delay or procrastinate as noted by one author who said to "take the plunge and write an article based on your dissertation which it is fresh in your memory." Finally, many authors reflected on the rewards and challenges of publishing, including the outcome of developing a sense of community among students and the need to pay attention to technical details.

Almost all journals use electronic processes for submission. One author experienced several challenges with the process and offered reflections while also advising others:

> Pay very close attention to the electronic submission process and the steps and double-check all the submission materials. It was easy to overlook that after spending so much time working on the paper and refining it and then getting to the submission, you're ready to just submit and get it off your to do list and in the reviewer's hands. It really was the technicalities of the process and the submission, which was the biggest stumbling block.

This author overcame these technical challenges, with the assistance of mentors and editors, and the manuscript made a fine contribution to this book.

Lessons Learned

Many of the responses about lessons learned also reinforced the processes and tips described in Chapter 1. Some reflected on the loneliness of the process, the need to be organized, the value of patience with the various steps, and the importance of not being defensive regarding feedback of editors and reviewers.

Representative verbatim comments from authors about the publication process follow:

- In many ways, the CCJRP is an anomaly – the peer review feedback was prompt, professional, and accurate. I learned that the peer review process can be very affirming and supportive, unlike other experiences.
- Publishing is a process. It cannot be done in one day. Writing an article takes plenty of research to be conducted, even before the research itself. Finding enough supportive/missing literature, to finding the right method to conduct your study, there are many steps. Once completed and accepted, however, there are still steps lie revising and formatting to the journal's guidelines, making any changes the reviewers mentioned, and then making changes the editors or publishers want.
- Patience about the process is important, and that self-care is essential. Take feedback seriously, but with a grain of salt.
- Be patient through each step. Some steps take longer than others but they all tie into the publishing process.
- I learned that the reviewer feedback can be helpful, confusing and frustrating all at the same time. I also learned that each revision makes the piece stronger, so I grew to become more comfortable with revising my paper.
- The process of publishing is humbling. Remember to not take anything personally. Each editor or reviewer may provide little or too much feedback. Multiple editor or reviewers can provide contradicting comments at first glance. It is best to sit on comments a couple of days before responding or devising a strategy to move forward. Then editors want to inspire work that can be held up to the greatest scrutiny.
- It can be lonely and a debilitating process even if you find guidance or people to help. Find a mentor early on in the process. Ask questions, do research, and read other articles to get a better feel for what this journal wants.
- As a result of the process, I learned to value my own voice as a scholar. It was so easy for me as a graduate student to see my professors and other published scholars as the "experts." But this process, along with the advice of mentors I received along the way, encouraged me to view my work as valuable and to speak with more confidence in my writing.

Concluding Thoughts

Research, writing, and publishing can be challenging for all who engage in scholarship, but the final published work brings a well-deserved sense of pride and joy. One graduate student author poignantly described the woes and joys of the publishing process by noting that "The process can be long and arduous, sometimes stretching into years, but producing work that will last forever is ultimately rewarding." And, another emphasized that "Publishing is not a one-time thing. Consider this a career long goal. There is always work to do."

No doubt, self-care, self-confidence, and surrounding yourself with those who believe in you is essential for successful writing for publication. This is essential for success since the process can be lonely and often filled with revisions and rejections. Seeking advice and support while also serving as an advisor and mentor is an important element for successful scholars. As one student stated, "Believe in yourself. Ask for help early in the process. Become a mentor yourself to pay it forward."

To all who have struggled with writing for publication and have benefited from mentors and colleagues who have supported them throughout this lonely process, we hope this book provides useful insight. Most of all, we hope that benefactors of mentoring will heed the advice to pay it forward and serve as a mentor to others. We all benefit when our community of scholars and colleagues offers helping each other throughout the publishing process. We believe this book is an example of a successful project featuring scholarly research as a result of effective mentor and mentee relationships. To those who have been mentored, now is the time to serve as mentors to others. *Pay it forward!*

Index

Note: **Bold** page numbers refer to tables; *Italic* page numbers refer to figures and page numbers followed by "n" denote endnotes.

Abbas, G. 19
Abelman, R. 113, 114
Abrica, E. 5
abstract liberalism 44
academic and career alignment 89
academic dishonesty behaviors 31, 38
academic transfer 91–92
accounting business course 145
Achieving the Dream (2017) 1, 144
administrative sanctions *see* punitive sanctions
advice about publishing 152
affordability 91–92
African American women in leadership 60
agreeableness 19
Aim & Scope 4
Allen, T.O. 120
Alletzhauser, H.L. 2
Americans with Disabilities Act (ADA) 126, 133
Amherst system 138
assistive technology 131–133
Astin, A. 143
Atoum, Y. 33
Author Services website 7, *8*
Avery, C. 111
Avery College 111

Bailey, T. 121
Banks, G. C. 19
Bass, B.M. 23
Bateh, J. 19
Bedford, W. 33
behavioral descriptive interviewing 45
Bell, D. 46
Berger, J.B. 98, 100
Bicak, I. 5
bicultural socialization theory 61, 66
Blumenfeld, W. 70
Boga, I. 19
Bommer, W.H. 17
Bonilla-Silva, E. 44

boolean searches 112
Bostic, D. 137
Bourdieu, P. 86, 93
Bowen, G.A. 139
Brawer, F.B. 43
Brazelton, G.B. 72
Brazier, E. 33
Brown, A. 33
Brown, J. 5
Burgos, D. 34
Burns, J.M. 23

calm behaviors 33, 38
campus climate 99–100
campus observations 62
Caple, R.B. 84
career advancement 60
career decision-making 87, 93
Carter, L. 114, 120
Case, C.J. 31
Cate, C.A. 98
Central Article Tracking System (CATS) 4, 10
checklist for authors 8–9
Chen, L. 33
Chennupati, K.R. 2
Ciez-Volz, K. 45, 46
Civil Rights Act of 1964 117
Civitas Learning 1
code of conduct 137–138; *see also* student conduct
Cohen, A.M. 43
collectivist theory of leadership 16
College Promise 1
color-blind ideology: codified language/fit 45, 49; disrupting in search process 50–52; diversity and 44, 48; Equal Employment Opportunity (EEO) 43, 49, 50, 52; pervasiveness 45, 52; racism among professionals 49–50; systemic racism 53; unmasking in search process 48–50; white supremacy 44

communication competency 20
Communities of Color 73
Community College Journal of Research and Practice (CCJRP) 1–4, 9
community college leadership frameworks *see* transformational leadership
community colleges and its leadership 59
community cultural wealth (CCW) 73
commuter campus syndrome 70
competencies for community college leaders: competencies framework 15–16; comprehensive leadership framework 15; epistemological position 16; focus areas 16; participatory leadership 16; transformational leadership 20–21
conscientiousness 19
construct proliferation 13, 15, 17, 25–26
Conway, K.M. 85
cost of college 92
Crandell, D. 2
Crawford, K. 60
crisis and opportunity framework 17
critical race theory (CRT): civil rights movement 46; communication of diversity 52; diversity and color-blind ideology 44; ethical decision-making 52; experiential knowledge 45; hiring practices 43; modified Stevick-Colaizzi-Keen method 46; racial justice through activism 53; racism in search process 46; systemic racism 53; tenants 46
Crossref Similarity Check Powered by iThenticate 9
cultural capital 73
cultural mediators and translators 64, 66–67

Dalessandro, A. 114
Davis v. Monroe County Board of Education (1999) 139
De Anda, D. 59, 61, 66
De Andrés, J. 127
Deaux, K. 60
Deferred Action for Childhood Arrivals (DACA): community resources 148–149; context 149; document analysis 148; emotionality 149; implications 149–150; institutional commitment 148; Institutional Undocu-Competence (IUC) 147; policy decisions 150; public institutional responses 148; public support and advocacy 149; rescind 148; social justice principles 147; Undocu-Competent Institutional Response (UCIR) Framework 149; undocumented students 147; visible and open advocacy 147
deficit thinking 73
degree advising 99
deGregory, C. 5
De Hoogh, A.H. 19, 21

Deinert, A. 19
Delgado Kloos, C. 34
Delgado, M. 5
Delgado, R. 43, 46
Devyer, M. 33
DeWaters, J. 127
Dewey, J. 143
Díaz, J. 85
Digital Object Identifier (DOI) 10
Dixon v. Alabama (1960) 138
document analysis 63, 136–137, 139, 148
domestic errands and children responsibilities 60
draft 7–8, *8*
dual-enrollment programs 32
Ducheny, K. 2
Dulebohn, J.H. 17
Dunbar, D.R. 67
Duree, C. 20

Ebbers, L. 20
economic status 85
Eddy, P.L. 21, 22, 24, 59, 60
editorial process 3–4
editorial screening 9
educational attainment 85
educational sanctions 137
Eggleston, L.E. 97
Eklöf, H. 33
eLearning 30–31; *see also* virtual proctoring
electronic and electrotonic journals 2
Elliott, K. 5
Ellis, M.M. 21, 22
Ensari, N. 19
Epstein, E. 5
Equal Employment Opportunity (EEO) 43, 49, 50, 52
equity in workplace 60
Erickson, W. 126, 127, 130, 132, 133
Espinosa, L.L. 121
ethical leadership 23–24
ethnicity 60
evidence-based research 1
evolving perspectives of value of degree 85
exam integrity 33
exchange manuscripts 4
existential threats 13
experiential learning: accounting business course 145; Achieving the Dream (2017) 144; advantages 144; Astin theory of student 143–144; completion rates of students 143, 144; course completion 144; educational practices 144; experiential learning cycle 143; findings 145; laboratory school 143; recommendations 145; research questions 145; student completion 144; support methods for course completion 143; Volunteer Income Tax Assistance (VITA) Initiative 145

INDEX

experiential learning cycle 143
extravertism 19

faculty development 114
faculty of color: abstract liberalism and avoidance 44; affirmative action policies 43; behavioral descriptive interviewing 45; benefit 42; community colleges *vs.* universities 45–46; critical race theory (CRT) 43, 46; data collection and analyses 48; diversity 44; Equal Employment Opportunity (EEO) 43; fit 45; hiring practices 43–44, 52; implications for future research 54–55; implications for policy 53; implications for practice 53–54; interview questions 45, 47; literature review 43–47; modified Stevick-Colaizzi-Keen method 44; NVivo 45; participants 47, **47**; phenomenological method 46–47; racial diversity of faculty 43; recruitment 44, 47, **47**; search committee 45; students of color 42–43; teaching demonstration 45–46; *see also* color-blind ideology
federal Pell grant program 119
financial independence 104–105
fit 45
Fitterer, A. 33
five-factor model (FFM) 4, 13, 19–20, 26
Flannigan, S. 45, 46
Flowers, C. 126–128, 130, 132
Foo, S. 2
Forever GI bill 98
Forman, T.A. 44
Forsyth, D. R. 19
four A's 7
four I's 18
Franklin, K. 71
Frazer, S. 70
Freeman, A. 46
Fujii, S.J. 44–46, 52
Fujimoto, E.O. 52
full range leadership theory 18

Garcia, L. 21, 22
gay-straight alliance (GSA) 72, 74, 75, 78, 80
Gonzalez, G. 137
Gosetti, P.P. 114, 121
Government Issue (GI) bill 84, 97–98
Graduate Students' Research About Community Colleges 3, 10
Grashow, A. 21
Green, D.W. 45, 46
Grove-Heuser, J.R. 18
guardrails 103–104

habitus and field concept 86, 93
Hackett, S. 127
Hannay, M. 32

Harper, K.A. 127
Harris, O.D. 114
Harry W. Colmery Veterans Education Assistance Act of 2017 98
Hawkins, C. 20
hearing officers 140
Heifetz, R.A. 21
Heyliger, W. 19
higher education learners 31–32
Hispanic women in leadership 60
Historically Black Colleges and Universities (HBCUs) 110
Historically Black Community Colleges (HBCCs) 5; antebellum period 111; Avery College 111; benefits 110; boolean searches 112; Civil Rights Act of 1964 117; current list 116, **116**; data and variables 115–116; empirical studies 112; faculty development 114; false dichotomy 113; federal Pell grant program 119; history 111–112, **112**; institutional advancement 114; institutional spending 114–115; Integrated Postsecondary Education Data System (IPEDS) 115–116; mission statement 114; Morrill Land Grant Act in 1890 116; organizational characteristics 116; organizational considerations and outcomes 114–115; *Plessy v. Ferguson* 111; policymakers 121–122; professional work and careers 121; quantitative analyses 121; recommendations for future research 120–121; replicating studies for HBCC 120; research area 113; state funding 119; student experience 113; student outcomes 113–114; student populations 120; student success and attainment 120–121; students with learning disabilities 113; Temporary Assistance to Needy Families (TANF) 113; theoretical frameworks to apply to studies 120; time-invariant characteristics 116–117, **117**; time-variant characteristics 117, **118,** 119–120; tuition and fees revenue 119–120; village pedagogy 114; vision statement 114
Hoch, J.E. 17
home and work culture 59, 61, 65–67
Hsu, S.D. 33
hybrid coding method 101

identity characteristics 105–106
immediate labor returns 90
immigrant community college students 5; academic and career alignment 89; academic transfer 91–92; affordability 91–92; bachelor degree 83–84; career decision-making 87, 93; conceptual framework 86; cost of college 92; data analysis 88; data collection 87; economic status 85; educational attainment 85; evolving perspectives of value of degree 85; G.I. Bill in the 1940s 84; Great Plains region 87;

habitus and field concept 86, 93; historical influences 84–85; immediate labor returns 90; immigrant students and community colleges 85; methodology 87; Morrill Act of 1862 84; participants 87, **88**; perception of college 84–85; positionality 86–87; qualitative research study 87; research questions 84; two-year *vs.* four-year environments 91; utility and viability of college degree 83, 86, 92–93
institutional advancement 114
institutional spending 114–115
institutional supports for veterans 99
Institutional Undocu-Competence (IUC) 147; *see also* Deferred Action for Childhood Arrivals (DACA)
Integrated Postsecondary Education Data System (IPEDS) 115–116, 125, 128
Internet technologies and web accessibility 125, 127, 128
Ivory, B.T. 70

Jabbar, H. 5
Jefferson, T. 137
Johnson, J. 59
Joliet Junior College 12
Judge, T.A. 18

Kanade, T. 33
Karim, M. 33
Kayes, P.E. 45
Kelly, B. 127
Kim, E. 85
King, D.L. 31
Kinnersley, R.T. 67
Kite, M. 60
Kolb, D. 143
Kolski, T. 4
Kouzes, J.M. 18
Kroeck, K.G. 18

Laanan, F.S. 97, 100
Lara, L. 4
Larson, M.B. 2
Latinx 42, 44, 55n1
leadership behaviors 18–19
learning organization 23
Lechuga, V.M. 2
Lee, S.Y. 45
Leonard, J. 33
lesbian, gay, bisexual, transgender, queer, and/or similarly-identified (LGBTQ+) Students of Color: alienation and marginalization 79; campus climate 71–72; at community colleges 70–71; community cultural wealth (CCW) 73; commuter campus syndrome 70; data collection **74,** 74–75; future directions 80; gay-straight alliance (GSA) 72, 74, 75; identity and interpersonal relations 72–73; implications 79–80; Latinx 71, 80n1; limitations 76; limited visible representation 76–77; memos 75; navigational capital 78–79; NVivo 75; participant **74,** 74–75; positionality 75; purposive sampling 74; recommendations 79–80; sampling methods 74; social capital 77–79; structural support for 72; transformative paradigm 73–74; trustworthiness 75–76
lessons learned 153
Li Liew, C. 2
Lim, B.C. 19
Linsky, M. 21
Liu, A.X. 33
Liu, O.L. 34
Liu, X. 33
Lorca, P. 127
Lowe, K.B. 18
Lyrén, P.E. 33

Ma, J. 85
managerial focused leadership approach 18
manuscript 3–4, 7
Marcus, A. 33
Martínez, A.B. 127
McKinnon-Crowley, S. 5
McNair, D.E. 24, 25
Mcneill, A.L. 2
Meléndez, E. 113, 120
memos 63, 101–102
mentor-mentee relationships 152
mentorship 3, 64–65, 153–154
military-affiliated students: campus climate 99–100; in community colleges 97; conceptual framework 100–101; data analysis 101–102; data collection 101; degree advising 99; educational funding 96–97; financial independence 104–105; Forever GI bill 98; guardrails 103–104; hybrid coding method 101; identity characteristics 105–106; implications for practice and future research 106–107; institutional supports for veterans 99; limitations 102; memos 101–102; methods 101; military benefits in United States 97–98; participants 101; Post-9/11 GI bill 98; social capital 100; structure hypothesis 100–101, 106; transfer capital 97, 106; transfer rates 97; transfer student capital 100, 104; transition to higher education 98–99; veterans benefits 97, 107n1; Yellow Ribbon program 98
military benefits in United States 97–98
Miller, A. 5
Mirza, N. 34
mission statement 114
Mjoni Mwale, H. 2
modified Stevick-Colaizzi-Keen method 44

Montgomery GI Bill 98
Moreton, A. 67
Morrill Land Grant Act in 1862 84, 97, 138
Morrill Land Grant Act in 1890 116
Moser, K.M. 97, 100
Moten, J. 33
Moustakas, C. 48
Murray, J.P. 45

navigational capital 78–79
neuroticism 19
Nevarez, C. 21, 23, 42
Newvine, T. 32
Nguyen, D.J. 72
Nicolazzo, Z. 73
Northouse, P.G. 67
NVivo 45

O'Boyle, E. H. 19
Offstein, E.H. 2
O'Mara, K. 72
online exam proctoring *see* virtual proctoring
open access mission 12, 13
open-door policy and programs 59
openness to experience 19
Opp, R.D. 114, 121
organizational characteristics 116
organizational culture 22–23
Ozuna, T. 5

Padilla, M. 5
Pardo, A. 34
Parmanto, B. 127
participatory leadership 16
Pasco, A.H. 2
peer review process 9, 9–10
Pegg, M. 143
People of Color 4–5
Phelan, D.J. 21, 22
Piccolo, R.F. 18
Plessy v. Ferguson 111
Ployhart, R.E. 19
policy and curriculum 5
positionality 75, 86–87
Posner, B.Z. 18
post-9/11 GI bill 98
postsecondary educational opportunities 12
practitioner-scholars 1
professionalism competency 21
publication process: Aim & Scope 4; call for papers 3; CCJRP special issue 2–3; Central Article Tracking System (CATS) 4; copy editing 4; editorial process 3; exchange manuscripts 4; graduate students 3; Historical Black Community Colleges (HBCC) 5; immigrant community college students 5; manuscripts 3–4; mentorship 3; People of Color 4–5; policy and curriculum 5; representative verbatim comments 153; review 3; scholarly and research full-length manuscripts 4; ScholarOne Manuscript management system 3; self-identified LGB Students of Color 5; student behaviors during virtual proctoring 4; technology 5; transformational leadership and five-factor model 4
publishing: academic talent 1; Author Services website 7, 8; Central Article Tracking System (CATS) 10; checklist for authors 8–9; Crossref Similarity Check Powered by iThenticate 9; Digital Object Identifier (DOI) 10; draft 7–8, 8; editorial screening 9; faculty mentors 6; fee-based editing services 7; four As 7; graduate programs 6; graduate students 6; journal selection 7–8; manuscript preparation 7; mentor 153–154; peer review process 9, 9–10; practitioner-scholars 1; professional associations 6; reader feedback 10; readership 10; recent graduates 6–7; recommendations for mentors 5–7; ScholarOne Manuscripts management system 9; tips 7–10, 8, 9
punitive sanctions 137
purposeful sampling 61, 62
purposive sampling 74

race-neutrality 46, 50, 53
racism and sexism 60
Rankin, S. 70
reader feedback 10
readership 10
recommendations for mentors 5–7
Rehabilitation Act of 1973 125–126
remote proctoring *see* virtual proctoring
Renn, K.A. 72
representative verbatim comments 153
Respondus LockDown Browser 34
Respondus Monitor 33–35
Rhoads, R.A. 60
Ridley, D. 14
Rios, J.A. 34
Robison, G.E. 18
Romero-Zaldivar, V.A. 34
Ruffins, P. 113, 120

Sagaria, M.A.D. 60
Salinas, C. Jr. 5
Schneider, T.R. 2
scholarly and research full-length manuscripts 4
ScholarOne Manuscript management system 3, 9
Schudde, L. 5
Scott-Clayton, J. 100, 106
search committee 45
Section 508 of the Rehabilitation Act of 1973 125–126

INDEX

self-identified LGB Students of Color 5
Senge, P. 23
Servicemen Readjustment Act of 1944 97
Shino, M. 33
Sivasubramaniam, N. 18
Smith, D. 60
social capital 77–79, 100
socialization 1, 2
specialized office for student conduct 140, 141n2
Stanton-Salazar, R.D. 73
Staples, E. 34
Starobin, S.S. 97
Statistical Package for the Social Sciences (SPSS) 36, **36**
Stefancic, J. 43
Stenlund, T. 33, 38
Story, P. A. 19
structure hypothesis 100–101, 106
student conduct: Amherst system 138; code of conduct 137–138; in community colleges 136, 141n2; court of law 137; data collection 139; *Davis v. Monroe County Board of Education* (1999) 139; definition 137–138; *Dixon v. Alabama* (1960) 138; document analysis 136–137, 139; educational sanctions 137; future research 140–141; hearing officers 140; history 138–139; implications for practice 140–141; *in loco parentis* 136, 138, 141n1; method 139; mission statements 137–138; punitive/administrative sanctions 137; qualitative research 139; specialized office 140, 141n2; student disciplinary issues 136; university policy 136–137; values and mission 137
students with disabilities 125–126; *see also* web accessibility
students with learning disabilities 113
Suárez-Orozco, C. 85
Suárez-Orozco, M. 85
systemic racism 43, 44, 46, 48, 50, 52–55

Tapia-Fuselier, N. 5
Tarker, D. 4
Taylor, Z. 5
Tedrow, B. 60
Temporary Assistance to Needy Families (TANF) 113
Tenon™ accessibility software 128, 130
Teranishi, R.T. 85
test anxiety and coping mechanisms 38
Thompson, T. 127, 130, 133
time-invariant characteristics of HBCCs 116–117, **117**
time-variant characteristics of HBCCs 117, **118,** 119–120
Title IV institutions 126, 128
trait activation theory 19
transfer student capital 100
transformational leadership 4; in AACC framework 20–21; authentic leadership and ethical leadership 17; and change 21–22; collaboration 17; communication competency 20; community college leadership training 25; competencies for community college leaders 15–16; construct proliferation 13, 15, 17; contemporary themes 21; crisis and opportunity framework 17; data analysis 14–15; ethical leadership 23–24; and faculty feelings 19; and five-factor model 19–20; four I's 18; full range leadership theory 18; future research 24; inclusion and exclusion criteria 14; and innovation 19, 21–22; interconnectivity and interdependence 17; leadership behaviors 18–19; learning organization 23; limitations to study 25; managerial focused leadership approach 18; methods 14–15; organizational culture 22–23; organizational effectiveness 18–19; professionalism competency 21; recommendations for practice 24; relational approach 18; results 13; search methods 14; vision 23
transformative paradigm 73–74
Trump, D. 147
trustworthiness 63, 75–76
Tsukada, A. 33
Turner, C.S.V. 44, 45

Undocu-Competent Institutional Response (UCIR) Framework 5, 149
undocumented students 147; *see also* Deferred Action for Childhood Arrivals (DACA)
utility and viability of college degree 83, 86, 92–93

Vacchi, D.T. 98, 100
Valenzuela, J.I. 147
Van Cott, D.L. 2
veterans benefits 97, 107n1; *see also* military-affiliated students
village pedagogy 114
virtual proctoring 4; academic dishonesty behaviors 31; assessment of student learning 32; calm behaviors 33, 38; cheating behavior 38; data analysis 35–36, **36**; data collection 35; definition 31; dual-enrollment programs 32; examinee behaviors 34; exam integrity 33; findings 36–37; frequency of behaviors 37; higher education learners 31–32; identified behaviors 37; implication 38–39; participants and setting 34–35; Respondus LockDown Browser 34; Respondus Monitor 33–34; similar behaviors 36–37; Statistical Package for the Social Sciences (SPSS) 36, **36**; technology-enabled assessments 32; technology support and instructor availability 37–38; test

anxiety and coping mechanisms 38; tools and instruments 35; use of 32–34; valuable resource 33
visible representation 76–77
vision statement 114
Volunteer Income Tax Assistance (VITA) Initiative 145

Walker, C. 5
Warshaw, J. 5
Watson, R.T. 14
web accessibility: Americans with Disabilities Act (ADA) 126, 133; assistive technology 131–133; cross-continent comparison 127–128; data collection and analysis 128–129, **129, 130**; delimitations 129–130; embedded search tool 131–132; errors **129, 130**; evaluation tool 130; homepages 130–131; hyperlink 131, 132; "id" attribute 132; implication 132–133; Integrated Postsecondary Education Data System (IPEDS) 125, 128, 129; Internet technologies 125, 127, 128; keyboard-focused assistive technology 131, 132; lawsuits 133; literature review 127–128; metadata 131–132; population and sample 128, **128**; research questions 126; sample size 129–130; Section 508 of the Rehabilitation Act of 1973 125–126; Tenon™ accessibility software 128, 130; Title IV institutions 126, 128; WCAG 1.0 standards 127; web accessible websites 133; web-based Bobby™ accessibility tool 127; Web Content Accessibility Guidelines (WCAG) 2.0 standards 126, 127
web accessible websites 133
web-based Bobby™ accessibility tool 127
Web Content Accessibility Guidelines (WCAG) 2.0 standards 126, 127
Weber, G. 70
Webster, J. 14
Weible, J. 4
White, C. D. 19
Whitehead, M. 5
Wilkinson, J. 33
Wisdom, J.R. 127
women in leadership 59–60
women of color: African American women 60; bicultural socialization theory 61, 66; campus observations 62; career advancement 60; challenges 67; community colleges and its leadership 59; cultural background 65–66; cultural mediators and translators 64, 66–67; data analysis 63; data collection 62–63; document analysis 63; domestic errands and children responsibilities 60; equity in workplace 60; ethnicity 60; Hispanic women 60; home and work culture 59, 61, 65–67; implications 66–67; interviews 62; in leadership 60; memos, analytic 63; mentorship 64–65; multiple responsibilities 65; open-door policy and programs 59; participant 61–62, **62**; pathways 68; purposeful sampling 61, 62; racism and sexism 60; role models 65, 67; site selection 61–62; success 67–68; Texas community college 58–59; theoretical framework 61; trustworthiness 63; vocational training 59; women in leadership 59–60
Woodford, M.R. 72
Wood, J.L. 21, 23, 42
Wu, D. 17

Yellow Ribbon program 98
Yosso, T. 73
Young, J. 5

Zagoršek, H. 23